PRAISE FOR *INTERNATIONAL BRAND STRATEGY*

Sean writes from the perspective of someone who has pondered the vagaries of product naming while standing in a shop in rural Ethiopia, reimagined adapting automotive ad copy sitting in a sleek conference room in Sweden, and walked the streets of Beijing to meet with engineers to find insights on a client's QA testing. He's a practitioner who knows what works and why, and any marketer who wants to sell internationally or adapt a global brand locally would do well to follow his lead.

Jonathan Salem Baskin, President, Arcadia Communications Lab and Author of *Branding Only Works on Cattle*

Value is as perceived in the eyes of the buyer, as the L'Oréals, Nestlés, Unilevers and P&Gs of the world have discovered and learned to exploit. Sean Duffy shows you the way to do it too! He has condensed his 30 years of handling strategic marketing and brand development exercises over six continents in a slim, practical but comprehensive book. It provides a framework of understanding the issues, analysing the options, and developing the actions needed to avoid the pitfalls in carefully crafted chapters.

Sanjay Kumar, Strategy and Operations and Professor, Delhi School of Business

Sean Duffy removes all the fuzziness from marketing and brand management with his new book. He clearly demonstrates how to grow brands and how to grow as marketers. Several classes of my MA students have developed into skilful marketers implementing the ideas from this book. Recommended reading for anyone serious about building brands and business.

Veronika Tarnovskaya, International Marketing and Researcher and Lecturer, docent, Lund University School of Economics and Management

This book is very practical with useful methodologies and concrete case studies. I'm really eager to see the Chinese edition quickly, so it will be a timely gift for those Chinese companies and marketers who are planning to run or are already operating businesses abroad. Marketers can take this book as a 'marketing bible' for international market entry and operations.
Edward Zhang, Founder of ZEN.EST Public Relations

You could argue that this book is like its author: all at once highly entertaining but also serious, deeply structured and brimming with practical tips. If you are a marketing practitioner, it will become your bedside reading with pen and paper to jot down those new ideas in the middle of the night. If you are a top executive discover how you can build brand equity, intentionally. And if you are a business student, this may well be your passport to a successful international career!
Donovan Hawker, Founder, Hawkers & Partner and Lecturer, Sorbonne University (CELSA)

Sean has captured both the 'how' and, more importantly, the 'why' in building successful multinational marketing efforts. I'm happy that TAAN Worldwide has played a supporting role over the years as Sean traversed the globe acquiring the wisdom he is now sharing with everyone.
Peter Gerritsen, President, TAAN Worldwide

Today global marketers don't hesitate to turn to independent agencies for international work. Sean Duffy, CEO of one of the most proficient, explains how. If you are looking for the definitive hand guide on how to successfully market your brand across borders, this is it.
Elliot Polak, Chief Consultant, Social Dividend Global

Sean Duffy's book is truly a gem. A must-read for every marketing and business leader growing their company across borders.
Nataly Kelly, VP of Localization, HubSpot and Author of Found in Translation

The hyper-practical (and uber-inspiring!) guide to taking your brand global. (Hint: It's way more than running your website copy through Google Translate!)
Ann Handley, Chief Content Officer, Marketing Professors and Author of Everybody Writes

You're just about to enter a new market with your brand. Excited? Consider this: the odds are high that you will fail… So if you don't want to become another sad statistic, then this book is a must-read!
Dr Ana Iorga, CEO and Chief Neuroscientist, Buyer Brain, and co-editor and author of *Ethics in Neuromarketing*

International Brand Strategy

A guide to achieving global brand growth

Sean Duffy

KoganPage

Publisher's note

Every possible effort has been made to ensure that the information contained in this book is accurate at the time of going to press, and the publishers and authors cannot accept responsibility for any errors or omissions, however caused. No responsibility for loss or damage occasioned to any person acting, or refraining from action, as a result of the material in this publication can be accepted by the editor, the publisher or the author.

First published in Great Britain and the United States in 2021 by Kogan Page Limited

Apart from any fair dealing for the purposes of research or private study, or criticism or review, as permitted under the Copyright, Designs and Patents Act 1988, this publication may only be reproduced, stored or transmitted, in any form or by any means, with the prior permission in writing of the publishers, or in the case of reprographic reproduction in accordance with the terms and licences issued by the CLA. Enquiries concerning reproduction outside these terms should be sent to the publishers at the undermentioned addresses:

2nd Floor, 45 Gee Street	122 W 27th St, 10th Floor	4737/23 Ansari Road
London	New York, NY 10001	Daryaganj
EC1V 3RS	USA	New Delhi 110002
United Kingdom		India

www.koganpage.com

© Sean Duffy 2021

The right of Sean Duffy to be identified as the author of this work has been asserted by him in accordance with the Copyright, Designs and Patents Act 1988.

ISBNs

Hardback   9 781 78966 631 1
Paperback 9 781 78966 629 8
Ebook   9 781 78966 630 4

British Library Cataloguing-in-Publication Data

A CIP record for this book is available from the British Library.

Library of Congress Control Number

2020950524

Typeset by Integra Software Services, Pondicherry
Print production managed by Jellyfish
Printed and bound by CPI Group (UK) Ltd, Croydon CR0 4YY

To the memory of Dr Paul E Duffy

CONTENTS

List of figures and tables xiv
About the author xvi
Preface xvii
Acknowledgements xxvii

PART ONE
Managing market complexities

Introduction 1

Missing the target 1
Success as a foregone conclusion 2
Compromised values 3
Technical difficulties 5
Price perception 7
Adapting to the market 9
Under-estimated competition 11
What can we learn from this? 12
Preparing for departure 14
Part One overview 14
Notes 16

01 Why brands fail abroad 18

The importance of knowing what you don't know 18
The nature of foreign markets 19
The nature of failure 20
The nature of marketing 21
The nature of competence 24
The nature of knowledge asymmetry 26
The nature of assumptions 26
Conclusion 29
Notes 30

02 Domestic vs international marketing 31

The difference between marketing domestically and abroad 31
The role of marketing 33
Language 35
Culture 36
Value proposition 37
Position 39
Media environment 43
Market intelligence 44
Documentation and codification 45
Conclusion 46
Notes 47

03 Reducing risk 49

Managing risk begins by acknowledging it 49
Overcoming cognitive bias 50
Success begins close to home 52
The ABCO case 54
Putting risk in perspective 57
What to include 58
Keep things moving 59
Idea 60
Phase I: Framing 60
Phase II: Strategy development 63
Phase III: Implementation 63
Phase IV: Management 64
Exit ramps 64
Conclusion 65
Notes 67

04 Defining your approach 68

Global integration vs local responsiveness 68
Embracing complexity 70
The Unilever approach 72
Multinational corporation structure 74

Conclusion 78
Notes 78

05 Being understood in foreign markets 79

The power behind your promotion 79
The role of language 80
The link to sales 82
Working with multiple languages 83
How to translate promotional material 84
Writing for the translator 85
The art of adaptation 85
Localization 87
Conclusion 90
Notes 91

06 Alternatives to translation 92

How to manage language barriers fluently 92
The right name for the right job 93
The right resource for the right job 94
Adaptation: The best of both worlds 97
Adaptation checklist 99
Conclusion 102
Notes 103

07 Planning for departure 104

Bon voyage 104
Planning checklist 106
The eight inputs required to localize your marketing mix 112
Conclusion 116
Notes 116

PART TWO
Creating and delivering value

Introduction 117

The problem with quality 117
What can we learn from this? 122

Building value in foreign markets 123
Part Two overview 124

08 Balancing short- and long-term growth 126

Building sales vs building a brand 126
The case for B-to-B brands 129
Blurring the lines 131
Conclusion 135
Notes 136

09 Developing a competitive advantage 139

The case of EMCO 139
How to avoid mirage marketing 142
Building an advantage from strength to strength 144
Preparing for competition 147
Conclusion 151
Notes 152

10 Defining a strategy to compete 154

Home-field advantage 154
Planning for profit 157
'But we don't have any competitors' 159
Competing on price 160
Competing on differentiation 162
A final note on strategy 164
Conclusion 165
Notes 166

11 Building brand equity 168

The mechanics of building brand equity 168
Brand management and brand equity 169
Adding insight to your net promoter score 171
Brand equity in action: The CrayOffs example 172
Conclusion 183
Notes 183

12 Net perceived value 185

Planning for profit 185
Value in action 186
Creating scarcity within a category 189
Understanding value 191
Identifying value 193
Ask why 196
Conclusion 197
Notes 198

13 Creating value 200

How buyers assess value 200
All products are 3-D 201
All value is relative 206
Value requirements change over time 213
Reducing cost 214
Sources of value 217
Conclusion 220
Notes 221

14 The commodity caveat 223

Commodity as a choice 223
Even commodities have perceived value 223
The VICO case 226
Conclusion 229
Notes 229

Afterword: Time to get started 231

Index 235

LIST OF FIGURES AND TABLES

FIGURES

Figure 2.1	Marketing Contribution Model	34
Figure 3.1	The four generic phases of marketing work that follow ideation when entering a new market	60
Figure 4.1	Integration–responsiveness grid: Bartlett and Ghoshal's model for finding the right balance between integration and responsiveness	75
Figure 10.1	Likely outcomes when pitting your strategic skills against those of local competing brands	155
Figure 10.2	The value loop	165
Figure 11.1	The Duffy Brand Equity Cycle, modelled from the consumer's perspective	173
Figure 11.2	Companies receive two types of value from markets, and should manage both	182
Figure 12.1	Percentage increase in operating profit based on a 2 per cent increase in price	187
Figure 12.2	The Net Perceived Value Model. The mental scales people use to assess the value of your offer	194
Figure 13.1	The 3-D Product Model	201
Figure 13.2	Rolex watch 3-D Product Model	208
Figure 13.3	Tesla automobile 3-D Product Model	208
Figure 13.4	iPhone smartphone 3-D Product Model	210
Figure 13.5	IFO fuse 3-D Product Model	210
Figure 13.6	Nokia vs Ericsson	212
Figure 13.7	Value lifecycle – how the relative importance of the three value categories can evolve over a category's lifecycle	213

Figure 13.8   The 3-D Cost Model 215
Figure 13.9   Bain & Company's Elements of Value®
              for B-to-C 218
Figure 13.10 Bain & Company's Elements of Value®
              for B-to-B 219

TABLES

Table 5.1   Various levels of localization 89
Table 6.1   Options for translating text from one language to
             another 95

ABOUT THE AUTHOR

Sean Duffy is an international brand strategist. Over the past three decades he has worked with dozens of global brands including IKEA, the United Nations, Volvo, VF Corporation, Absolut, Pfizer and GSK in over 40 countries across six continents. Originally from Greater Boston, Sean has lived and worked in Boston, London, San Francisco, Copenhagen and Stockholm before founding Duffy Agency in 2001.

Duffy Agency is a marketing consultancy and part of the TAAN Worldwide network. The Agency helps CEOs, CMOs, brand managers and ad agency planners see the world through the eyes of their target audiences around the world. Having done that, Duffy Agency then helps them create and execute marketing strategies to drive sales, maintain margins and build brand equity globally.

Outside Duffy Agency, Sean serves as Adjunct Professor of International Strategic Marketing at the Lund University School of Economics & Management in Sweden. He has also served as mentor in the Masters Program in Entrepreneurship at Lund University. Sean is an active member of TAAN Worldwide, where he has served two terms as the European Governor. Established in 1936, TAAN Worldwide is a global network of over 50 independent marketing agencies with annual billings of $1.5 billion USD.

PREFACE

What could go wrong?

When people think about cross-cultural marketing blunders, what usually comes to mind are the funny translation gaffs. You've probably come across a few of these yourself, like the list that *Inc* magazine published[1] with examples like:

- Paxam, the Iranian company, whose laundry soap was called Snow in Farsi. It wanted to launch in English-speaking countries and so translated the brand name to Barf, which appeared on all its packaging.
- Nike added some styling to its shoes intended to look like a flame, but after it was released, it was noted that the graphic resembled the Arabic word for Allah and the products were recalled.
- Swedish company Electrolux marketed its vacuum cleaners in the US with the tag line: 'Nothing sucks like an Electrolux.'
- US air carrier Braniff International wanted to advertise its new leather seats in the Mexican market. When it translated the US headline 'Fly in Leather' into Spanish it read 'Fly Naked'.
- Clairol launched a curling iron called 'Mist Stick' in Germany and decided not to translate the product name. Unfortunately, 'mist' is German slang for manure.
- Many companies have struggled with Mandarin, including Coca-Cola. In its first marketing attempt in China the name was translated to the equivalent of 'Bite the Wax Tadpole.'

While amusing and well circulated on the internet,[2] these are not the types of things that ruin businesses. These are the small hiccups that occur when executing a campaign in a foreign country. While these blunders can be embarrassing, their effects are usually fleeting so long as they are corrected in short order. To my knowledge, none of the brands mentioned in these online anecdotes have suffered any lasting consequences as a direct result of their cultural faux pas.

The marketing problems we'll address in this book are far less amusing, far more damaging and, for the most part, invisible. They afflict consumer-oriented brands as well as business-to-business brands, from small startups to large corporations.

Prepare to defy the odds

In 2005 Thomas L Friedman echoed Theodore Levitt in declaring that the world is flat.[3] Both were referring to a world where people, communication, goods and services flowed effortlessly over borders. When Friedman wrote his book, the internet was just approaching 100 million users globally. Today there are over 4.5 billion people online. This has triggered a boom in low-cost, modular, turnkey solutions for online retailing sites, automated merchandising and customer relationship management, global logistic support, payment processing and even live customer support. Add a co-working subscription and you'll have a downtown office space in practically every major market on Earth. The world has never seemed smaller nor the allure of foreign markets more pronounced for businesses large and small. Then why is it that so few businesses venture abroad, and of those that do, why do so few manage to succeed?

Although the average failure rate for new product launches is often estimated to be as high as 95 per cent,[4] the accuracy of this estimate is questionable.[5] More conservative estimates, like the median failure rate of 52.5 per cent suggested by Stevens and Burley,[6] are probably closer to the truth. Even still, 50/50 is not great odds. It bodes even worse for companies that are looking to expand abroad. That's because the failure rates most often quoted are based on domestic launches. International launches have more moving parts that make them more prone to failure than domestic launches.

In this book we'll see that, no matter how strong the brand is at home or how well the launch was funded, there is always the chance that the market may simply not take to it. It's the amorphous nature of this threat that makes brand acceptance the trickiest issue to deal with and a major source of business risk when entering a new market. What could account for this abysmal failure rate? The reason most often cited by those practitioners closest to the frontlines, myself included, is lack of adequate preparation.[7] This is good news because, of all the things that could go wrong, this is completely within your control. With foresight, a little discipline and the advice from this book, you can keep your brand from becoming another sad statistic. This book provides concrete steps and practical advice marketers can follow before, during and after launch to ensure enthusiastic acceptance of their brand and growth of their business in foreign markets.

This book assumes that you are entering new markets not simply to sell but also to build equity for your brand, value for your customers and profits for your company. It assumes that you want to grow as a marketer. It assumes you want to make a difference.

If you follow the path I lay out in this book, you will be able to outperform your competitors, large and small, both at home and abroad. That is an opinion, but it is based on first-hand work with hundreds of marketing departments across six continents spanning three decades. The reason I'm confident you will succeed is that most marketing departments today are glutted with data yet starved for insight. They excel at tactics yet flounder with strategy. Their contribution is clear when measured by web analytics and re-tweets but less so when it comes to operating profit and brand valuation. The advice in this book will enable you to set yourself and your company apart.

The power of perspective

Data and tactics do the most good when they feed insight and inform strategy. For that to happen, you will need more than research and analytical skills. You and your team will need to cultivate the skill of thinking from your target's perspective – to see the world as your buyer does. If there is an art to marketing, this is it.

Being able to strategize and communicate from the target's perspective is the primary skill of marketing, but this skill is not as easy to master as it may sound. Let me illustrate. Picture your buyer on the other side of a pane of glass, like a sliding patio door. You are inside with a fresh whiteboard marker in your hand. They are outside on the patio looking in at you. At first glance, communicating with them seems simple enough: you decide what you want to say and then write it on the glass. But consider things from their perspective. From the outside looking in, it all looks backwards. That's because it was written from your perspective, not theirs. The words you write on the window may be unintelligible from outside, but they still convey a strong message: 'I do not understand, or care, about your perspective.'

Find a pen right now and try to write the word 'bandages' backwards on a piece of paper. When you are done, turn the paper around and hold it up to a light to see how you did. I think you will find it's not that easy and that was just one word. Imagine writing an entire ad, brochure or marketing plan like that. Now imagine doing that in a foreign language with a foreign alphabet. If nothing else, it would be an amazing feat of discipline and concentration.

This is a simple metaphor for what is perhaps the biggest challenge facing companies who are looking to grow their business abroad. By default, most companies communicate to buyers from their own corporate perspective. This applies not just to messaging, but also to all aspects of how your company conducts business, such as:

- product features that reflect the company's priorities, not the target's
- return policies that increase efficiencies inside the company but make it impossible for customers
- product naming systems that make sense internally but not to outsiders
- web content on topics in which the target has no interest

It happens all the time. Why? Because it would require an amazing feat of discipline and concentration to do otherwise. Our brains aren't wired to function this way, but they can be trained. Most companies simply are not up to it. If you are, then you will have an advantage.

That is my objective with this book. I want to help you and your company create profit with a brand presence that offers clear and superior value from the target's perspective in every market you enter. One that reflects their reality, even if it does not necessarily reflect your own. This includes:

- a product offer that is aligned to their needs and options
- communication that reflects not only their language but also their culture and values
- positioning thaes it easy for them to understand how your product is different
- behaviour that earns their loyalty because they believe you understand their perspective

About this book

The first half of this book will help you plan for new market entry. It will lay the groundwork for sustainable success in foreign markets with practical guidance and examples. Use it to prepare your brand for departure, or catch up if you have already launched.

The second half will focus on creating value once your brand has arrived and begins competing with local brands. Although it is written with the international marketer in mind, I think you will find most of the examples and advice in this part apply to domestic marketing as well.

I introduce six heuristic models in this book that will have practical application when launching and managing brands in foreign markets:

- The first is the Marketing Contribution Model, explained in Chapter 2, which shows the three types of value that the marketing department should provide to their company and against which the department's budget should be set and performance assessed.

- The 'Eight Inputs' Model is introduced in Chapter 7. This model serves as a mini-guide to the eight central elements you'll need to customize your marketing mix for any market you enter.
- The third is the Duffy Brand Equity Cycle introduced in Chapter 11. It models how brand equity is built from the buyer's perspective and the steps required by companies to take a person from unacquainted, to a customer, to an advocate, as measured by the net promoter score (NPS) metric.
- In Chapter 12 I introduce the concept of net perceived value with a simple scale metaphor to help you visualize value and how marketers can manage it.
- Chapter 13 includes two models adapted from of Philip Kotler's Three Layers of Product Model that I call the 3-D Product Model and the 3-D Cost Model.

Organizations have many stakeholders, from current and prospective employees and customers to investors and the community. Brand management will affect them all. I use the word 'buyers' as opposed to 'customers' because the latter implies that the individual already has established a relationship with the brand. I intend 'buyers' to be more inclusive, referring to both current and potential customers. This word has its limitations. For example, it is not a good fit for non-profit organizations, whose product is an idea that is not exchanged for currency. However, I think you will find the principles still apply despite the sub-optimal word choice.

This book is written for companies that sell their product to consumers (B-to-C) as well as for those who sell to other businesses (B-to-B). I draw on examples from both types of buyers. Furthermore, the book applies equally to companies selling products or services. For the sake of simplicity, I use the one word 'product' to refer to both the products and/or services a company offers. Where I use the word 'product' or 'offer' I am referring to the three levels of product defined in Chapter 13. Similarly, when I refer to the 'cost' of a product, I do so in accordance with the definition provided in Chapter 13.

I have written this book with mid-sized companies in mind (annual revenue US $10 million to $1 billion) because this is where I have seen the most need. However, the lessons in this book apply to businesses large and small.

The book, and most of my experience, is focused on developing brand equity in foreign countries. In one sense, 'foreign' simply means a country other than one's own. That's easy enough to deduce by looking at a map. But 'foreign' also means outside one's own context and conventions. This can apply to addressing a new segment of your home market as much as a new segment on the other side of the world.

Finally, although it may sound counterintuitive, this book also applies to companies that feel they do not compete with other brands at all. In Chapter 14 I make the case that companies selling commodity goods have the most to gain from the advice in this book. If you're in the commodity business and are not convinced, I suggest you skip to Chapter 14 right now.

Brands: Separating the benefits from the babble

If hearing marketers drone on about the ethereal nature of brands and the mysterious activity of 'branding' makes your head spin, I feel your pain. The word 'branding' has always been a nebulous concept in marketing. It typically served as a catchall phrase for all things emotional, intangible, and unquantifiable. Then in the 1990s, these sentiments were packaged and turned into the brand consulting industry. The assertion that emotional, intangible and unquantifiable forces can impact a business is valid. The deluge of models and remedies produced by marketers to defend that position, less so. As Chris Kenton put it, 'an entire generation of marketers has found a way to obscure the obvious, to make the brand more fantastic, to make it hard enough to understand that you need consultants to help you figure it out'.[8] At the risk of adding to that dubious body of work, this book will address brands from a buyer-centric, operationally relevant point of view.

If you search the internet for a coherent definition of 'branding' or 'brand' you will find an impressive assortment of pithy truisms that sound nice but say little. Definitions like 'The intersection of promise and expectation', 'The art and science of managing consumer expectations', or my favourite, 'Everything', are the norm.[9] As my career evolved from copywriter, to creative director, to planner, and then to strategist and agency owner, my perspective on 'brand' and 'branding' changed. I am no longer comfortable with the fuzzy logic used to define and defend these terms. The contradictions and ambiguity surrounding them became most apparent when I started creating projects to help my own clients with their brands. That's because, to do my job, I need to define 'brand' and the activity of improving it in terms of concrete objectives, deadlines and steps. The right human resources must be allocated to each step. Unambiguous roles need to be established. Cost and time estimates must be determined. Each step must be placed on a timeline in proper sequence linked by clear dependencies to all other steps. Routines need to be defined to maintain the work after the initial setup is completed. Specific metrics need to be defined to measure the success of the work. Further, these activities and their value to the business must be quantified, explained in detail and justified to the people who are paying for the project. At this level of granularity, the contradictions and ambiguities found in most definitions of 'brand' and 'branding' render them useless because they simply can't be operationalized.[10]

In my contribution to the book *Brand Theories*, I wrote a chapter called 'Making sense: A practical guide to speaking about brands'.[11] I defined what a 'brand' is and why 'branding' is not an activity. For clarity's sake, it may help to recap some key terms from that work here.

- **Brand** is defined as, essentially, a trademark – a name and/or symbol (typically presented with a specific design treatment, phrase or combination of these) in which an organization invests to differentiate its products or organization from others in the same category. It serves as a store for the value generated from marketing activities.

- **Brand identity** refers to how the organization would like its brand to be perceived in the market. This identity is informed by the overarching marketing strategy and crafted to positively differentiate the brand. This identity works best when it is firmly rooted in the truth and not simply fabricated to appease a market segment.
- **Brand image** is how the brand actually is perceived in the market. This includes the values, traits, personality and other associations people make with the brand. Brand owners would like the brand image to correspond exactly with the brand identity they have crafted, but that is rarely the case.
- **Brand implementation strategy** refers to how the organization will overcome obstacles to operationalize its brand identity. That entails training and constant reinforcement with staff to ensure that brand values are practised uniformly by all employees, in all departments. If this is achieved then brand values will be conveyed convincingly to the target and shape the brand's image.
- **Marketing strategy** defines the company's goals and provides overarching guidance for how the company will overcome obstacles to achieve them. It defines how market share will be won and defended along with the specifics of market segmentation, competitor segmentation, targeting, product position, value proposition and support points.

In this taxonomy, there is no such activity as 'branding' per se. To ensure the brand identity is conveyed to the target audience, everyone in the company simply does their job in compliance with the brand identity as well as the guidelines and training established as part of the brand implementation strategy.

This type of strategy development, along with investment in and management of brands, requires talent, budget and time. This probably explains why companies fixated on short-term profits seem to avoid brand development activities like the plague. Could such companies be selling their business short in the mid- to long-term?

You certainly do not need to build brand equity in a foreign market to sell your products there. You could simply sell your product 'white label' to local companies who would then sell it under their own brand name. You could also sell through a distributor, like the medical device company cited in Chapter 7 where, even though the products have your logo imprinted on them, you are not making investments in the market to support that name. Choosing not to develop your brand in foreign markets reduces complexity, risk and cost. So why bother developing a positive brand image abroad in the first place?

A positive brand image gives you more ways to compete for customers in the market that you are entering, rather than relying on core features and price alone. In a tight labour market, it can also help you compete for employees without having to coerce them with inflated salaries. Above all else, it allows you to capture more value from the market. Companies that understand this don't just strive to gain more customers, they strive to gain more advocates. They know that fostering brand loyalty in addition to sales helps support the premium price they charge and increases the probability of future sales – all of which increase the value of the company. So the ability to recruit more easily, charge more and increase the value of your business are fairly compelling reasons for you to consider investing in your brand as opposed to simply selling products. The introduction of strategy combined with proper brand management can transform businesses. This applies to all companies, whether they are selling to consumers or to other businesses.

ACKNOWLEDGEMENTS

Creating a book, I discovered, is like crowdsurfing – you can't do it alone. In case you plan on writing a book yourself, I thought I'd make a handy list of the eight people you will need:

1. My mother to help you deal with deadline pressure. My first experience with a deadline was in second grade. I was working on a book report for *The Ugly Dachshund (A Little Golden Book)* by Carl Memling. I procrastinated, and the day before it was due I was still reading. I was terrified that I would have to tell Sister Bernadette I had failed. My Mom taught me what could be accomplished at a kitchen table with a little structure and a lot of compassion. I got an A on the report. Thank you Mom.

2. Someone to draw you a map. Nine months after my father died I attempted to recreate the Christmas lighting extravaganza he produced on our front lawn every Holiday Season. I found the Christmas lights all neatly organized in the garage. On top was a hand-written map of the entire yard with exacting details on which strand went on which bush, plugged into which outlet. This was one of several instructions my siblings and I would discover with a smile as we adjusted to life without him. I'm grateful to my father for imparting the value of planning and process and for providing me with the maps, written and otherwise, that I use to navigate each day.

3. A friend who knows you well enough to explain to you what you're trying to say. I met Rick during the first day of freshman orientation at Colby College in Maine. He was studying business and economics, I was studying biology and literature. Our common ground has always been humour, high jinks and a reverence for logic. After an early retirement from Wall Street, Rick moved his family to a mountain top in Vermont. From there he insisted on

reading every word I wrote and helped me understand what I was really trying to get at with this book. Thank you Rick Hauser for your sharp logic, straight feedback, and time away from your family to make this a better book.

4 A teacher to ask the tough questions. In September 2008 I gave a talk called 'The Seven Deadly Sins of International Marketing'. During the Q&A I received a barrage of excruciating questions from the same person. On stage, I could not see my tormentor, but I'm grateful I sought her out afterwards. She invited me to lecture at Lund University School of Economics and Management (LUSEM) in Sweden and thus began our professional collaboration and friendship. I owe Veronika Tarnovskaya and the graduate students I have had the privilege of teaching and mentoring at LUSEM a special debt of gratitude. I suspect I have learned as much from them as they from me.

5 A boss who inspires you. I met Christine in 1991 shortly after I moved from San Francisco to Sweden. She was working for an ad agency in Stockholm that would soon be part of the Interpublic Group (IPG). We hit it off and she hired me to work on the Scandinavian Airlines global account. Christine provided my introduction to international marketing. For the next ten years we worked side-by-side, having a blast and developing the agency's international business until 2001 when I left IPG to start Duffy Agency. Thank you Christine Björner for your faith, friendship and inspiration.

6 An attack helicopter pilot to watch your back. I wrote most of this book in a secluded spot by a lake in northern New Hampshire, USA. I had three adversaries there: the cold, cabin fever and distraction. Aside from providing transport and dropping off fire wood, each day the former Green Beret turned Chief Warrant Officer would check in to see how I was doing. He prefaced our chats with the same question: 'How much have you written since yesterday?' If the page count was not to his liking I got a verbal boot in the ass. Thank you Ekim Yelnoc for your support in writing this book and for four decades covering my six.

7 A family to help you celebrate when you finish. Thank you to Erika, Liam and Ryan for your constant love and support, even when family time became writing time. I love you madly and could not have written this book without you. And boys, not to worry, I haven't forgotten my promise to crack open the kiddie champagne when this is published.

8 You. I'm told no one reads the acknowledgements, so I'd like to acknowledge you for bucking the trend. I've written this book to provide value to you and your company. I don't expect you to agree with every idea, but I invite your feedback and hope you will share your perspective on the topics I raise. Connect with me on LinkedIn to continue the conversation.

This section would not be complete without expressing my gratitude to everyone at Kogan Page for encouraging me to write this book in the first place and for taking this journey with me. Thank you to my clients past and present for your trust and for providing me with the real-life challenges and lessons that I share in this book. I'm thankful to each of the experts I cite in the book and to Professor Sanjay Kumar at Delhi School of Business for sharing their insights. Thanks also to my colleagues at Duffy Agency and TAAN Worldwide for their support, particularly Grant Adams who for the past several months has had the unenviable task of trying to schedule my work in and around my writing.

Notes

1 G James, 20 epic fails in global branding, Inc, 29 October 2014. www.inc.com/geoffrey-james/the-20-worst-brand-translations-of-all-time.html (archived at https://perma.cc/T6SS-TVZ7)

2 Marketing translation mistakes, www.i18nguy.com, undated. www.i18nguy.com/translations.html (archived at https://perma.cc/DAY6-A7NN)

3 TL Friedman, *The World is Flat: A brief history of the twenty-first century*, Farrar, Straus and Giroux, 2005.

4 C Nobel (2011) Clay Christensen's milkshake marketing, Working Knowledge, 14 February 2011. https://hbswk.hbs.edu/item/clay-christensens-milkshake-marketing (archived at https://perma.cc/F7Y5-MKF9)

5   G Castellion and S K Markham, Myths about new product failure rates, *Journal of Product Innovation & Management*, 30, pp 976–79, 25 October 2013. https://newproductsuccess.org/new-product-failure-rates-2013-jpim-30-pp-976-979/ (archived at https://perma.cc/LB9U-WZ43)

6   G Stevens and J Burley, 3,000 raw ideas = 1 commercial success! *Research Technology Management*, 40, pp 16–27, 1997. www.researchgate.net/publication/281980914_3000_Raw_Ideas_1_Commercial_Success (archived at https://perma.cc/BK5P-PLK5)

7   J Schneider and J Hall, Why most product launches fail, *Harvard Business Review*, April 2011. https://hbr.org/2011/04/why-most-product-launches-fail (archived at https://perma.cc/88ZL-HK9A); K Schroeder, Why so many new products fail (and it's not the product), The Business Journals, 14 March 2017. www.bizjournals.com/bizjournals/how-to/marketing/2017/03/why-so-many-new-products-fail-and-it-s-not-the.html (archived at https://perma.cc/6HS3-HGHB); H Umbach, The biggest reason product launches fail, Medium, 24 January 2019. https://medium.com/@heathumbach/the-biggest-reason-product-launches-fail-fb82fe348457 (archived at https://perma.cc/2SHY-WG3A)

8   C Kenton, What, exactly, is a brand? Bloomberg, 15 March 2005. www.bloomberg.com/news/articles/2005-03-14/what-exactly-is-a-brand (archived at https://perma.cc/L5BZ-HFZT)

9   B Kessel, What is a brand? Quora, 17 December 2017. www.quora.com/What-is-a-brand (archived at https://perma.cc/U5E2-NM58)

10 J Bertilsson and V Tarnovskaya (eds), *Brand Theories: Perspectives on brands and branding*, Studentlitteratur, Lund, Sweden, 2017.

11 J Bertilsson and V Tarnovskaya (eds), *Brand Theories: Perspectives on brands and branding*, Studentlitteratur, Lund, Sweden, 2017.

PART ONE: MANAGING MARKET COMPLEXITIES

Introduction

Missing the target

On the morning of 18 March 2013, an exuberant yet slightly haggard young man stood before a small group of hastily gathered reporters in the Devonshire Mall in Windsor, Ontario, Canada. Dressed conspicuously in a tan blazer, red tie and red-and-white striped shirt, he had invited the journalists to show off the new Target department store which, it had just been announced, would open the following day.

Founded in 1962, Target is one of the largest retailers in America, trading on the promise of 'Expect More. Pay Less.' On this particular morning, the retail giant was embarking on its first international venture into neighboring Canada. Leading the charge, and the store tour, was a 38-year-old American named Tony Fisher, Target Canada's CEO.

The first three Canadian stores had opened two weeks earlier. The Windsor store was the fourth of a planned 124 Canadian stores to open over the next nine months. Already, it had been a rocky start for Target, and it showed in Mr Fisher's frenetic replies to the reporters' questions about everything from pricing and selection to empty shelves and unannounced openings.

As Tony Fisher began his tour that morning, something extraordinary happened outside. The temperature in Windsor, already at freezing point, plummeted to −18°C (0°F) in a matter of minutes. If a greater power were trying to give Tony Fisher and his employer a sign, it went unheeded.

Within 14 months, Tony Fisher and the US CEO who hired him would both be fired as a prelude to the announcement on 15 January 2015 that Target would exit Canada altogether. All told, 17,600 employees lost their jobs as Target closed all 133 Canadian locations. According to Canada's *Financial Post*, the misadventure was estimated to have cost Target $5.4 billion CAD ($5.5 billion USD) in pre-tax losses.[1]

Fortune Magazine concluded that 'Target failed to entice shoppers in Canada, a country of 36 million people with a way of life similar to Americans' but with habits different enough to make it a potential minefield for US retailers.'[2] As a primer on why brands fail abroad, Target Canada is a textbook example.

Success as a foregone conclusion

Target's ill-fated launch in Canada has become a staple in any discussion of international marketing. This is partly because of how completely the endeavour failed, but mostly because it was so unexpected.

On paper, Target seemed to have everything in its favour. To start, Target's birthplace and headquarters is in Minneapolis, Minnesota, just 360 kilometres (225 miles) from the Canadian border. It had a 50-year track record of sound business and, specifically, marketing decisions. With annual revenues topping $70 billion USD, Target had grown steadily across the US, becoming the second-largest discount retailer behind Walmart. The company demonstrated a deep understanding of its shoppers and impressive business acumen. With over 1,800 US stores, it was estimated that 75 per cent of the US population lived within 10 miles of a Target. It is understandable that it would consider expanding outside its home market.

Prior to 2011, Target had expressed interest in global expansion. Its main US rival, Walmart, had done so with stores spanning North and South America, Asia, Africa and Europe. Starting in Canada must have seemed like an easy first step for Target.

Target's value proposition of a large selection at low prices seems like it would travel well. And it wasn't as if Canadians needed to be educated about the Target brand. About three-quarters of the entire Canadian population live just 160 kilometres (100 miles) from the US border. As a consequence, almost 10 per cent of the Canadian population were already regular Target shoppers and many more knew of the brand. A survey conducted about eight months before Target's Canadian launch showed that 83 per cent of Canadian shoppers were aware of the Target brand and four in five expressed an interest in shopping there.[3]

It's uncommon for a brand to enter a foreign market with the advantages Target possessed. So how did things wind up going so poorly? The complete list of factors that have been attributed to Target's failure in Canada is extensive. An overview of the top five reasons may give the flavour.

Compromised values

The whole foray seems to have been triggered by a real estate deal. Target had been eying Canada for years, but had rejected the idea of gradually building up stores in Canada. It wanted to enter with a national presence all at once. However, the amount of retail-friendly real estate required to do that in Canada is hard to come by. So when Target was given the opportunity to compete with Walmart in bidding for 220 leases across Canada from Zellers Inc (a failing Canadian discount retailer), it saw a clear opportunity to pursue its international ambitions. Seventeen years earlier, Target's rival Walmart got its start in Canada when it purchased 122 stores from the Woolco division of Woolworth Canada.

Ironically, Zellers also had a similar start in 1931 when it took over the stores of the faltering US retailer Schulte-United. Zellers was more downmarket than Target, but unfortunately had adopted the same red-and-white corporate colour scheme. The Zellers stores were about half the size of Target stores, and many of them were located in areas that bore little resemblance to where Target situated its US stores.[4] Despite all this, on 13 January 2011 Target's CEO Gregg Steinhafel paid CAD $1.825 billion for the leases after Walmart passed on the deal.[5]

Once the leases were purchased, the clock was ticking. Steinhafel had committed the company to opening stores as quickly as possible to avoid paying rent on empty retail space. This resulted in the very ambitious plan to open 124 stores by the end of 2013 and to be profitable within its first year of operations. It took Target almost 20 years to reach 124 stores in the US. In Canada they gave themselves half as many months to do the same.

If there was one decision that sealed Target's fate in Canada, it wasn't that of purchasing the over-priced leases; it was the subsequent decision to, at all costs, avoid paying rent on vacant retail space. That priority overrode Target's core business strategy and brand values, expressed in the company's tag line 'Expect More. Pay Less.' The Target US brand had built enormous success with a single-minded mission: To provide an unequalled discount shopping experience to its guests. In allowing short-term financial goals to eclipse the company's core values in Canada, Target unwittingly neutralized its only competitive advantage there. This is a good example of 'be careful what you wish for': Target got 124 stores open at all costs – a cost that included their customers and business.

Abandoning the corporate mission in pursuit of a financial objective in Canada was a seismic shift in corporate ethos for Target. No one ever came out and said as much, but they didn't need to. It manifested itself in four years of myopic dedication to opening stores no matter what type of shopping experience they offered guests. Although Tony Fisher and others dutifully recounted the corporate line about putting shoppers first, it was clear that their focus was elsewhere – simply getting the stores to a minimally viable state so they could be opened.

Just three weeks after the Canadian launch, Tony Fisher spoke at the Canadian Club in Toronto. His speech provides insight into the organization's priorities in Canada. He said, 'Speed has been at the essence since we started this process because it was important to get stores open as quickly as possible so we could start providing a return on Target's investment.' He went on to say that one consequence of speed was, 'We knew from the beginning we wouldn't be perfect immediately, but our minimum expectation was to be very good.' Mr Fisher admitted that providing a customer experience that was not up to Target's usual standards was hard to get used to, but felt it was the best approach for Canada. Most of his 30-minute speech focused on the operational challenges of opening so many stores in so little time. Fretting over the finer points of shopper experience is a luxury when you're wrestling with the nuts and bolts of building basic supply chain infrastructure.

The moment the Canadian organization prioritized opening stores ahead of delighting customers, the Canadian brand entered new territory veering sharply away from the American brand values and blazing its own path in Canada.

Technical difficulties

Modern retail depends on the interaction of many software systems to ensure an uninterrupted supply chain and positive customer experience. In the US, Target had developed its own proprietary software to order products from vendors, process them through warehouses, and get them onto store shelves in a timely manner. This system had been refined over decades and worked well in the US. But the system was never set up to work internationally. For instance, it was incapable of dealing with different currencies and languages. Given the ambitious deadline, there would not be time to adapt the system, so Target thought it could save time by buying new 'off the shelf' supply chain software for its Canadian operations.

Of course, the system had to be adapted to Target's needs, manually populated with data on 75,000 items, and integrated with all Target's other systems and processes – to say nothing of training. This would have been a challenge under any circumstance, but in this case no one in the organization had experience of using this new software. As a result, many mistakes were made. Product dimensions were entered in the wrong order, so height was mistaken for width or depth. Inches were used, which the system interpreted as centimetres. Items were entered with the wrong currencies, and much information was simply missing altogether. As a result, about 70 per cent of the data in the Canadian system was deemed erroneous compared to the typical 1–2 per cent in the US system.

The operational consequence of these mistakes was a highly dysfunctional supply chain. Joe Castaldo of *Canadian Business* magazine interviewed almost 30 former Target employees after the closure. His article, 'The last days of Target',[6] provides an insightful, behind-the-scenes look at what went wrong. Castaldo summarizes the supply chain woes the company suffered from the moment it tried placing orders through its new supply chain software:

> Items with long lead times coming from overseas were stalled – products weren't fitting into shipping containers as expected, or tariff codes were missing or incomplete. Merchandise that made it to a distribution centre couldn't be processed for shipping to a store. Other items weren't able to fit properly onto store shelves. What appeared to be isolated fires quickly became a raging inferno threatening to destroy the company's supply chain.[7]

Castaldo chronicles how other systems suffered a similar fate. Due to supply chain woes, bare shelves were the norm in Target Canada stores. This shocked consumers and was widely publicized in the press and on social media. At the same time, Target's Canadian distribution centres were overflowing with products to the point where additional warehousing needed to be secured. That's because another software system that controlled forecasting and replenishment of the distribution centres filled them with far more products than were needed. It turned out that this new software required years of historical data to operate properly. Unlike the US stores, the Canadian stores had no historical sales data for the software to effectively run its algorithms.

Yet another system that controlled point-of-sale functions was also purchased having never been adequately vetted or trialled. It too was a disaster. Self-checkout returned the wrong change and the system would frequently freeze or provide the wrong price. Sometimes a transaction would appear to go through, but after the customer had left with their purchases, the payment would fail to process and the entire transaction would be invalidated.

Price perception

Low prices are at the core of Target's offer and the 'Expect More. Pay Less.' promise the brand made to Canadians for two years building up to the 2013 launch. In fairness to Target, it did deliver. Several price surveys found its prices, on average, to be on par with other local discount retailers like Walmart. But the public didn't see it that way.

Target's prices in Canada were noticeably higher than in the US. Since many Canadians shop at Target in the US, they compared prices to the US stores. Given the price disparity, Canadian shoppers concluded that Target had abandoned its low-price promise in Canada. The disappointment of the Canadian shoppers seems to have coloured their view of the Target brand in general. Even though Target's prices were competitive in Canada, consumers perceived the prices to be higher than those of other discount retailers in the Canadian market.

From day one, Target had been hammered by the press and social media on the topic of price. In response, Target's Canadian CEO cited the facts:

> Transportation costs are higher, distribution costs are higher, fuel costs are higher, wage rates vary across the country, the tax rates are different, cost of goods are different, the duties – I think the scale we have here in Canada is quite different from the incredibly different, densely populated US marketplace.[8]

The problem was that you didn't need to open a store in Canada to know these things. Price disparity between the US and Canada and its causes had been an issue in Canada for years. In fact, just a few weeks earlier, Canada's largest daily newspaper had run a story on the topic citing how Canadians felt 'ripped off' by higher retail prices in Canada.[9] The story cites a Bank of Montreal study from 2012, which found that, on average, Canadian retail prices run 14 per cent higher than in the US for many of the reasons Tony Fisher mentioned.

On 30 October 2013, almost eight months after Target's launch in Canada, Tony Fisher and Target's US CEO, Gregg Steinhafel, spoke with analysts in Toronto. They had to account for lower than expected performance and admitted that they were struggling to change consumer behaviour in Canada. Despite consumer outcry, he maintained that Target Canada's prices were competitive with Walmart and didn't need to change. Holly Shaw, a reporter for Canada's *Financial Post*, captured Steinhafel's assessment:

> 'We are right on where we need to be here in Canada,' Mr Steinhafel said, adding that trying to compare prices at Target Canada with that of certain Target stores in the US 'would be like comparing prices in Boston to prices in rural Iowa. There are wide price variances between different US markets, he added. 'We focus on being priced properly in each and every trade area that we operate in, [and] the same approach holds true in Canada.'[10]

What Mr Steinhafel is saying here, essentially, is that the Canadian consumer's price perception problem is illogical and therefore he will continue to follow Target's logical US pricing policy, no matter what. But consumers have their own logic that, right or wrong, dictates their purchase decisions. Marketers need to look beyond their market constructs and assumptions and see the world the way their customers do. This was second nature for Gregg Steinhafel in the US, where he had proven himself adroit at understanding the perspective of the American shopper.

The way that Mr Steinhafel defined 'trade areas' seems based on a top-down, US-centric view of the market. Canadian consumer behaviour dictates their 'shopping areas', which in many instances violate the boundaries of Target's trade areas. Shoppers in Windsor can just drive to the next town, Detroit in the US, to shop in that trade area. That tendency of Canadians to shop outside the lines of Target's preconceived trade zones was recognized by Target's executives. But that recognition was limited to the positive effects that cross-border shopping had on brand awareness and image in Canada. What Target overlooked, at its peril, were the glaring brand-perception challenges that such shoppers would pose for the company were it to venture across the border.

Shaw reports that Target 'did not anticipate consumers would expect the retailer to match its US pricing, leading to some alienation and confusion'. Yet this was not difficult to see in advance. In fact, a report published in the summer of 2012 by the Canadian market research firm Vision Critical flagged the issue outright.[11] Its survey of over 1,000 Canadian consumers found that Target's tagline, 'Expect More. Pay Less.' was fuelling excitement for low prices among 70 per cent of shoppers. The study concluded:

> While two-thirds (65 per cent) of Canadians believe the shopping experience at Target Canada will be comparable to the US, it's paramount that Target be prepared to explain any potential major differences in pricing and promotions to Canadian shoppers to proactively avoid disappointment.[12]

The same company surveyed 1,500 Canadian shoppers in 2015 and found that a whopping 89 per cent of Canadians felt Target failed to deliver on its promise 'Expect more. Pay less.' These types of local consumer insights are not difficult to find, but you have to first see the value in going out and looking for them. You will not find them in typical market analysis reports written from a 10,000-metre (30,000 foot) perspective.

Adapting to the market

Target also seemed to enter Canada determined to change the market rather than adapt to it. It expected Canadian shoppers to conform to its needs with regard to pricing, locations, selection and shopping behaviour.

For instance, Canadian shoppers tend to cherry-pick from the perceived strengths of different stores depending on what they needed to buy. So, they may pick up household staples at Walmart, beauty and healthcare items at Shoppers Drug Mart and groceries at Loblaw.

Seventeen years of prodding from the world's one-stop-shopping leader Walmart had not changed this habit. Yet part of Target's plan was to make itself a one-stop-shopping destination in Canada. About eight months after launch, Mr Fisher explained, 'This requires us to redefine the perception of what a trip to Target means, so we can fundamentally change habits in a market where consumers are accustomed to visiting many other competitors to accomplish all of their shopping.'[13] This is the antithesis of marketing. Expecting foreign buyers to adapt their priorities and behaviour to suit your brand is not realistic. In this case, it's made more absurd because, at that point, Target wasn't offering enough perceived value to move people into their stores, much less move the entire market's shopping behaviour.

The fact that Target said it was struggling to change Canadian shopping habits in the October 2013 analysts meeting is telling. Tony Fisher described how Target's business model was fine-tuned to compete in the American retail environment by adapting itself to the needs and habits of the American shopper. Target entered the Canadian retail environment with this same US-centric business model apparently expecting the Canadian shoppers to adapt to it. The organization said it was surprised to learn that Canadian shoppers expected the same prices as they received in the US when this was, quite literally, public knowledge. Having made the realization, management claimed the fault lay with the Canadian consumer's expectations, not their strategy. At the analyst's meeting, Steinhafel delivered his message in Canada on behalf of a Canadian corporation to a Canadian audience, but did so from an entirely US perspective, right down to his choice of Boston and Iowa as examples. This behaviour is consistent with an organization that has not yet mastered the skill of seeing the world from the perspective of its foreign buyers and then adapting to their perspective.

Nine months after announcing its exit from Canada, Target re-entered the Canadian market in October 2015, this time with a Canadian version of its website to encourage online shopping. The news was met with enthusiasm by Canadians – until they tried to shop on the site. Unlike domestic orders made from the US site, there were stiff shipping charges and duties in Canada. The result is that an item like a $25 CAD blanket cost the Canadian online shopper almost $70 CAD after shipping and duties were added. Predictably, this was met with outrage by the Canadian press and shoppers. The Canadian Broadcasting Corporation ran the headline 'Target now shipping to Canada, but shoppers dismayed by cost'.[14] Ironically, the site's homepage proclaimed 'We Love Canada.' This online shopping experience further reinforced the notion that Target struggled to see the world from the perspective of the Canadian shopper.

Under-estimated competition

When your corporate tag line is 'Expect More. Pay Less.' you create certain expectations on which you need to be prepared to compete. Target was not properly prepared when it came to Canada.

Of course, Target knew it needed to offer low prices and a wide selection. But 'low' and 'wide' are relative terms. 'Low and wide compared to what?' is what a marketer should ask. And the only person whose answer matters is the consumer's.

Target Canada was the victim of fierce competition against one of the world's most savvy marketers. Had Target questioned its own assumptions about the market and invested more time in understanding the Canadian consumer, then it could have easily identified the competitive challenges that ultimately led to its demise and created strategies to deal with them.

The savvy competitor that Target Canada never acknowledged was not Walmart. It was Target US. From the start, Canadian consumers were not comparing Target's prices to other local discount retailers. They were comparing Target's prices to Target's own prices across the border. That, combined with the chain's core promise 'Expect More. Pay Less.', created a price expectation that Target simply was not able to meet in Canada.

On 26 March 2013, when asked about price disparities with Target US, Mr Fisher replied, 'I still work for Target, we are not trying to compete with ourselves – we want to come in and compete with the retail landscape here.'[15] No doubt that is what Target wanted to do, but this fails to take into account the perspective of the local target audience. Despite what Target wanted, Canadian shoppers *did* see Target competing directly with itself. The failure to recognize this and other differences between US and Canadian consumers put Target at odds with its customers.

In several interviews, Target Canada's CEO would remind us that 'I work for Target…' and then describe the situation from that perspective. That mindset, on its own, accounts for a lot of Target's poor decisions in Canada. As he presented the new Windsor store to reporters on that chilly March morning in 2013, something Tony Fisher said stuck with me. When asked if it mattered to him whether shoppers visited this new store or hopped over the border to shop at Target in the US he replied, 'This is nothing against the Windsor market, but I work for Target, and I think for me whether they shop in our Target US stores or Target Canadian stores, it's all Target to me.'[16]

It should have mattered to him because it obviously mattered to his shoppers. In the final analysis, Target was competing with itself and lost.

What can we learn from this?

Tony Fisher and Gregg Steinhafel were two of the brightest stars at one of the most successful companies in history. They were both accomplished, world-class retailers who got themselves into an impossible situation. Target's Canadian adventure has been cited as a textbook case of how not to enter a foreign market. But I see it as a cautionary tale of how sharp marketers who are skilled, experienced and successful in their home market can go off the rails making rookie mistakes when they venture abroad – even to a neighbouring market with a common language. In the case of Target this was writ large, but I see this same scenario played out every day by equally brilliant marketers as they take businesses large and small across borders.

Hindsight is 20/20, but even so, some of the mistakes Target made would be obvious to a first-semester Master of Business Administration candidate. For perspective, let's go back to 2011 and imagine that

Tony Fisher and Gregg Steinhafel were having a friendly lunch with an executive from a Canadian retail brand that wanted to launch in the US. Assuming they wished her well, would Fisher or Steinhafel condone the Canadian executive's plan to:

- Pay almost $2 billion for sites that were not quite on-brand?
- Commit to open 124 stores in under nine months – an unprecedented launch schedule that no one believed in?
- Put someone in charge who was extremely capable but had no experience in the local market and never opened a single store from scratch on their own, no less 124 at once?
- Decide to keep to the original schedule even after it was discovered that none of the systems that actually run the stores could be functional in time for opening?
- Dissuade shoppers from crossing the border with the promise of 'Expect more. Pay less.' and then provide less selection and higher prices?
- Decide to open stores with empty shelves knowing that they would offer shoppers a truly disappointing, social-media-rant-inducing brand experience?
- Re-enter the market with an online shopping site that proclaimed, 'We Love USA' with prices that were 280 per cent higher than prices they would find in the US bricks-and-mortar shops?

I think we can safely assume the answer to most, if not all, of the questions above would be a resounding 'No.' No prudent marketer would do any of these things, especially a marketing organization as skilled as Target. Likewise, I doubt that Tony Fisher or Gregg Steinhafel would ever have made these types of blunders in their home market. Which leaves us with a question: Why did these two extremely talented executives do all of the above in Canada?

I hope the answer to this question will present itself throughout the course of this book. But the takeaway here is that if it could happen to Tony Fisher and Target it could happen to you and your brand.

Preparing for departure

Whether your brand is about to enter a new foreign market or is under-performing abroad, this book will help you. In Part One, we explore how experiences in your home market can blind you to threats and opportunities in new markets and how to adjust your vision for success. It will provide you with insights and a practical framework to help you plan your entry into foreign markets.

Part One addresses the most persistent challenges I see facing companies when marketing abroad. They persist because they are deceptive in their appearance. Adequate preparation, research and planning are things business people do every day. In the case of international marketing, however, these terms belie a level of complexity that most domestic marketers are not prepared, or willing, to embrace. But embrace we must, and the first part of this book will provide some practical advice to deal with that complexity and succeed.

We started the book with the case of US retail giant Target and their ill-fated foray into Canada. This provides a textbook example of how badly things can go wrong – even when you are not taking your brand that far from home. I use Target Canada as a reference case study throughout Part One of this book.

Part One overview

How can we prevent the types of problems that led Target astray in Canada? The easy answer is better preparation. In Chapter 1 I explore the paradox of why smart, skilled marketers consistently make rookie mistakes when they leave their home markets. This is a persistent problem. I take the time to define its roots so that you, as a smart person yourself, might avoid the calamitous mistakes made by so many smart marketers before you.

How is marketing internationally any different from marketing domestically? It's difficult to appreciate the extent to which foreign markets are different from our home market. Our view of foreign markets is skewed by assumptions formed at home. This can obscure obstacles and opportunities alike. In Chapter 2 I list seven of the most relevant differences between marketing domestically and internationally that marketers need to be mindful of when venturing abroad.

What can you do now to mitigate risk and avoid the pitfalls of marketing abroad? We've already identified poor planning as a problem. I don't believe any marketer purposely enters a market unprepared. It's more likely they have the wrong idea about what proper planning looks like. To reduce the ambiguity, in Chapter 3 I discuss the risks involved in entering a foreign market and what a plan to mitigate them look like.

A key decision will be how you organize to succeed abroad. Should you manage things from headquarters? Should you let the local team call the shots? The answer for most companies lies somewhere in between. In Chapter 4, we'll explore different approaches so you can find the set-up that works best for your brand.

How will your brand be understood in foreign markets? Just as important, how well will you understand the market? One of the most obvious differences between foreign markets is language. Adapting your marketing communication to the local language is important. That will get your message understood. Far more challenging is adapting to the local culture. That will get your message believed and trusted. In Chapter 5 and 6 I deal with the dual challenges of working with foreign languages and cultures.

How will you know if you are ready to launch abroad? In Chapter 7 we'll end Part One with some final tips on how to prepare for success. This includes the Eight Inputs Model, which breaks down the elements that shape the marketing mix.

To begin, then, in Chapter 1 I will explore why international marketing makes us more vulnerable to failure and what you can do to ensure success.

Notes

1. Financial Post Staff, Target Corp: A timeline of the retailer's failed Canadian experiment, *Financial Post*, 15 January 2015. https://financialpost.com/news/retail-marketing/target-corp-a-timeline-of-the-retailers-failed-canadian-experiment (archived at https://perma.cc/A2U2-AKCX)
2. P Wahba, Why Target failed in Canada, Fortune, 15 January 2015. https://fortune.com/2015/01/15/target-canada-fail/ (archived at https://perma.cc/ZRH5-C3TG)
3. D St Louis, Canadians look forward to Target, if price is right, Vision Critical, undated. www.visioncritical.com/news-events/canadians-look-forward-target-if-price-right (archived at https://perma.cc/MUZ3-KM99)
4. I Austen, Target push into Canada stumbles, *The New York Times*, 25 February 2014. www.nytimes.com/2014/02/25/business/international/target-struggles-to-compete-in-canada.html?_r=0 (archived at https://perma.cc/39FM-CBUC)
5. J Tilak, Update: 2-Target to enter Canada with Zellers deal, own plans, Reuters, 13 January 2011. www.reuters.com/article/target-canada/update-2-target-to-enter-canada-with-zellers-deal-own-plans-idUSN1326316220110113 (archived at https://perma.cc/NV5M-X3YG)
6. J Castaldo, The last days of Target: The untold tale of target Canada's difficult birth, tough life and brutal death, Canadian Business, undated. www.canadianbusiness.com/the-last-days-of-target-canada/ (archived at https://perma.cc/29N6-4UJN)
7. J Castaldo, The last days of Target: The untold tale of target Canada's difficult birth, tough life and brutal death, Canadian Business, undated. www.canadianbusiness.com/the-last-days-of-target-canada/ (archived at https://perma.cc/29N6-4UJN)
8. H Shaw, 'Quite different' markets: Target Canada president addresses price gap with US, *Financial Post*, 26 March 2013. https://financialpost.com/news/retail-marketing/quite-different-markets-target-canada-president-addresses-price-gap-with-u-s (archived at https://perma.cc/7MYU-7GZM)
9. D Flavelle, Here's why things cost more here than in the US, *The Star*, 6 February 2013. www.thestar.com/business/personal_finance/2013/02/06/canadaus_price_gap_senate_report_due_today.html (archived at https://perma.cc/G7Z9-45HG)
10. H Shaw, Target Canada still plagued by price perception problems as sales fail to meet expectations, *Financial Post*, 30 October 2013. https://financialpost.com/news/retail-marketing/target-canada-still-plagued-by-price-perception-problems-as-sales-fail-to-meet-expectations (archived at https://perma.cc/9DAD-G9CQ)

11 D St Louis, Canadians look forward to Target, if price is right, Vision Critical, undated. http://webcache.googleusercontent.com/search?q=cache:https://www.visioncritical.com/news-events/canadians-look-forward-target-if-price-right (archived at https://perma.cc/53CH-VZ6P)

12 D St Louis, Canadians look forward to Target, if price is right, Vision Critical, undated. http://webcache.googleusercontent.com/search?q=cache:https://www.visioncritical.com/news-events/canadians-look-forward-target-if-price-right (archived at https://perma.cc/46Q9-E8HD)

13 H Shaw, Target Canada still plagued by price perception problems as sales fail to meet expectations, *Financial Post*, 30 October 2013. https://financialpost.com/news/retail-marketing/target-canada-still-plagued-by-price-perception-problems-as-sales-fail-to-meet-expectations (archived at https://perma.cc/9DAD-G9CQ)

14 S Harris, Target now shipping to Canada, but shoppers dismayed by cost, CBC, 22 October 2015. www.cbc.ca/news/business/target-canada-online-sales-1.3282848 (archived at https://perma.cc/7Z67-JUTK)

15 Canadian Club of Toronto, Tony Fisher, President, Target Canada [Audio], 2013. www.mixcloud.com/canadiancluboftoronto/tony-fisher-president-target-canada/ (archived at https://perma.cc/64YB-554H)

16 CBC News, Target won't entice cross-border shoppers to stay home, CBC News, 18 March 2013. www.cbc.ca/news/canada/windsor/target-won-t-entice-cross-border-shoppers-to-stay-home-1.1317162 (archived at https://perma.cc/6UCW-QGXT)

01

Why brands fail abroad

The importance of knowing what you don't know

Anyone who's spent sufficient time with a five-year-old can attest that sometimes it's the most obvious questions that prove the most difficult to answer, like 'What is time?' or 'Why is darkness black?' In 2010 I was asked such a question that led me down a path of discovery that I share in this chapter.

I had been invited to guest-lecture and mentor at the Master's programme in Entrepreneurship and Innovation run by the Lund University School of Economics & Management in Sweden. It is one of Europe's top entrepreneurship programmes and attracts students from all over the world. I find this work particularly rewarding because of the calibre of students enrolled and the innovative ideas that each brings to the programme. In one of my very first lectures on international brand management, a young entrepreneur asked me, 'Why do brands fail abroad?' We discussed several studies that cited things like insufficient awareness, lacklustre marketing, poor planning, misguided assumptions, failure to understand the target audience, poor project management, inadequate funding… the list goes on.

'But those are the same reasons that marketing initiatives fail domestically,' she said. 'What reasons are specific to international?'

I answered with a question: 'Don't you think that dealing with a different buyer in a different culture in a different language could be the reason?'

'No,' she replied. 'I see how that would require extra competencies to manage, but marketers are always faced with new segments of the population that they need to understand, and they have the tools to do so. Language and culture are known quantities. I can't see how they would pose a significant obstacle.'

She was correct. I felt that I should be able to answer her question directly. But I couldn't. None of the studies or citations I had prepared could provide a satisfactory explanation. Having gone as far as my professorial skills could take me, I replied as a practitioner.

'Here I can only offer a reflection, although it is based on decades of direct observation. Yes, brands fail abroad for exactly the same reasons they fail domestically but there is one glaring difference. The people who make those mistakes.'

I explained how novice or unskilled marketers might be expected to make more mistakes whether marketing at home or abroad and even the most skilled marketer is bound to make mistakes from time to time, regardless of the market. But what was less explicable were the skilled marketers I had seen making mistakes in foreign markets that I simply couldn't see them making in their home market, the case of Target in Canada being a good example. That was a mystery. So, yes, language and cultural factors are novel obstacles when entering a foreign market but they are knowable, and a skilled marketer surely has ample tools and methods to navigate them successfully. Which led us to the obvious follow-up question, 'Then, why don't they?'

I wasn't able to answer that question in class, but I'd like to try here. This chapter will explore why international marketing makes us so vulnerable to failure and how we might avoid it.

The nature of foreign markets

Launching a brand in any market is a complex endeavour with a lot of interdependent moving parts. It's not surprising that it can fail. What is surprising is the rate of failure. Domestically, about half of all new product launches fail.[1] Those odds are not reassuring although they are a lot better than the 95 per cent failure rate often wrongly ascribed to Clayton Christensen of The Harvard Business School.[2] In any event, it's clear that launching a brand in your home market is a risky proposition.

Now consider launching in a foreign market. Even if your product and brand have been sold domestically for years, it will be a new product and brand in the country you are entering. So, presumably you will face many of the same challenges as a domestic launch, with the addition of things like language, culture, logistics, regulations, etc. Each new variable introduces more risk, but, as my student pointed out, these additional variables are not beyond the realm of knowledge. They can be predicted, studied and managed.

Cases like Target are easy to write off as extreme examples of incompetence. In fact, any competent marketer who reads them could be forgiven for feeling immune to such calamity. But the staggering failure rate of new business ventures would suggest otherwise. The reason we feel immune is because hindsight affords us a clear view of all the obstacles. This raises a question: How is it that otherwise highly capable business people, like Target's ex-CEO Gregg Steinhafel, so often do not see these towering obstacles and navigate around them?

To answer this, it's worth taking some time to understand the source of failure and what we can do to avoid becoming one more data point in the grim statistics of international marketing.

The nature of failure

To understand the nature and causes of failure, take 20 minutes to read 'Toward a theory of medical fallibility.'[3] In this paper from 1975, philosophers Samuel Gorovitz and Alasdair MacIntyre explore the fundamental nature of failure framed in human fallibility. They make the point that there are limits to what we know on a given subject. We can't know everything. What we do know, however, allows us to attempt things like predicting the weather, repairing a heart valve, or building brand equity in a foreign market. The paper offers a premise that in such endeavours, all failure can be boiled down to two factors: ignorance and ineptitude.

Ignorance is the condition where the knowledge required to succeed in the endeavour simply does not yet exist. It is beyond our ability to know. Ineptitude is when the knowledge does exist but we fail to use it. The gist of their argument is captured in the quote below. If you replace the word 'science' with 'international marketing' you'll get the point:

> Predictive failure in science can only have two sources: factual ignorance as to the relevant laws or as to just which properties are present in a situation; or inferential error, such as when conclusions are drawn carelessly from the laws and descriptions of properties. Thus, where we are not ignorant, any inadequacy in our predictive powers must be attributed to the predictor, to his willfulness or his negligence.[4]

Gorovitz and MacIntyre's paper was featured in Atul Gawande's book *The Checklist Manifesto*.[5] It is a book about failure written by a surgeon whose resume has to qualify him as one of the most successful humans on Earth. Gawande took Gorovitz and MacIntyre's insights and applied them to medicine and commerce. He maintains that the volume and complexity of what we know today has surpassed our ability to use the information at our disposal. In other words, ineptitude has surpassed ignorance as the driver of failure. His research concluded that the use of checklists dramatically reduces failure in complex endeavours. Launching your brand in a foreign market would surely qualify as a complex endeavour and so would benefit from the use of checklists. But checklists can only work where there is a) willingness to use them and b) agreement on what a quality outcome looks like and what standard operating procedures are best to achieve it.

The nature of marketing

So, it seems that having standards for outcomes and procedures to achieve those outcomes could be an important part of the puzzle. If we had them, then we could create checklists to ensure we are working to a standard. Both Gorovitz and MacIntyre's paper and Gawande's book draw on examples from disciplines where there is an organized body of knowledge, established standards, and professional practitioners. This forms the foundation from which checklists can be created and implemented.

Unfortunately, marketing lacks this foundation because marketing is not a profession. 'Profession' has a real meaning beyond any group of people who have similar job titles. If we look at the characteristics of a profession, it is clear to see that marketing does not make the grade. Those characteristics are:

- rigorous academic training
- exclusionary vetting process
- licensed practitioners
- common body of knowledge
- unified vocabulary
- unified best practices
- common ethical guidelines
- reasonably unified job descriptions
- professional governance

We recognize these characteristics as the hallmarks of fields like medicine, law, accounting and civil engineering but, collectively, marketing practitioners can claim few of them, if any. Based on that, I'd maintain that we are surely a business discipline, but not a profession.[6]

In the case of civil engineers, for example, we expect that they work in accordance with a common body of engineering knowledge and are skilled at the application of that knowledge in adherence with the laws of physics and material science as well as accepted best practices. We expect they share common underlying principles, a body of accepted research and have a coherent professional vocabulary. We also expect that if an overpass fails, an objective investigation will take place and be shared, so that the profession as a whole improves and failure rates decline over time. We would expect the same from lawyers, pilots, surgeons and accountants. The same cannot be expected of marketers.

That's not to say that there are no highly skilled marketers. There are plenty, and you may be one of them yourself. But not having the infrastructure of a true profession to support you makes achieving excellence that much harder. Marketing has its gurus, research and common practices, but it lacks uniformity of standards and best practices, which makes it tough for those who practise it. As a result, many marketers are forced to make it up as they go along. Although they use many of the same terms (brand, mission, value, position, etc), there is wild variation in how these terms are defined and applied to operations. Even as a discipline, marketing itself is defined differently from one company to the next. This all helps explain why failure rates in the 80 to 90 per cent range have been the norm for decades, without much sign of improvement. It also throws a huge wild card into the equation with regard to our ability to predict the success or failure of an international marketing endeavour.

Gorovitz and MacIntyre's paper makes it incumbent upon the practitioner to be aware of all that is known relative to the topic they are working with, or at least to be aware of, the most recent findings. Failure to do so would be considered incompetence. This is not impossible for marketers, but surely it is more difficult to achieve widespread awareness of, and access to, knowledge outside the knowledge transfer infrastructure afforded by a profession.

To overcome this, you can create a micro-profession within your organization. Define your marketing ecosystem (eg your workgroup, department, or if you are really ambitious, your entire company) and then create a common set of standards, a body of knowledge, vocabulary, ethics, etc. This is not a new idea. Forward-thinking marketers like P&G, Kellogg's, Unilever, etc, have been doing this for decades. Having helped create these micro-professions for several clients, I've seen the positive difference it makes. Once in place, preventative measures like checklists, post-mortem analysis and knowledge sharing can be employed to reduce the risk posed by ineptitude. This feudalistic approach to marketing professionalism surely is not ideal, as it leaves gaps among the different micro-professions, but it is a pragmatic place to start.

The nature of competence

Since we've zeroed in on Gawande's definition of ineptitude as the main cause of failure, it's worth noting that its opposite, competence, is not a binary concept but seems to exist along a scale. This scale was defined in 1969 by management trainer Martin Broadwell. He called his model 'the four levels of teaching'. Over the next decade his ideas were refined by Noel Burch of Gordon Training International (GTI) into what has also become known as 'the four stages of competence.'[7] I find these stages relevant because I see them played out so often working with many different individuals on international marketing initiatives. These phases are:

1 **Unconscious incompetence**

    We don't know what we don't know. At this level we are inept, as Gorovitz and MacIntyre define it, yet unaware of it. As a result, we don't recognize our lack of knowledge or skill as a deficit. If we are made aware of it, we may deny the usefulness of that skill or knowledge. To move on from here we must recognize both our own limitations and the value of the new skill or knowledge.

2 **Conscious incompetence**

    Here we still do not possess the skill or knowledge but at least we see that as a problem. Recognizing both our own limitations and the value of the new skill or knowledge at this level makes us receptive to learning.

3 **Conscious competence**

    Here we have acquired the new skill or knowledge and understand its value but are not yet proficient in its use. Checklists are particularly useful here.

4 **Unconscious competence**

    With enough practice, we reach a state where the knowledge or skill is second nature and we employ it without even thinking about it. Also known as fluency, it's at this level that we can start teaching others.

In my experience, I have found unconscious incompetence to be the biggest contributor to failed international marketing efforts. Fortunately, it's also one of the easiest to solve if it is recognized. The problem is that most leadership teams don't see that they have a blind spot. And the worst offenders in this regard can be the marketers who have achieved the most success domestically. They have strong marketing skills developed in their home market but they fail to appreciate the differences in the foreign market. These marketers struggle when strategies and tactics that have worked so well at home don't produce the same results abroad. As we explore several cases in this book, I think you may recognize this type of marketer, found across all different types of brands and sizes of companies. The hardest part for any company is transitioning from unconscious incompetence to conscious incompetence, where they accept that they have a marketing blind spot and are receptive to solutions. For someone leading an international marketing initiative, once they get to the conscious incompetence phase, they don't necessarily need to strive for unconscious competence. They can save time and effort by simply hiring someone who has reached that level. For international marketers, achieving conscious incompetence begins with accepting two foundational assumptions:

- Marketing internationally is a discipline, related to, but different enough from, marketing at home that it warrants international marketing expertise. I make the case for how they are different in Chapter 2.
- Foreign buyers are always different from one's domestic buyers, no matter how similar they may seem on the surface; therefore, you need to possess the requisite skills and resources in order to acquire a deep understanding of those buyers, or to find someone who can help you.

Adopting these two statements as truth, or at least as working hypotheses, will not resolve all the challenges you will face marketing internationally, but without them it is difficult to see how you could succeed.

The nature of knowledge asymmetry

Related to all of the above is the notion of knowledge asymmetry. Richard Barker from the University of Oxford's Said Business School tackled this issue in terms of management in general. He says that a generally accepted and relatively permanent knowledge asymmetry is the mark of the true profession. That is, people accept that you know more about a certain topic than they do and therefore trust your advice at face value. He also emphasizes the importance of a common body of knowledge as being at the crux of professionalism:

> If physicians cannot agree on how the human body functions, or lawyers on the nature of a contract, no discrete body of knowledge can be said to exist. The boundaries and consensus for any profession will evolve over time, but at any given moment they can be defined – which is what enables formal training and certification. Certification signals competence to consumers who would benefit from it.[8]

Recognizing a knowledge asymmetry is required for you to appreciate the value that people with skills other than your own can offer and thus include them in your team. An easy example of this is a translator. Most marketers can easily appreciate the knowledge asymmetry with regard to foreign language skills. As a result, they make an effort to fill this blind spot with someone who is qualified to translate their message into the target language (we will address translation at length in Chapter 6). In fact, novice international marketers often believe that translation is the only exogenous skill they need to succeed in international markets. If you share that belief now, then I hope I am able to move you to a higher level of competence over the course of this book.

The nature of assumptions

When approaching a new market, you are essentially an entrepreneur starting up a new business. This is true even if your company has been in business in your home market for decades. It helps, therefore, to adopt the mindset of an entrepreneur. The seminal attribute of such a mindset is being able to spot assumptions within a business strategy and question them. This is a valuable skill because, for the most part, we are blind to the myriad assumptions we make each day.

Assumptions are ideas that are accepted and acted upon as truth in the absence of evidence. In fact, they often seem so self-evident that it wouldn't even occur to us to seek evidence in support of them. For instance, I drive over a highway overpass assuming it can withstand the weight of my car. I do this routinely with no objective data on the structural integrity of the overpass in question. I assume it will not crumble beneath me because it looks like thousands of other overpasses I have crossed without incident. I make that assumption even though the consequences if I'm wrong are quite dire. The fact is, we make hundreds of decisions each day, some noteworthy, most trivial, and almost all unconsciously based on assumptions. It's a sort of mental shorthand that helps us get on with things. If we were to require proof for each decision, we would be immobilized.

For better or worse, making assumptions is an essential part of the human condition. When we say a business person has 'good instincts' we are saying that they are adroit at making assumptions. On the other hand, assumptions can be incredibly corrosive to society, as in the case of unfounded bias or discrimination against people who seem different from us for whatever reason.

The problem with assumptions in marketing is that we make them automatically based on our previous experience and enabled by our unconscious incompetence. In most cases, experience gained in one market will never be 100 per cent transferable to another market. That is, success in market A does not guarantee success in market B. That's why if there is one habit to develop as an international marketer, it is humility. Accepting that each new market presents a novel challenge will help you ruthlessly question your assumptions and take nothing for granted when developing your entry strategy. Despite your best efforts in this regard, even successful strategies can have some false assumptions. The idea is to minimize the number of false assumptions so they don't accumulate to a tipping point where they can tank the project.

When executives develop marketing strategies, they tend to gather the facts on the situation that they feel are most pertinent based on their experience, and then identify gaps. The gaps are filled with facts from the market. The leader then combines what they feel are the pertinent facts (that for which they have proof) with assumptions (that which they treat as fact without proof) to create a coherent and actionable narrative that can be shared.

In this scenario, everything that is not identified as a fact is an assumption. Strategies are basically dozens of proof points bound together by thousands of assumptions. It's the assumptions that serve as the glue to connect the facts and produce the 'full picture' of the situation. The resulting picture appears complete, but the accuracy of that picture is dependent on the validity of the untested assumptions that are woven through it. If the person making the decisions about a foreign market is not experienced in that market (or international marketing in general), then their assumptions are essentially being drawn from the wrong experience base. The resulting strategy is bound to be riddled with false assumptions that can create a very distorted view of the market. In the case of Target Canada, the 'full picture' of the launch included assumptions that both customers and the supply chain software would behave as they do in the US.

As I mentioned, all the assumptions in a strategy are never 100 per cent correct, but an effort should be made to keep them in check. Additionally, some assumptions are more important than others. If one or two key assumptions are off, or enough of the supporting assumptions are wrong, then failure is likely. For this reason, successful international marketers tend to assume less and thereby see more gaps in their understanding of a market. They have passed the first level of international marketing competence and, at least, know what they don't know. These marketers employ a process to identify, list and weigh the importance of the assumptions in their plan. Then they assess their confidence level in each key assumption to determine which require validation. These marketers tend to see more value in research and discovery at the project outset. This has direct time and cost implications for the project so they plan and budget accordingly.

A marketer with this level of competence can reduce the risk of entering a foreign market if the project sponsors share his level of competence. Unconscious incompetence among project sponsors expresses itself in a reluctance to provide the time, budget, or resources to perform the research and discovery required. They simply can't see the value in it, so they neglect to include it in the project timeline or budget. By the time someone with international marketing competence is called in to help, the project's own parameters, now etched in stone, work against their success. They will lack the mandate, time and budget to adequately test assumptions and gain the local insights required to succeed. In other words, failure is baked into the plan.

Conclusion

Brands fail abroad for many of the same reasons they fail domestically. Lack of target insight, poor planning, false assumptions and all the other maladies of weak marketing can doom domestic and international marketing efforts alike. The real question is, how is it that folks who have mastered these skills in their home market can fail like Target did when they go abroad? From a practitioner's perspective, I've seen that even highly skilled domestic marketers can make rookie mistakes when venturing abroad. This most often occurs when they fail to recognize international marketing as a special case requiring additional skill and expertise, and when they fail to respect the differences that are inherent in every new market they enter, even when they are not readily apparent.

If Broadwell and Burch are correct, it would seem that ineptitude in international marketing is a normal starting point for any marketer. We all start at a level where we don't know what we don't know. But we can learn. The determinants of success in a foreign market are completely within our control. However, learning requires that we move on from a state of unconscious incompetence. Once we do that, we'll also need to educate our project sponsors or find new ones. The fact that you are reading this book is an indicator that you are well on your way down this path. Next, in Chapter 2, I explore some of the key differences between marketing at home and abroad, and offer eight tips you can use to adapt.

Notes

1. G Stevens and J Burley, 3,000 raw ideas = 1 commercial success! *Research Technology Management*, 40, pp 16–27, 1997. www.researchgate.net/publication/281980914_3000_Raw_Ideas_1_Commercial_Success (archived at https://perma.cc/6HQP-LURC)
2. C Nobel, Clay Christensen's milkshake marketing, Harvard Business School Working Knowledge, 14 February 2011. https://hbswk.hbs.edu/item/clay-christensens-milkshake-marketing (archived at https://perma.cc/D5YV-J9GQ)
3. S Gorovitz and A MacIntyre, Toward a theory of medical fallibility, *The Hastings Center Report*, 5 (6), pp 13–23, December 1975. www.jstor.org/stable/3560992 (archived at https://perma.cc/X8VG-F5AQ)
4. S Gorovitz and A MacIntyre, Toward a theory of medical fallibility, *The Hastings Center Report*, 5 (6), pp 13–23, December 1975. www.jstor.org/stable/3560992 (archived at https://perma.cc/X8VG-F5AQ)
5. A Gawande, *The Checklist Manifesto: How to get things right*, Metropolitan Books, New York, 2010.
6. S Duffy, Sorry, you are not a marketing professional (and neither am I), Talent Zoo, 26 July 2010. www.talentzoo.com/news/Sorry,-You-Are-Not-a-Marketing-Professional-and-Neither-Am-I/7931.html (archived at https://perma.cc/JJJ3-8QAS)
7. J Flower, In the mush, *Physician Exec*, 25 (1), pp 64–66, 1999. https://pubmed.ncbi.nlm.nih.gov/10387273/ (archived at https://perma.cc/5BQT-JV73)
8. R Barker, The big idea: No, management is not a profession, *Harvard Business Review*, July–August 2010. https://hbr.org/2010/07/the-big-idea-no-management-is-not-a-profession (archived at https://perma.cc/5B2F-WWF5)

02

Domestic vs international marketing

The difference between marketing domestically and abroad

In Quentin Tarantino's World War II film *Inglourious Basterds*, a British spy disguised as a German army officer finds himself in a tavern behind German lines. A real German Major takes notice of him and sits at the spy's table. The Major grills him with a series of questions to ensure he is who he says he is. The British spy has studied German culture well and has all the right answers. The German Major seems satisfied, and the spy is relieved. A second later the spy is discovered when he orders a round of drinks for the table saying '*Drei Gläser*' (three glasses) to the bartender. His German is flawless. What gives him away is that he gestures 'three' by holding up his index, middle, and ring finger. A German would have held up his thumb, index, and middle finger. The Major reacts immediately with a drawn pistol, concluding he is an imposter. When trying to ingratiate into a new market, little things mean a lot.

If it's the first time you are taking a brand abroad, you may feel that your biggest challenge will be translation. That's understandable. Language is the most obvious difference between countries, and getting it right is absolutely essential. That can be tricky, but with the right process in place and team supporting you, translation can be solved. And once you solve it, you will wish that all the challenges facing you as an international marketer could be dispatched as easily.

Beyond language, there are a number of more subtle differences that threaten to disrupt your brand's smooth assimilation into the new market – although some people maintain that these differences between cultures are going away. This may be true, but I doubt you will see it in your lifetime. I'm fairly confident that when the first stone-age mariner struck out to sea in a dugout canoe, a stone-age pundit observing on the beach heralded the arrival of the global village. In more recent history, the term has been popularized by Marshall McLuhan in his 1962 book *The Gutenberg Galaxy: The making of typographic man*.[1] He cited the spread of global media as the unifying force. In 1983 Theodore Levitt published the article 'The globalization of markets',[2] asserting that the world was racing towards a state of complete homogenization propelled by technology combined with economies of scale and the universal desire for quality goods at a cheap price. 'The earth is round,' Levitt said, 'but for most purposes it's sensible to treat it as flat.' In 2005 political commentator and three-time Pulitzer Prize winner Thomas Friedman published *The World is Flat: A brief history of the twenty-first century*.[3] His reasoning was not far off from Levitt's but, of course, by 2005 he could add developments like the internet, collaboration software, and offshoring to support his argument. The book was popular with the public but, as with Levitt's article, drew its fair share of well-supported criticism.

One vocal critic of Levitt and Friedman has been economist Pankaj Ghemawat. With articles like 'Distance still matters: The hard reality of global expansion'[4] and 'Why the world isn't flat',[5] Ghemawat feels the case for global interaction and homogenization has been grossly overstated. He maintains that, although transportation and technology have made geographic distance more manageable, there are still significant cultural, administrative, political and economic divisions that have yet to be unified.

My own take on globalization is more in line with Ghemawat's. I agree that the growing interconnectedness of national economies, innovation in communication, advances in technology, and ease of transportation are flattening traditional economic barriers. I also agree that those developments have some effect on a societal level. When you adopt the broad view, it would seem that many of the tools required to dismantle cultural differences are in place. However, in marketing, as in physics, when you get to a culture's quantum level, the level of individuals, the standard models don't always apply. The differences between cultures become apparent when working with the quirky mental stew of beliefs, perceptions, identity, influences, attitudes, traditions, needs and motivations that define market segments. These differences are real, affect marketing outcomes, and should be addressed by your foreign marketing programme.

The risk posed by these differences can be mitigated with a little preparation on your part. In this chapter I discuss how cultural differences affect marketing strategy and suggest ways that you can manage these differences to your brand's advantage.

The role of marketing

Allow me to begin with one thing that doesn't change. The marketing function should be the same whether you market domestically or internationally. However, the role and responsibilities of the marketing department can differ quite significantly from one organization to the next. They can even be defined differently among individuals in the same organization. To avoid confusion at the outset of your international expansion, it helps to arrive at a common definition of marketing and the purpose it serves. To avoid any ambiguity here, I provide a definition of the role of marketing as it is used in this book.

The marketing department makes three fundamental contributions to the business, as shown in Figure 2.1. They can sometimes pull in opposite directions so it is important to find the right balance between these three objectives:

- **Sales: Increases the probability of sales today**
  This is an obvious objective – so much so that it can foster a very limited, short-term view of markets and the opportunity they hold. Of course, short-term sales revenue is vitally important since, for many businesses, it dictates cash flow and keeps the lights burning. But if business owners want sustained long-term profit and value in the business, then more is needed.

FIGURE 2.1 Marketing Contribution Model

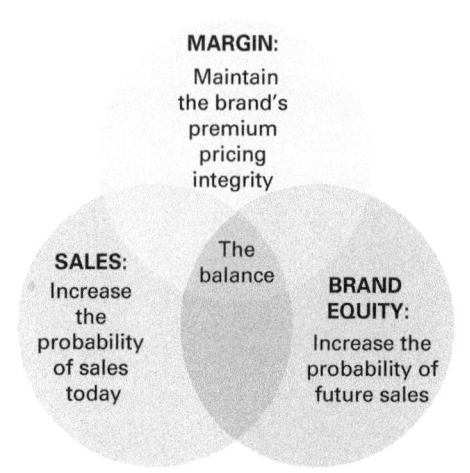

MARGIN: Maintain the brand's premium pricing integrity

SALES: Increase the probability of sales today

The balance

BRAND EQUITY: Increase the probability of future sales

The goal: sales, margin, *and* brand equity

- **Margin: Maintains premium-pricing integrity**
  The ability to maintain premium-pricing integrity is also known as pricing power. Warren Buffett identified pricing power as the single most important factor in evaluating the health of a business. That's because the ability to sustain small increases in price can yield far more profit than moderate gains in volume or reductions in cost. See more on this in Chapter 12.

- **Brand equity: Increases the probability of future sales**
  Compared to sales and margin, brand equity can seem less concrete. It is the sum of how much awareness, understanding, interest, trust, trial, belief, affinity, loyalty and advocacy a brand has among a defined segment in a particular market. Chapter 11 defines this concept in detail. Its function is to ensure long-term growth and profitability.

Accomplishing this balancing act requires the coordination of all aspects of the business, so close collaboration with the CEO and the rest of the leadership team is imperative for success. Many companies limit the role of their marketing department to promotion only, leaving the rest of the marketing mix (product, price and place) to other departments. To get the most return from marketing efforts, all four aspects of the marketing mix should be coordinated. For this reason, it is important that the marketing department is actively involved in shaping all of them.

If this does not resemble the marketing department in your company, you're not alone. The broad scope and power of the marketing department defined in this model is not something I see often in the field. Yet, I believe it's one towards which every company should aspire.

Language

| Domestic reality | You typically have one or two languages to work with and you and your team are familiar with those languages. |
| International reality | You will often need to communicate with the market in languages that are foreign to you and your team. |

This is a significant handicap that a translation service alone will not solve. Information is easy to translate but good marketing communication does more than convey information. It engages, motivates and inspires. To a large extent, it does this with the artful use of images and language. At a bare minimum, you need to be sure that the images and words are understandable, not offensive and not likely to be misinterpreted. This is often the ambition level of people who are translating their domestic materials for use abroad. But think about that.

This bare minimum approach will catch the misspellings, poor grammar and cultural faux pas but it does little to ensure that the communication has the desired effect on the foreign target – as in, persuade them to love your brand and purchase your product. This sets a pretty low bar for your communication. The bare minimum approach will help you save face in a foreign market but on its own will not bring your marketing communication to the level where it can compete. How will you communicate in a culture and language that is foreign to you and your team? It is a question you will need to answer for your marketing materials on a case-by-case basis. For instance, materials with relatively long production lead times like advertising and packaging will afford plenty of time to work with the language and assure proper approvals. In the case of communication with short lead times, like interacting on social media or customer support, you will need to think about other solutions.

Chapters 5 and 6 cover language and translation in some detail, but for now it's worth noting that it helps to have a well-defined methodology to handle the logistic, governance and quality-control issues that come up in the process of adapting marketing materials to a new language and culture. Having an adaptation project manager who is specialized in this type of work can save time and prevent costly errors and frustration. They should be backed by their own global network of copywriters, adapters and translators.

Culture

Domestic reality	You are operating in a culture that you and your team understand intuitively.
International reality	You will be on the outside looking into a culture where, even if you learn the highlights, you will still lack a feel for its nuance and texture. For better or worse, you will also be perceived, by default, as a foreigner by the local market.

As Quentin Tarantino's *Inglourious Basterds* illustrated, sometimes factual and linguistic fluency is not enough. It's cultural fluency that informs the substance of what the brand communicates through its words and actions.

Every culture is a unique and nuanced blend of shared verbal and non-verbal language, beliefs, values, history, norms, behaviours, cuisine, ideology and religious influences that are actively and passively learned and passed on from one generation to the next. That's a lot to get your head around, especially if you are dealing with multiple foreign markets. Most of these issues also have finer layers of complexity. For instance, norms establish the guardrails for acceptable behaviour in the culture. They can be formal, or informal unwritten norms. But not all norms are equal. Sociologist William Graham Sumner is credited with breaking down norms into mores and folkways. Folkways are conventions or customs that are socially accepted and that society expects to be followed, although breaking them is not morally offensive. This includes things like which digits one would use to gesture 'three' when ordering drinks in Germany. If you break these norms, you may be considered odd, foreign or rude. Mores, on the other hand, are also unwritten norms, but have a strong sense of morality. Those who violate mores can face outright rejection, if not retaliation, from a society.

It is not uncommon for marketers to create strategies in foreign markets that are heavily influenced by cultural clichés and distorted by ethnocentrism and cultural relativism – that is, interpreting a foreign culture through the lens of your own culture as opposed to understanding it on its own terms. The point is that achieving true mastery of a culture other than one's own is a daunting if not impossible task for most marketers. Nonetheless, the consequences of not being culturally in tune can be quite severe. This is true even for brands that self-identify as foreign. Foreign or not, you will be held accountable to cultural norms and rewarded for your ability to read and navigate them successfully. To do this, you will need guidance from locals who are immersed in the culture and fluent in the unwritten rules that govern all aspects of behaviour there.

Value proposition

Domestic reality	Your domestic value proposition was developed around the habits, needs and perceptions of your domestic target.
International reality	If the habits, needs and perceptions of your foreign target are not the same as those of your domestic buyers (they often are not), then your value proposition may not work in the market you are entering.

Your brand's value proposition is at the heart of generating interest in the market. It flags your brand's unique ability to address a buyer's under-served needs. The products that travel best are the ones that have a value proposition that is, more or less, universal. A sports drink like Lucozade can do that because it satisfies a universal need for hydration, and since humans share the same biology it has a similar effect on consumers globally. Engineering products like industrial heat exchangers also serve fairly universal needs, aided by the fact that the laws of thermodynamics do not change from country to country.

A product has many attributes but you should choose one with which to lead. For instance, Volvo, for many years, led with the value proposition of safety. Do car buyers base their purchase decision on safety alone? No, but that's not the point. A relevant value proposition sets your brand apart with a distinguishing trait for which it is recognized and remembered. It gives your brand a central theme and narrative around which to form your communication. Think of it as a conversation starter.

Before you venture abroad, be sure to revisit your value proposition. There is a good chance that it is biased towards the peculiarities of your home market. Strive to find the 'red thread' in terms of a *common need* shared by your target in your different markets and form a value proposition that addresses it. Take a moment to evaluate your brand's value proposition. Is it:

- singular in its focus?
- highly relevant to your target?
- believable (better yet, demonstrable)?
- not used as a value proposition by anyone else in your category?
- something you can own (even if you don't now) and defend?
- something around which you feel comfortable focusing product development?
- an area where you can be perceived best in category?
- something that is able to work in all your markets globally?

If you answered no to any of the questions above, then you may want to work to refine your value proposition. If possible, strive to have the same value proposition in all markets. This isn't always possible, but it makes building global brand equity and managing your global presence easier if you do. Some buyers may be exposed to your brand in different countries. Being exposed to different value propositions for the same brand can cause confusion and dilute brand identity.

Position

Domestic reality	A brand's position is defined to differentiate it in relation to other brands competing in the same domestic category.
International reality	In many cases, you will be faced with a different set of competitors in foreign markets and therefore may need to rethink your position there.

Think of a brand's positioning as the way that customers and prospects perceive its intended purpose relative to the other brands in the same category. Advertising pioneer David Ogilvy had this to say about it:

> This curious verb is in great favor among marketing experts, but no two of them agree what it means. My own definition is 'what a product does, and who it is for'. For instance, Dove has been successfully positioned as bars of soap for women with dry hands, vs a product for men with dirty hands.[6]

The difference between value proposition and position can be difficult to grasp. A well-managed brand like Dove provides clarity. At the time Ogilvy said this, Dove's value proposition was that it promoted beautiful skin. You can see the interplay between value proposition and position in his example. *Strategy* magazine published a 50-year retrospective of the Dove brand that chronicles how the same value proposition has been paired with different propositions and messaging over the decades to accommodate changes in the market.[7] We see the position shift from a bar of soap for women with dry hands, to a bar of soap for women seeking self-fulfilment, to a bar of soap for women who reject conventional beauty stereotypes. This is not dissimilar to how you may have to adapt your position and messaging to appeal to different foreign markets you serve.

Even the word 'position' begs the question: In relation to what? That's because positioning is a relative thing that has implications for international marketers. Position defines where you stand in relation to all other options – in the mind of the local consumer. The power of positioning is that it forces you to adopt the perspective of the buyer as they evaluate options. This idea has always been part of good marketing but was defined and popularized by Jack Trout[8] and Al Ries, who said, 'The basic goal of positioning is not to create something new and different, but to connect your product or service meaningfully to the mental perceptions that already exist in the mind of prospective customers.'[9]

Companies define how they want their products to be positioned with a positioning strategy. Then they work hard using the marketing mix to cultivate the desired perception in the market, so their brand compares favourably. Ultimately, however, it is the buyer, not the seller, who is the final arbitrator of your brand's position. When a company states their brand's position, be sure to clarify whether that is their desired position as determined by the marketing department or their actual position as determined by their buyers.

If you have experienced strong domestic growth you may be tempted to simply replicate your positioning strategy in other markets and hope for the same outcome. After all, why re-invent the wheel? The short answer is that the reason your current wheel works so well is because it is fine-tuned to the nuances of your market. As such, it is pretty much guaranteed not to be fine-tuned to the needs of new markets you are entering. This has two main implications for marketers.

First, while it's easier and preferable to have the same position in different markets, it is not always necessary or possible. Ask yourself what position would best suit your brand in the market you are entering (regardless of how it may be positioned in other markets). If the objective answer to that question is the same position that the brand has in its home market, then go for it. If it's not, be open to adapting the position to that market. Sometimes the position you have used domestically is already taken by an entrenched competitor in the foreign market, and sometimes the domestic position is simply not relevant to the new market.

Second, even if you do decide to establish the same position in the new market as you used in your domestic market, you will most likely need a market-specific strategy to achieve it. To illustrate, let me describe a prank I pulled when I was seven. It was Saint Patrick's Day, and in Boston many people celebrate that day by displaying the colour green. That morning, I got up before the rest of my family, found some green food colouring in the cupboard, and put it into the milk and orange juice. When my family gathered for breakfast, everyone was amused by the green milk and less amused by the brown orange juice. What I forgot to compensate for was that the milk and orange juice were different colours to start with. To make orange juice green I needed to add blue food colouring, not green, to achieve the same effect as with the milk. Since you are marketing to people who are not identical to your domestic buyers, there is a good chance that you will need to adapt your strategy to have the same desired effect on them with regard to your position. This explains why effective positioning strategies don't lend themselves easily to globalization. If you are managing a global brand, it is unlikely that the factors affecting your position will be the same in all markets you serve. For that reason you'll need to localize your strategy.

Position is usually built to complement, if not directly support, your value proposition. It takes that proposition and frames it in the context of the buyer and the market. You can think of it like the packaging in which the value proposition is delivered. For instance, in the Volvo example mentioned earlier, the value proposition was safety. The brand was then positioned in the US as a premium import brand for those buyers who are most likely to put a premium on safety: parents. Its price point and country of origin supported the premium import aspect. The content, placement, tone, and manner of their advertising and sponsorships signalled that this was a car for responsible, suburban parents. The idea is to nail down its unique value for the local buyers in a way that is highly relevant to them and differentiates your brand from competitors. This isn't just window-dressing. Once you have decided on the value proposition and position, you should focus the entire marketing mix on supporting it.

Since context is more prone to change than needs, the brand position tends to be more malleable than the value proposition. For instance, the sports drink Lucozade began in 1927 as a medical-hydration remedy made of glucose syrup and water sold by UK pharmacists.[10] The value proposition was hydration and energy. It was positioned in the UK as a treatment for the sick, and became a standard for children with dysentery. By the early 1980s, the need for hydration and energy spread to adults who had joined the new fitness craze. Beecham, the British pharmaceutical company that owned the brand, repositioned Lucozade in 1983 from a medical treatment for the sick to a sports drink for the healthy. They changed the tag line from 'Lucozade aids recovery' to 'Lucozade replaces lost energy' and pursued the fitness crowd. Sales tripled in the five years following the reposition.[11] Ironically, the current Lucozade labelling includes a warning that Lucozade is not appropriate for replacing the fluid lost to dysentery.

In the Lucozade example we have the same underlying value proposition since 1927 but a major shift in position to adapt to a new target and new competitive landscape. This is not unlike what you'll be faced with when you introduce your brand into a new market. Position is highly dependent on market context. That's why it is very likely that you will need to rethink your position in each market. As a rule of thumb, do your best to create a value proposition that can work in all the markets you intend to enter and then tweak the position as needed to suit the local environment. To use the sports drink example, you could create the value proposition of 'increased stamina' for global use but then position it in Finland as the drink preferred by hockey players, in the US as a basketball drink, and in Brazil as the choice of soccer players.

Media environment

Domestic reality	You compete for share of voice in a media environment that is familiar, in your language and where you have built a presence.
International reality	You compete for share of voice in a media environment that is foreign, often in a different language and where you have no presence.

In 1990, John Philip Jones published results of a global study examining the relationship between media spend and sales.[12] He found that a brand's share of voice in any given market is perhaps the single most accurate correlate to share of market. Brands that achieve a share of voice that is above their share of market tend to see share of market increase to close the gap. If you're entering a crowded category without significant product differentiation, then the relationship between share of voice and share of market favours the category incumbents, and is often used as an effective barrier to entry for newcomers.

That same year, building off Jones' work, James Schroer made a compelling case for why it is an economic folly to enter a new market and attempt to overtake the entrenched leaders who understand the local media market.[13] Both these researchers focused on consumer categories with relatively undifferentiated products (eg soap, coffee and beer). However, more recent research by Binet and Field in 2019 supports Jones' findings and has found that business-to-business (B-to-B) brands can likewise grow market share by increasing share of voice.[14] No matter what type of brand you are managing, share of voice is important because it seems to be a strong determinant of share of market. As a new entrant, you would be wise to leave your domestic media strategy at home and study the new media environment with fresh eyes to define the best channels and the optimal media spend in the new market.

Related to this is the online marketing environment. Online advertising and social media can be an effective way to boost share of voice in the new market if you can use them effectively. Aside from the fact that the platforms may be different, how they are used and the language spoken on them is likely to be different as well. Keywords used for online advertising or search engine optimization (SEO) will need to be re-thought in the local language and culture, which usually requires more thought and insight than merely taking your domestic keywords and running them through Google Translate. Again, you will need local expertise to navigate the media landscape and effectively develop you brand's share of voice in your new market.

Market intelligence

Domestic reality	You are typically passively aware of changes to your market as a matter of course, and acquiring impromptu market intelligence is relatively swift, accurate and inexpensive.
International reality	If you are not living in the market and/or don't speak the language, it is easy for significant shifts in the market to occur 'under the radar', and acquiring impromptu market intelligence can take longer, and be less reliable and more expensive.

When most people think about marketing, they think promotion: talking to the market. To the strategic marketer, an even more important function of marketing is providing the marketing team with new intel and insights from the market. Markets are constantly changing and it is the marketer's job to anticipate those changes and adapt the marketing mix in a timely manner. Keeping so closely in tune with a market can be difficult when it's thousands of kilometres away. This is yet another factor that can create a home-team advantage for local players.

Compared to your domestic market, working in foreign markets will make it much more challenging for your team to keep on top of shifting buyer perceptions, competitor activity and overall market conditions. It's best to accept this at the outset as a potential blind spot and take active measures to compensate. I suggest setting up a 'market intelligence programme' for each market that will assess buyers, competitors and market conditions on a regular basis. Ongoing programmes like

Net Promoter Score and web analytics can be supplemented with deeper dives to understand buyer sentiment using interviews and focused surveys. For some brands, an annual deeper dive may be sufficient. For others, it could be needed quarterly. The important thing is that your team receives a steady flow of timely information about the market variables that matter most to your business in each market. Many small to mid-sized companies balk at the cost of this investment since they have already succeeded at home without this sort of structured approach. That brings us to our final point, the increased need for documentation and codification when working abroad.

Documentation and codification

Domestic reality	Your marketing programme grew organically over time, largely through trial and error, in your home market. Today, your success can be attributed to a vast trove of undocumented institutional knowledge held by your team.
International reality	You will need the cooperation and contribution of many professionals who are outside your team, often at a great distance, speaking different languages, with different business practices and who have no understanding of your brand, your strategy, or your processes.

I have seen some fantastically successful brands operate domestically with almost nothing of their brand identity, marketing strategy or processes committed to paper beyond the annual marketing budget. These are typically very tight teams where all the players know the script and simply get on with their jobs. This is commendable, but relying on the same type of intuitive teamwork becomes implausible as you enter new markets.

Succeeding abroad will require the cooperation of many people who exist outside your team, not to mention outside your market and culture. Coordinating their activities and focusing their energies will require clarity and a lot of rapid knowledge transfer. Things you simply do as a matter of course will now need to be explained to someone five thousand kilometres away in a manner that makes sense to them. Processes that were once as simple as handing a document to the colleague sitting next to you and having a quick chat can involve many more people and steps when working in foreign markets. This is to say nothing of practicalities like time differences, business norms, work habits, language barriers, holiday schedules, etc.

The best way I've found to maintain both quality and agility is to document and codify. This starts with creating a marketing ecosystem with your extended team that includes basic terms and principles as discussed in Chapter 1. It will also help if you can break down the components of your brand identity with a brand codification so that it can be easily learned and operationalized by those who are not familiar with it. Similarly, brand strategies and operating procedures, from the adaptation of ads, to document naming and version control, to the regular gathering of marketing intelligence, should be written down and systemized – even if these measures are not required for your domestic operations. Creating structure and clarity will yield better results in less time and make managing foreign markets a lot less taxing on the organization as a whole. This is not as daunting as it sounds. My team has walked clients through this process and had them up and running in short order, often avoiding setbacks that could have cost the organization months or years.

Conclusion

The main take-away from this chapter is that using a cookie-cutter approach based on your home market will not work when building a brand overseas. No matter how similar it may look on the surface, every new market you enter is its own special case and needs to be treated that way. That's why the executive who succeeds in building your brand domestically might actually be the worst choice to head up your entry into a foreign market. Success in the home market can blind them and equip them with experience that may not be transferable. This makes it so much more difficult for that individual to see the market with new eyes. This can be exacerbated by pressure from management for a repeat performance. I saw this with a pharmaceutical executive who launched a drug with moderate success in the US and was immediately promoted to head up the launch of the same drug across Europe, where he had no experience. It was clear to everyone, including the executive, that management expected him to repeat the feat in the European Union (EU) using the same approach he used in the US. Against all advice to the contrary, he applied the US strategy and the drug floundered in every EU market in which it was launched, for many of the reasons listed above.

The overarching difference between marketing domestically and internationally is complexity. International marketing introduces complexity that most domestic marketers are not prepared to acknowledge or deal with. In most cases, this is because they never saw it coming. Fortunately, you have. As you prepare to take your brand abroad, take the time to ensure everyone in your company is clear on what role marketing plays and consider the seven differences outlined in this chapter. This will not eliminate the risks inherent in launching abroad, but it will put you and your team in a much better position to mitigate them. In the next chapter I look at those risks and how to manage them as part of your routine work flow.

Notes

1. M McLuhan, *The Gutenberg Galaxy: The making of typographic man*, University of Toronto Press, Toronto, 1962.
2. T Levitt, The globalization of markets, *Harvard Business Review*, 613, pp 92–102, May 1983.
3. T L Friedman, *The World is Flat: A brief history of the twenty-first century*, Farrar, Straus and Giroux, New York, 2005.
4. P Ghemawat, Distance still matters: The hard reality of global expansion, *Harvard Business Review*, September 2011. https://hbr.org/2001/09/distance-still-matters-the-hard-reality-of-global-expansion (archived at https://perma.cc/65RA-V6JP)
5. P Ghemawat, Why the world isn't flat, Foreign Policy, 2009. https://foreignpolicy.com/2009/10/14/why-the-world-isnt-flat/ (archived at https://perma.cc/XTV2-7NPZ)

6 D Ogilvy, *Ogilvy on Advertising*, Crown, New York, 1983.

7 L Saddleton, The evolution of Dove, Strategy, 1 December 2007. https://strategyonline.ca/2007/12/01/tributedove-20071201/ (archived at https://perma.cc/QY59-7EJF)

8 J Trout, 'Positioning' is a game people play in today's me-too market place, *Industrial Marketing*, pp 51–55, 1969.

9 A Ries and J Trout, *Positioning: The battle for your mind*, McGraw-Hill, New York, 1981.

10 Superbrands case studies: Lucozade, Campaign, 14 January 2005. https://www.campaignlive.co.uk/article/superbrands-case-studies-lucozade/232378?src_site=brandrepublic (archived at https://perma.cc/P6QB-85XH)

11 Lucozade, *Wikipedia*, undated. https://en.wikipedia.org/wiki/Lucozade (archived at https://perma.cc/WM6T-6Y9D)

12 J P Jones, Ad spending: Maintaining market share, *Harvard Business Review*, January–February 1990. https://hbr.org/1990/01/ad-spending-maintaining-market-share (archived at https://perma.cc/Z8XV-4WRZ)

13 J C Schroer, Ad spending: Growing market share, *Harvard Business Review*, January–February 1990. https://hbr.org/1990/01/ad-spending-growing-market-share (archived at https://perma.cc/NAD6-ZEH2)

14 L Binet and P Field, The 5 principles of growth in B2B marketing, The B2B Institute, 2019. https://business.linkedin.com/content/dam/me/business/en-us/amp/marketing-solutions/images/lms-b2b-institute/pdf/LIN_B2B-Marketing-Report-Digital-v02.pdf (archived at https://perma.cc/YEB6-E7Q4)

03

Reducing risk

Managing risk begins by acknowledging it

On the afternoon of 24 October 1901, a 63-year-old woman and her cat climbed into a wooden pickle barrel on Goat Island in upstate New York. The barrel was sealed and cast into the Niagara River where the current carried them over the edge of the 57-metre waterfall. Why would someone do this? For the same reason many business owners want to enter foreign markets. Money.

The woman's name was Annie Edson Taylor. She was a widowed American schoolteacher whose fear of winding up in the poorhouse was greater than her fear of being smashed to bits at the base of a waterfall. Niagara Falls is not the highest waterfall in the world but it is surely one of the most violent. With nearly 115 thousand cubic metres of water flowing over its precipice each minute, it boasts the greatest flow rate of any waterfall on Earth. Mrs Taylor survived the ordeal. As she was plucked from the frigid waters at the base of the Falls she said, 'If it was with my dying breath, I would caution anyone against attempting the feat... I would sooner walk up to the mouth of a cannon, knowing it was going to blow me to pieces, than make another trip over the fall'.[1] While the stunt didn't make her rich, it did help her achieve her goal of avoiding the poorhouse, as she traded off her notoriety for the next 20 years until her death. Mrs Taylor's stunt unwittingly triggered a cottage industry among daredevils seeking fame and fortune. 16 such individuals have gone over the Falls since then, and 11 of them have survived.

I often tell this story when teaching business leaders or students of international marketing. After I describe Mrs Taylor's exploits, I ask who in the class would go over the Falls in a barrel if the 20-minute ordeal would earn them a million dollars? Behind me, projected on a screen, is a very intimidating picture of the Falls with a wooden barrel caught in the current. No hands go up. I feign surprise. 'Why not?' I ask incredulously. 'Too risky,' they reply. I then relate a realization I had when visiting the Falls' daredevil exhibition just prior to starting my first business overseas.

Near the Falls was a small venue displaying memorabilia and stories of the souls who had attempted the drop. Inside the exhibit, a friend asked me if I'd go over the Falls for a million dollars. My immediate response was '*No!* What kind of idiot would...' but then I paused mid-sentence, because as I spoke it occurred to me that the plunge I was about to take launching my business in Europe had a much lower survival rate than going over the Falls. Historically, the average survival rate at Niagara has been 69 per cent. Considering that all the literature I'd read up to that point put the survival rate of new brands around 10 per cent, going over the Falls started to look like a much saner way to earn a living.

I raise this point to people who are considering entering a new market, not to dissuade them, but to have them first acknowledge the very real business risk they face in the hope that it will motivate them to do the hard work required to mitigate that risk. Entrepreneurs who are in love with their creation or executives who suspect they have spotted a new opportunity are most inclined to ignore these risks.

Overcoming cognitive bias

The tendency to ignore or grossly underestimate risk is not an isolated behaviour. In his 2001 article 'Distance still matters: The hard reality of global expansion', Pankaj Ghemawat provides one answer to the question of why businesses fail abroad with the case of Australian businessman Rupert Murdoch's efforts to grow Star TV across Asia. Ghemawat deemed those efforts a 'high-profile disaster' and said the failure was typical of companies who seek global expansion 'Because, like Star, they routinely overestimate the attractiveness of foreign markets. They become so dazzled by the sheer size of untapped markets that they lose sight of the vast difficulties of pioneering new, often very different territories.'[2]

Nobel Laureate, psychologist and behavioural economist Daniel Kahneman believes this tendency is hard-wired into the human condition. He and Amos Tverske coined the term 'planning fallacy' to describe it.[3] It's a cognitive bias shared by all of us that makes us irrationally optimistic when it comes to estimate time and costs associated with our own projects. We habitually and wildly underestimate. This bias is also stubbornly resistant to factual evidence that contradicts it. The odd thing is that it only applies to predictions about one's own tasks. When independent observers produce an estimate of someone else's project, they show a pessimism bias. In his book *Thinking, Fast and Slow*,[4] Kahneman provides examples, like a 2002 survey of US homeowners who, on average, estimated the cost to remodel their kitchens at $18,658. In reality they wound up paying, on average, $38,769. Anyone who can relate to examples like this should take note.

Even when warned, Kahneman's cognitive bias combined with a sense of urgency and exuberance often leads managers to conclude that there is no need and/or no time to look before they leap. Gorovitz and MacIntyre would classify this behaviour as ineptitude. As discussed in Chapter 1, they assert that all failure can be traced back to one of two possibilities. The first is the natural limitation of what is known or knowable in a particular discipline, which they label 'ignorance'. The second cause of failure they identify as wilfulness and negligence on the part of the practitioner, which they label as 'ineptitude'. 'Wilfulness and negligence will arise when those motives that are to be restrained by external norms of natural science – ambition, impatience, competitiveness, a great anxiety to do good in the world – are allowed to override the internal norms.'[5] This to a great extent defines the driving forces behind the failure of international expansion initiatives described by Ghemawat and others. In the case of marketing, the 'internal norms' that keep our baser instincts in check refer to objective research and analysis.

Richard Tedlow provides further insight into the pervasiveness of ineptitude in business in his book *Denial: Why business leaders fail to look facts in the face – and what to do about it*. The book explores the question we posed at the end of the previous chapter: Why do sane, smart leaders often refuse to accept the facts that threaten their companies and careers?[6] He finds the tendency of business leaders to resist inconvenient or painful truths is 'the biggest and potentially most ruinous problem that businesses face, from start-ups to mature, powerful corporations'. Of course, resisting the truth may not always be as bad as it sounds. If every entrepreneur took failure rates to heart then we might not have many entrepreneurs left. So, perhaps a little bit of wishful thinking can help grease the wheels of success and help us prevail against the odds. Tedlow quotes Orwell who coined this tendency 'protective stupidity' but cautions that 'In business, pretending that things are better than they are virtually ensures failure.'

Even the best managers have a natural tendency to underemphasize complexity and risk and to avoid information that could pose an obstacle to their wishes. This is not because they are bad at their jobs. It's because they are human. This is good and bad. Bad, because it means this behaviour is the normative state for all managers and invites significant risk to global expansion. Good, because knowing that, it is completely avoidable. If we are aware of our own cognitive biases and destructive behaviours then we can take measures to counter them.

Kahneman suggests the antidote for the planning fallacy is to adopt an 'outside view' of the project, summarizing as much reference data as is available into a forecast. For us, that starts with the independent creation of a business case for our international initiatives.

Success begins close to home

When faced with the notion of entering a foreign market, managers often begin by looking outward to the market, assessing gross domestic product (GDP) growth and other economic factors, collecting sales and demographic data, crunching numbers and making projections to justify the expansion (and their cognitive bias). In their article 'Does your company have what it takes to go global?' authors Douglas Quackenbos, Richard Ettenson, Martin S Roth and Seigyoung Auh maintain that while external factors like those listed above are important to understand, they are just the tip of the iceberg. Over a ten-year period, they studied over 100 international organizations. What they found was a pattern of over-eager managers entering foreign markets based solely on their desire for growth and the identification of external market factors that seemed compatible with their ambitions. This is a common recipe for disaster because it glosses over all the other requirements a brand needs to succeed in a foreign market. The authors concluded that:

> External factors only set the stage for an international opportunity; they are just one part – and not necessarily the most important one – of global expansion success. And while companies recognize the need for internal capabilities such as language and cultural adaptation skills in a new market, they tend to overlook other, less obvious internal requirements, only to discover too late that they are ill prepared for what awaits them.[7]

Amen to that.

There is a helpful step to take before looking outward, which will protect you from your own cognitive biases. A company should begin the process of international expansion by looking inward at their own company, product, motivation, assumptions, resources, historical data and risk tolerance. This is done by developing a business case for international expansion.

A business case forces corporate leadership to look before they leap. It systematically and objectively lays out the reasons for initiating a project or task in the first place. With regard to entering a foreign market, it clarifies why the business needs to do this and quantifies the expected value, costs, and risks to the business drawing on historical data and cases where possible. As such, it is done before any decisions are made. At least, it should be.

According to project management experts Elizabeth Larson and Richard Larson, projects are often started without a proper business case. They describe the consequences when companies neglect this vital step. They include lack of clarity with regard to objectives, timing and cost, which result in scope creep, cost and scheduling overruns, delays and rework. Projects that lack a strong business case also fail to anticipate changes in the business environment that can put the project in jeopardy. Ultimately, such projects are often scrapped altogether because they lose the support of the project sponsors. 'The net effects of cancelled projects and unused products are wasted investments, lost opportunity costs, and more pain and frustration.'[8]

The ABCO case

I saw the consequences defined by Larson and Larson first hand when a successful EU-based company, we'll call it ABCO (not their real name), hired my company to help them develop their first consumer brand. ABCO had built a strong business-to-business brand in hospitality supplies and was already selling its products to businesses around the globe. It wanted to enter a number of markets with a consumer-facing e-commerce brand. The project had been underway for the better part of two years when they hired my company to develop an international brand identity and marketing strategy. Initially, my team was confused by the request. First because of the odd chronology – the marketing strategy and brand identity are typically done at the outset of such a project, not two years in. Even more peculiar was that this initiative didn't fit ABCO's core competence, brand profile or business model.

To help my team understand the situation, I asked to see the business case. I was told that there wasn't one. I asked why the project was initiated. The sales and marketing director said ABCO had been able to secure exclusive rights for two years on a machine that could personalize certain party favours – small gifts given to guests at a party. Personalized party favours were growing in popularity with consumers at the time. The CEO had seen projected sales for this category and wanted to cash in on the trend with the new machine. I told the sales and marketing director that I was having a hard time seeing the fit and asked him to allocate a modest portion of our budget to conduct a preliminary business case analysis to support the marketing strategy (albeit after-the-fact).

Completing the preliminary business case analysis took three weeks. Our research and analysis revealed a number of challenges ABCO had not anticipated:

- ABCO initiated the project on the assumption that the product for which it had negotiated exclusive production rights was unique and that it would have little competition in the markets it was entering. Neither assumption was true. There were two formidable competitors with strong consumer brands in the markets in which they were interested, not to mention scores of smaller brands. The two largest competitors had hundreds of personalized party products but did not offer the new products that our client was planning to launch. A little more digging revealed that some of the other competitors had used different technology to produce the same personalized products as our client. Except the competitors' products had faster turn-around time and higher resolution graphics at a lower price!
- Our client had planned to sell a very limited range of personalized party products, which meant that the customers would be forced to buy the rest of their party supplies elsewhere. But this is not how customers purchase these products in the markets they planned to enter. Consumers there want a one-stop-shopping solution.
- The CEO had based his decision on projections for all sales in the category. As it turns out, online sales accounted for less than 15 per cent of that figure, the rest were bricks-and-mortar purchases.
- The allocated media budget was about one-tenth of what would be required to drive enough traffic to meet their sales goals.
- Worse still, because the project had run into constant cost and time overruns, the exclusivity agreement on the production machinery was due to expire two weeks before the e-commerce site was scheduled to launch.

A month after we presented these findings, ABCO's CEO cancelled the project, having already spent two years and millions of dollars on it.

In this instance, the two initial facts that sparked the project were both valid. Yes, the market for personalized party favours was growing strongly in the geographies they targeted, and yes, ABCO did have exclusive rights to a machine that produced such goods, but those facts alone proved insufficient to support a decision to launch a consumer brand. That's because those two facts on their own provided no insight into either the likelihood of commercial success or the strategies that would be required to achieve it. Even the most rudimentary business case analysis would have revealed this at the outset.

Equally surprising is that a much more plausible alternative was overlooked: using its existing B-to-B model and expertise to sell their exclusive personalized party favours to one or both of the existing companies that dominated the market. This approach would have offered immediate access to the market with negligible risk and cost. In this way, it could extract the most business value from the two-year exclusivity agreement on the production method.

In the case of ABCO, the company had already been selling to businesses in the markets where they planned to launch their consumer brand. So, in a sense, those markets were not foreign to it since it had ongoing operations there. But those operations were B-to-B sales operations. Now it was considering establishing a consumer brand. Although the country was not foreign to them, the market certainly was. ABCO had absolutely no experience developing consumer brands or strategic marketing. The consumer market it wanted to enter was clearly outside their area of competence. Unable to see that, it applied methodologies and assumptions shaped by their direct sales experiences to this new venture. It wasn't until my team understood this that a certain underlying logic was revealed.

The baffling series of decisions it had made began to make sense when we understood that it was approaching this consumer marketing launch in the same way it had successfully approached B-to-B sales campaigns in the same countries. It suffices to say that many assumptions formed through one-on-one sales experience with purchasing departments are not readily transferable to strategic mass marketing to consumers. The preliminary business case helped ABCO realize that it was entering a foreign market in a familiar country.

Putting risk in perspective

If a board informed its CEO that in six months' time they would be stuffed into a pickle barrel and sent over Niagara Falls with a 30 per cent chance of failure, you can be sure that the ensuing 24 weeks would be spent feverishly studying water flow patterns on the Niagara River, testing multiple barrel designs with the aid of experts in material science, fluid dynamics and human physiology, consulting with meteorologists to define environmental facts to be considered, etc… The CEO would immediately recognize the gaps in their knowledge. Moreover, they would scrutinize and challenge even the most mundane assumptions to ensure the greatest possible chance of success. They would do this because they have a visceral appreciation for the completely foreign nature of the risks they would be facing and the limits of their competence in addressing them.

In the same sense, I've routinely seen CEOs charged with entering a foreign market with a 50 per cent plus chance of failure, balk at the idea of investing any time and budget to develop a business case before committing to the project and, more importantly, setting its parameters. In these instances, I've found it's not the money that's the issue as much as the time required. Having spotted an opportunity to enter a market, leadership understandably wants to get on with things. Distractions like business cases and research just seem like needless delays.

Conducting the business case analysis shouldn't feel as if it's slowing the momentum of the initiative. Instead of being seen as a distraction to the process, these measures should be seen as the vital first steps in that process. Below I outline an approach for assessing opportunity, risks and costs that are seamlessly incorporated into the market entry process from the start and not treated as an optional provision.

What to include

Business cases can take many forms, but they are all intended to provide an objective reality check to ensure management enters new ventures with a clear view of what they are getting into. To start, let's take a look at the main components. An excellent resource to learn more on this topic is the Project Management Institute (PMI). It is an international not-for-profit professional organization that advocates for standards in project management. At PMI's 2009 Global Congress, members Brian Herman and Jay Siegelaub provided a sensible framework that, with a few modifications, I've found useful for creating business cases. It is built around five main topics:

- **Reasons:** Defines the objective and expected benefit the business is seeking with the project and explores the problem that the project will solve as well as the context that produced the problem in the first place.
- **Options:** Identifies different ways that the problem could be solved given the objectives and resources of the organization. It highlights the pros and cons of each and the rationale for why one approach was chosen over others.
- **Benefits and negative consequences:** Defines expected benefits, how long it will take to achieve them and how they will be measured. This is not just a matter of listing deliverables. It looks deeper into the business value being created. It also explores the ways that the project can hurt or strain the organization and how those facts can be minimized.
- **Timescale and costs:** Knowing how long a project will take to finish and the costs involved are vital to making a go/no-go decision. Here those elements are explored using as much historical reference data as possible so that the organization has a clear idea of the resources required.
- **Major risks and opportunities:** What factors inside or outside the company threaten the project, and which are likely to contribute to its success? How are these factors likely to change over the

course of the project and beyond? Weighing these factors will help management decide if the project falls within their risk tolerance. This approach asks the investigator to dig into each of these keys areas and define the reality as it is today. However, the context and business environment can change over the course of a major project so Herman and Siegelaub also ask that the investigator consider how future changes could affect these five factors and alter the foundational assumptions.

There are dozens of business case templates available online and through consultants. You should be able to find one that suits your organization and project or modify what you find to create your own. I've found it useful to adapt these templates to the specific needs of the project.

Keep things moving

If everything stops while the business case is being developed, then the opportunity that necessitated it in the first place could pass before the analysis is delivered. To avoid that, as well as build momentum and keep sponsors engaged, I suggest integrating this work into the market entry phases defined in Figure 3.1. The development of the business case should not be seen as something peripheral or separate from the core process the company follows leading up to market entry. Launching a new brand or product in a foreign market starts with the idea then typically unfolds in four main work phases for marketers. This work is coordinated with all other functions in the company – not least IT, production and distribution. Since no two companies have exactly the same process, I've taken the liberty of sketching out the four broad work phases that follow ideation in Figure 3.1. Working from this model, we will be able to identify the most sensible way to integrate the business case criteria outlined by Herman and Siegelaub into the work process.

FIGURE 3.1 The four generic phases of marketing work that follow ideation when entering a new market

IDEA	I. FRAME	II. DEVELOP	III. IMPLEMENT	IV. MANAGE
Define need	Define solution	Develop solution	Implement solution	Create value

Idea

The first time you hear an idea for a major marketing initiative, like entering a new market, give it a quick sanity check and ask the obvious. The earlier you can flag issues or opportunities with a new idea, then the easier it is to shape the direction that idea will take. This requires no research, just your common sense and experience. Take, for instance, the ABCO case. The CEO had an idea to use their two-year exclusivity on manufacturing to sell direct to consumers in several countries. Had someone asked the obvious questions, like how long it would take to establish a consumer brand in those markets, or why the company wasn't going to sell to retailers who already had strong consumer brands instead of competing with them, then ABCO could have been spared two years of wasted resources.

Phase I: Framing

This is the critical step that is most often skipped. To use a medical analogy, it is the initial diagnosis. Performing open-heart surgery on a patient without first conducting a diagnosis would be negligent. It's the same when launching a major business operation. Use Herman and Siegelaub's criteria to start to tease out what, exactly, you are trying to achieve with the initiative and the risks, opportunities and implications entailed. If, for instance, the idea is to enter a predetermined market, then this phase serves to flag potential implications of that choice. If you are considering multiple markets, then the framing should make it clear which ones will best meet the organization's objectives. In the event where multiple countries are selected for entry, then the markets are prioritized and ordered chronologically in terms of ideal entry sequence. The next three steps would then be repeated for each country where the company plans to launch its brand.

A good doctor makes an initial diagnosis by looking at the problem to be solved from multiple perspectives. The result is a recommendation on how to proceed and what further tests will be required. In the case of marketing diagnosis, the result is a recommendation on how best to move the project forward based on the initial assessment. The recommendation includes an action plan that spells out the steps required for phase II, along with ballpark timelines and cost estimates. If the company decides to move forward based on the framing report then the ballpark estimates are tightened up for final approval of phase II.

Below I've included the outline of a framing document, by way of example. I am not recommending this as a strict template since this document should be customized to suit the specifics of your company, its objectives and situation. This framing exercise is for a robotics firm that serves a global market with on-the-ground operations in over a dozen countries. They have grown rapidly though a number of acquisitions and now find themselves with a portfolio of corporate and product brands each with different levels of brand equity in different countries and categories. The new CMO is a sharp strategic marketer who is looking for a global brand architecture, marketing strategy and brand identity programme that will help the company create synergy between its brands, and be better able to compete for employees, clients and investors. After a quick sanity check, we conducted a framing exercise. My team's hope with this exercise was to cover Herman and Siegelaub's criteria as well as build consensus in the leadership team. The main sections of that report include:

- **Problem:** A definition of the business problem we are trying to solve with the project, along with its effect on the business and the key internal and external contributing factors.

- **Options:** The most viable options for addressing this problem with the marketing mix. This includes an analysis of how competitors and customers are dealing with similar challenges.
- **Solution:** A recommendation of which option seems most viable, including a rationale for the choice vs other options.
- **Value:** The value that achieving that objective will bring to the business. This also includes the value to customers, employees and investors.
- **Assumptions:** The main assumptions upon which the recommendation was made and the initiative's success depends.
- **Confidence:** Key assumptions are rated by the degree to which the investigators feel they are valid. This is a judgement call informed by the degree to which the assumptions are supported by research and the validity of that research.
- **Risk:** Risk factors are identified and recommendations made on how to mitigate them. This includes all key assumptions that were flagged as low confidence.
- **Scenarios:** Scenario planning to anticipate the effect of known variables on the project moving forward and monitoring to keep those effects from derailing the project.
- **Next steps:** The scope, timeline and resources required to develop a strategy based on the recommendation. This includes a discussion of cost and time requirements to implement and start generating value for the organization.
- **Appendix:**
  - glossary;
  - SWOT analysis;
  - competitor analysis and comparison;
  - work breakdown for phase II;
  - framing methodology.

Phase II: Strategy development

Once we know what country and issues to focus on, we can perform in-depth research into the market, competitors and buyers so that a credible strategy can be developed. If our enquiries raise significant unforeseen questions, additional primary research may be recommended at this point to address them. This contingency should be included in the planning of the discovery phase. When completed, this phase provides a fairly granular view of the marketing terrain that exists between where the company is today and where it wants the market expansion to take it.

Working off this information, the strategy defines the route that offers the best chance of success in the selected market. It details how the organization will use the marketing mix to navigate the terrain and achieve its business objective. This includes a ballpark estimate of the time, budget and resources required, including any external expertise. If the company decided to move forward with the strategy then the ballpark estimates are tightened up for final approval of phase III.

Phase III: Implementation

Implementation is where the specific tactics required to deliver on the strategy are developed. This includes customizing the marketing mix, which may involve modifications to product and pricing. In most cases it will include work to developing the supporting marketing infrastructure by modifying or creating things like apps, websites, content programmes, advertising, media plans, events, sales support material, etc. As a rule, we also strive to establish methodologies and processes to monitor progress of the marketing efforts and receive a steady stream of input from the market.

Implementation in foreign markets can involve a greater number of external specialists than domestic launches. This can include a range of third parties, from ad agencies and web developers to adaptation and research firms. In my own case, my company outsources much of the implementation work to our network of trusted global partners, but we remain heavily involved in overseeing the work to ensure that all the players are coordinated and remain on strategy. You will need to do the same thing.

Phase IV: Management

Fourth is the launch and management of the programme you have developed. This starts with a marketing plan that details activities on a weekly basis for the next 12 months. This plan also specifies the people who will be responsible for each activity, the best practices and standard operating procedures they will follow, and how their progress will be measured and reported. How you handle this will depend on the operating structure you choose, as outlined in Chapter 5.

Exit ramps

Eager executives often commit to the specifics of market entry prematurely before the facts have been adequately and objectively assessed. And once these edicts are made, the rank and file treat them as sacred. This was clearly the case at Target Canada and at ABCO where, soon after the CEO put the project in motion, it gained so much momentum that no one dared question it; they were too busy trying to accommodate the CEO's mandates. Given this tendency, it's important to build clear exit ramps into your path to market and establish them in advance as best practice.

An exit ramp is a point in the development process where leadership stops, assesses the situation and makes a go/no-go decision to move onto the next phase. If the decision is no-go, it doesn't necessarily kill the initiative. It just means that under its current incarnation the idea won't fly and either needs to be revamped or abandoned. These exit ramps should be built into the process in a highly visible way, not only allowing but also encouraging anyone on the team to raise a red flag at these junctures.

The first is the sanity check. If the idea has obvious flaws they should be called out early and given back to the person who had the idea to resolve before the idea is entertained further – even if that person is the owner or CEO.

The second exit ramp is at the end of the framing process. At this point you will not have a detailed account of the total cost for the project because that is highly dependent on the strategy that is developed. However you will know enough to get a rough idea of the costs and if your company can afford them based on the estimates provided for phase II and on the costs of similar projects your company or its partners have completed in the past.

Conclusion

Even the best managers will have a natural inclination to underestimate the risk, cost and time required by the projects they manage. They will also actively resist information that contradicts their view. This makes them, by far, the biggest obstacle to the success of your international expansion. Defining a market for your product and backing that with positive economic data does not constitute due diligence when entering a foreign market. The existence of potential buyers in a robust economy offers virtually no predictive value of brand success. Before you seriously consider launching your brand abroad, make a proper business case for doing so.

Today many governments and larger businesses are now requiring business cases to be made for major initiatives like new market entry. Some businesses may forgo a true business case if much of the required analysis is accomplished in documents such as cost–benefit analysis (CBA), financial justification, return on investment analysis (ROI), a project feasibility study or framing exercise. What you call it isn't that important. What is important is that, before you make the decision to enter a foreign market, you take the time to conduct an analysis that includes the five criteria recommended by Herman and Siegelaub.

Target assumed its IT systems could work in Canada, or at least be replaced in time. ABCO assumed it could launch a consumer campaign with the same budget it allocated for its trade campaigns. In ABCO's case, it was able to see the obstacles soon after it hired external consultants to provide an objective, outside perspective. In Target's case that perspective came much later, provided by its customers after launch. When a company spots an opportunity abroad it typically reacts like Target and ABCO did. It skips the tedium of developing a proper business case. Instead, it embarks on a quest to justify the decision it's already made with consumption trends and market growth data. This is a mistake.

Target's CEO Gregg Steinhafel had talked about taking the company international years before it actually did so, but apparently he didn't see the need to commission a feasibility study to see what the implications might be. When he was given the opportunity to purchase Zeller's retail leases in Canada, he didn't hesitate. He leapt in with both feet. He set bold objectives and fostered a 'gung ho' work environment. It was only after launch that he began to realize the implications of his decision.

Over the course of his 35 years with Target, Gregg Steinhafel had proven himself an exceptionally competent executive. I suspect he would have achieved his bold objectives had he chosen to open 124 stores at once in the US. The IT systems would have worked, there would have been no duties and other new regulations to sort out, no different units of measure, no changes in price, and no foreign attitudes and consumer behaviour to accommodate. Having never opened a store outside America, he and his team were blind to these differences and their significance.

The gaps in their knowledge and planning seem obvious to us now, but at the time they were concealed by false assumptions. In this sense, Target's deep experience doing business in its home market actually worked to its detriment abroad. It provided a false sense of security and blinded the company to the reality before it. Fortunately, Target was big enough to absorb the losses that came with that mistake and survive. Many smaller companies do not have that luxury.

If Target's example teaches us anything, it is that there is no opportunity so great and no time pressure so extreme that is justifies proceeding without a business case. Before you leap in, pause and evaluate the opportunity objectively. If you make a strong case, then you have taken the first step. New market entry may never be as safe as going over the Niagara Falls in a barrel, but with a proper business case, you'll be that much closer to making it so.

Figure 3.1 defines the four broad phases of marketing work that lead up to market entry. The last phase in that process is management. In the next chapter, I review the different approaches that companies take to manage their foreign marketing operations.

Notes

1 N Berton, *Niagara: A history of the falls*, Anchor Canada, Canada, 1992.
2 P Ghemawat, Distance still matters: The hard reality of global expansion, *Harvard Business Review*, September 2001. https://hbr.org/2001/09/distance-still-matters-the-hard-reality-of-global-expansion (archived at https://perma.cc/SCC3-E7P4)
3 D Kahneman and A Tversky, Intuitive prediction: Biases and corrective procedures, Decision Research, June 1977. https://apps.dtic.mil/dtic/tr/fulltext/u2/a047747.pdf (archived at https://perma.cc/GX3G-Y2QL)
4 D Kahneman, *Thinking, Fast and Slow*, Farrar, Straus And Giroux, New York, 2011.
5 S Gorovitz and A MacIntyre, Toward a theory of medical fallibility, *The Hastings Center Report*, 5 (6), pp 13–23, December 1975. www.jstor.org/stable/3560992 (archived at https://perma.cc/4VP9-V84U)
6 R S Tedlow, *Denial: Why business leaders fail to look facts in the face – and what to do about it*, Portfolio, New York, 2010. www.hbs.edu/faculty/Pages/item.aspx?num=32392 (archived at https://perma.cc/74E6-G2Y9)
7 D Quackenbos, R Ettenson, M S Roth and S Auh, Does your company have what it takes to go global? *Harvard Business Review*, 11 April 2016. https://hbr.org/2016/04/does-your-company-have-what-it-takes-to-go-global (archived at https://perma.cc/6Y5E-TPES)
8 R Larson and E Larson, Creating bulletproof business cases, Paper presented at PMI® Global Congress 2011: North America, Dallas, TX, Project Management Institute, Newtown Square, PA, 2011.

04

Defining your approach

Global integration vs local responsiveness

I was visiting a rural village in Ethiopia for work and stopped at a local shop to get a drink. There were several local options that were new to me and one called ኮካ-ኮላ that I recognized immediately. That's not because I speak Amharic. I recognized the drink because of the bold white letters against the cherry-red background and distinctively shaped bottle. It was Ethiopian Coke. Not only did I recognize it, but I also knew exactly what it would taste like if I bought it. That's because Coca-Cola is a brand that uses a global approach to the markets it serves. The Atlanta-based company has gone to great lengths to standardize its brand and its product in the 150+ counties where it is officially marketed. It occasionally modifies the language on the label and replaces cane sugar with high-fructose corn syrup in some markets. By and large, however, the Coca-Cola Corporation strives to make the buyer's experience with the brand identical, whether it's purchased in Atlanta or Addis Ababa. It would seem that the appeal of Coca-Cola as a soft drink is universal, which, no doubt, creates profit-boosting efficiencies for the Coca-Cola Corporation.

The American food processing company HJ Heinz has chosen a different approach to its markets. Collectively, Heinz's portfolio of 20 brands is as globally pervasive as Coke. Unlike Coca-Cola, Heinz actively alters its food products to adapt to local markets. Even the recipe of its iconic ketchup is adapted to suit local tastes around the world. While you might recognize the Heinz label in a foreign grocery store, you could not be 100 per cent certain that the product inside would be the same as similarly labelled products from your home market.

Could the product you sell benefit from the type of global standardization that Coke pursues, or do you feel you could best achieve your business goals with a more localized approach like Heinz? As you look to market your brand beyond your home market, you will start to feel the tug of two opposing forces. On the one hand, you have the pressure for global integration on operations and strategies. The benefit here is economies of scale, cost reductions and simplicity. On the other hand, you have the pressure for local responsiveness to better compete by satisfying the needs of local buyers, accommodating different distribution systems and complying with local norms, laws and regulations. Too much of either is not good for business, so you'll need to define your own comfort zone.

Dealing with multiple markets brings new decisions that company leadership have to make. Basically, you need to sort out how decisions are made, and what stays the same and what is customized to suit local markets. As with most things in marketing, there is no one-size-fits-all solution because the challenges faced by each particular brand in each particular market are unique. The good news is that management consultants have been developing models for the past half-century to help. You can choose from global, international, multinational, transnational and multi-domestic approaches, to name a few.

For large multi-national corporations (MNCs), the approach they choose towards their markets is well thought through and a central part of their overall business strategy. For small to mid-sized businesses looking to grow abroad, it can easily fall to the periphery. These companies often decide on their approach to international markets in a binary manner, choosing between either centralized or decentralized management and standardized or localized products. This choice is typically made at an administrative level based on what is most convenient and least costly at the outset. There's nothing wrong with making the decision based on those two criteria, but the mid to long-term implications of that choice should at least be considered and discussed. Marketing is one of several functions in the company that will be directly affected by the approach chosen. As such, marketing leadership should be actively involved in that decision, along with the heads of other affected functions.

This chapter can't answer the question of which approach is best suited for your company. That's because there are legal, operational, taxation and other considerations on which I'm not qualified to offer advice. I will only be commenting from a marketing perspective. In doing so, I shed light on the implications that the different approaches have for marketing strategy and brand identity.

Embracing complexity

One of the seminal texts in cross-border management is *Managing Across Borders: The transnational solution* by Christopher Bartlett and Sumantra Ghoshal.[1] I think they best captured the transition from domestic-market focus to international when they described it as adding a third dimension to your business.[2] Although the book was first published in 1989 (an updated second edition was published in 1998), I recommend reading it. The book's focus is management more than marketing specifically, but the two are so intertwined that marketers should find its examples, analysis and advice highly relevant.

Their work was based on discussions with over 250 managers working in nine MNCs. They found patterns in the thinking of these executives that I myself have observed working with companies expanding abroad. Many of the MNCs Bartlett and Ghoshal describe took a similar trial-and-error line over decades to arrive at a market approach that worked best for them. I'd argue that many CEOs today could spare themselves some of that trial and error by learning from the examples that Bartlett and Ghoshal present and applying those lessons to their own organizations.

The evolution of market approach among MNCs that the authors describe is still played out within companies today. It often starts with a binary, two-dimensional view of their options. Managers faced with internationalization feel as if they have to make sweeping edicts with regard to choices between whether to employ a system of centralized command and control or allow for greater autonomy in their subsidiaries, whether to standardize the marketing mix or be more responsive and adapt it to local markets, and whether key assets and resources like research and development (R&D) or manufacturing should be centralized or decentralized.

Bartlett and Ghoshal found three universal assumptions that MNC managers from all industries, countries and management cultures made when making decisions about how to approach their markets:

1 The first was the assumption that MNCs need a uniform and symmetrical management approach across all units, in all countries, and across all functions in those units.

2 The second was that the MNC needs clearly delineated relationships between all units, defining each as either dependent or independent of the other.

3 The last was the assumption that, in an MNC, the principal role of management is to institutionalize decision making and simplify the mechanisms required to exercise control.

If you hold any of these three assumptions, you're not alone. They were considered by all the managers they interviewed to be fundamental to success when working across borders to the point that they were rarely discussed, let alone questioned. They came from what the authors saw as an intrinsic need to reduce organizational and strategic complexity shared by all the executives. Presumably, they were trying to constrain complexity, at least to the same levels that were experienced in the cosy confines of their home market. After all, that was the only blueprint for success these corporations had as they ventured abroad.

The authors, however, make the case that the decision to go international in itself multiplies a company's organizational complexity. There is no way around this. Increased complexity is part of the price you pay when you commit to growing your business over borders, no matter what approach you take. Trying to eliminate that complexity is counter-productive. Companies must instead strive to understand and embrace it. The first step is to toss out the three assumptions defined above and replace them with new thinking.

MNCs that thrive do just that. Instead of seeking uniformity and symmetry in management practices, they strive to understand differences between units, markets and functions and systematically differentiate their approach to address those differences. They replace the dependent vs independent mentality by striving for interdependence instead. They replace the command-and-control mentality with a desire to coordinate and co-opt. Companies that have mastered this approach are what Bartlett and Ghoshal refer to as transnational companies, a highly competent subset of MNCs characterized by their ability to maintain high levels of global cooperation while at the same time being highly responsive to the market environments in which they operate.

The Unilever approach

For example, working under the three assumptions above, Unilever had a long history of decentralized responsibility, allowing national subsidiaries to make their own decisions. However, over time, this blanket approach became increasingly difficult to manage on a global scale. The authors cite the example in the 1970s when Unilever's rival, Proctor & Gamble (P&G), launched a laundry detergent based on a new formula that was developed centrally and sold by P&G's national subsidiaries. Most of Unilever's autonomous national subsidiaries acted independently, addressing the threat on their market. They developed 13 different formulations and launched them in their markets. The cost of re-inventing the wheel 13 times over was substantial. Worse still was the realization after that work had been done that not one of the 13 new formulations was as good as the formula Unilever had developed centrally and which all 13 markets had passed on, opting instead to develop their own solution. This experience led Unilever to rethink its approach.

Instead of decentralizing everything, Unilever acknowledged that some product categories would benefit from less global coordination and more national differentiation than others. For instance, their detergent business might benefit from less autonomy and local product variation, while its food business might benefit from more autonomy and product localization. But that didn't necessarily apply to all the functions within those businesses.

On a functional level, Unilever realized that research and development for detergents would benefit from a highly centralized global cooperation where marketing for detergents would benefit from a more autonomous approach with more national differentiation. They didn't stop there. They took it down to a geographic level for each function in each business area. In the example above they determined that with regard to marketing for detergents, countries like Germany, the UK and France would benefit from both high global coordination and localization of marketing efforts, as opposed to Brazil and India, where localized marketing worked best with very little global coordination. This case-by-case assessment replaced simplistic dichotomies of global vs domestic, standardized vs customized, centralized vs distributed. Transnational companies don't ask which of these approaches is best. They ask which is best for specific functions of specific product categories in specific geographies. They accept that choosing one approach over the other for everything is a losing proposition. They embrace complexity.

To thrive as an MNC, managers should consider replacing the two-dimensional thinking that works in one's home market with a three-dimensional perspective that accommodates the complexity introduced by going international. The authors found that changing this thinking was very difficult for MNCs that had been operating under the three assumptions. That's good news for those of you who are starting your international journey, since you have an opportunity to shape your organization for international growth now and avoid the pain and cost of trying to retrofit it later.

Multinational corporation structure

To help provide some easy landmarks by which to navigate your approach to the market, let's define an MNC as any company that trades in multiple foreign markets and makes investments in those markets, also referred to as direct foreign investment (DFI). DFI can range from simply marketing there to opening offices, shops, or manufacturing or distribution operations. From there we can use Bartlett and Ghoshal's model to label three basic approaches that MNCs use toward their markets: global, transnational and transdomestic. These are identified in an integration-responsiveness (IR) grid (Figure 4.1). The vertical axis of the grid represents low to high global integration. This indicates pressure for centralized control and standardization. The horizontal axis represents low to high local responsiveness. This indicates pressure for autonomy and differentiation to best suit local market conditions. Note that one of the approaches in the grid, 'international approach', involves no DFI and therefore no local brand development.

There are dozens of overlapping terms used to define the different approaches companies take when they do business outside their home market. These terms are also used in an inconsistent manner from one author to the next. For the purposes of our discussion, the finer points of taxonomy used to describe the various approaches below are not important. The objective of all these approaches is the same: To strike the right balance between reaping efficiency gains through standardization and centralization while at the same time being responsive enough to buyers, competitors and overall market conditions to compete successfully. What marketers can take away from these approaches are that trade-offs will need to be made between the efficiency gains made through standardization, centralization and economies of scale vs the competitive gains made by localization, autonomy and adapting to the nuances of the local market. There are solutions at each end of that spectrum and a range of options in between. The approaches defined below each fall neatly into different boxes. In practice, however, MNCs often combine aspects of different approaches to create their own hybrid solution or

FIGURE 4.1 Integration–responsiveness grid: Bartlett and Ghoshal's model for finding the right balance between integration and responsiveness

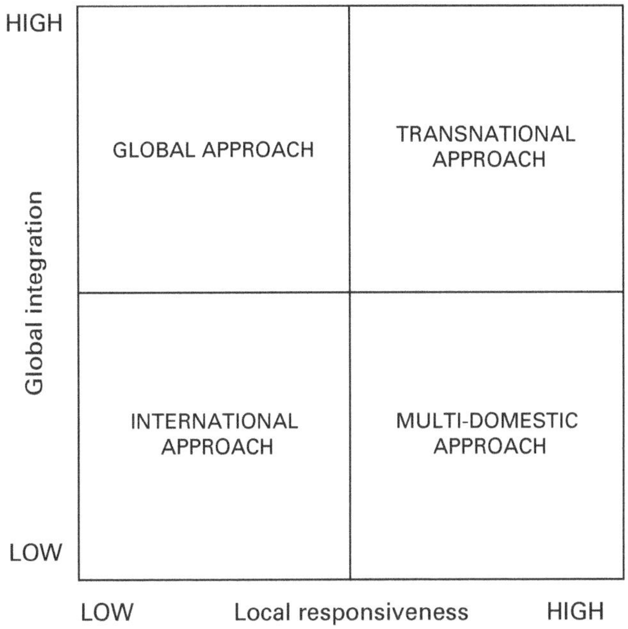

	Local responsiveness LOW	Local responsiveness HIGH
Global integration HIGH	GLOBAL APPROACH	TRANSNATIONAL APPROACH
Global integration LOW	INTERNATIONAL APPROACH	MULTI-DOMESTIC APPROACH

use different approaches for different products. You will need to decide which combination of forces will affect your business in the markets you are entering and develop your approach in response.

The global approach

Global integration: High

Local responsiveness: Low

The global approach strives to achieve maximum cross-border efficiencies through standardization with minimal adaptation to local markets. Here control is highly centralized and very little, if any, autonomy is given to the local subsidiaries. Decisions are centralized at the global headquarters, which is often but not always situated in the market where the company was founded. These companies strive to standardize the product, pricing model (not the actual price), distribution and promotion as much as possible. They adapt to local needs only when deemed absolutely necessary. This is often the case with regard to the use of language in the product or promotion. Even in regard to promotion, however, the aim is to produce global campaigns that are readily adapted to the local language. Under this definition, examples of MNCs that lean towards the global approach with highly standardized products and brands include Coca-Cola, Gillette and Microsoft.

The multi-domestic approach

Global integration: Low

Local responsiveness: High

This is the opposite of the global approach. MNCs that adopt this approach are different from global companies in that they routinely adapt their products as needed to suit local market conditions and preferences. Companies taking this approach are typically under great pressure to adapt to different needs, tastes, regulations or other market factors in the different countries where their products or services are sold. In order to compete, they gravitate towards autonomy in both their management and marketing mix. Efficiencies are often sacrificed in return for greater responsiveness. This can be tricky to pull off if the company also strives for an identical brand identity. A global law firm would be likely to follow this model since the laws and legal norms in each market would be very different. In this case it would want to ensure that the core brand values and, if possible, value proposition are upheld by the different offices despite the differences in legal code. Of course, the ultimate expression of a multi-domestic approach would be to develop different brands for the local markets as well.

The transnational approach

Global integration: High

Local responsiveness: High

These companies have the most difficult job of all. They strive to be highly responsive to the local market while at the same time reaping the efficiencies of high integration. In this sense, trade-offs are made on a business area by business area, function by function, and location by location basis. Yes, it's complex, but it allows these companies to have the best of both worlds. In addition to deft management, the transnational approach requires very well codified values, brand identity and product requirements to ensure that the system does not devolve into a portfolio of different products that are similar in name only. While the various subsidiaries around the world may or may not be controlled centrally, they do fall under some centralized constraints with regard to the brand and the product. For instance, Nestlé's Kit Kat bar is sold in Nestlé's home market of Switzerland as chocolate layered between cookie wafers. In Japan, however, the Kit Kat bar has been completely re-invented to suit the local market. The Japanese Kit Kats are offered in a range of colours, with both sweet and savoury flavours like baked potato, wasabi, cheesecake and green tea. In fact, there have been over 300 different limited edition flavours launched in Japan. Nonetheless, the brand name, logo, shape, packaging material, general manufacturing process and cookie wafers are the same. For Kit Kat in Japan, this approach works. It has made Kit Kat the number one confection in the country.

The international approach

Integration: Low

Responsiveness: Low

Companies that use this approach sell to buyers from different countries but make no direct investments in those countries. These international companies are often called exporters. They only have operations in their home country and make their product or provide their service from their home country. Their buyers, on the other hand, can be from outside their home country. This could be a contract manufacturer in China that produces bicycle parts for other companies globally. It could be a chateau in Bordeaux that exports its wine around the world. In any event, these companies do not invest in developing brand equity in any of the foreign markets where their buyers reside. For that reason, they fall outside of our focus.

Conclusion

How should you choose between global integration and local responsiveness for your business? You shouldn't.

1 Don't choose for your business as a whole – choose for each business function, in each geographic area and for each business line.
2 Don't make binary choices – explore the range of possibilities in between the two extremes to find the sweet spot for specific functions in specific markets for your specific business.

That's the way to approach it if you want to be highly responsive to your markets (which will help you compete better) while gaining the efficiencies of global integration (which helps you profit more). Of course, a ball bearing, aspirin or semiconductor may require very little market adaptation compared to a restaurant chain, comedy podcast or legal textbook. You will have to assess the forces at play on your business in the markets you are entering and make the best call.

This chapter has laid out a theoretical framework to help you formulate an approach to the market. In the next chapter I take a more operational stance and provide a few practical suggestions on how to deal with differences in language and culture.

Notes

1 C A Bartlett and S Ghoshal, *Managing Across Borders: The transnational solution*, Harvard Business School Press, Boston, 1989.
2 C A Bartlett and S Ghoshal, Managing across borders: New organizational responses, *Sloan Management Review*, 29 (1), pp 43–54, Fall 1987.

05

Being understood in foreign markets

The power behind your promotion

It was advertising legend David Ogilvy that said, 'I don't know the rules of grammar... If you're trying to persuade people to do something, or buy something, it seems to me you should use their language, the language they use every day, the language in which they think. We try to write in the vernacular.'[1]

Ogilvy wasn't referring to international marketing specifically, but rather to effective promotional copy. His words capture the tension behind any effort to get promotional concepts from one language to another. It's the struggle between the marketer's fear of making a stupid mistake in the spelling, grammar or syntax in a foreign language, and their desire to write text that persuades the target audience to the brand's point of view. This tension also extends to the struggle between being faithful to the source text, and saying things in a way that sounds natural in the local context and will cause the same desired effect in the recipient.

In this chapter I hope to relieve some of the tension by exploring the role of language in marketing and how to preserve the essence of good writing when taking promotional concepts from one language to another. At the outset, I'd like to introduce the concept of source vs target text, language and culture. When you have created a promotional text in your native language that you wish to have translated into another language, we refer to that text as the source text, which was written in the source language from the perspective of the source culture. The source text is then translated into a target text that reflects the language and culture of the intended recipient.

The biggest challenge in any writing is to accurately convey emotion. But does this matter to marketers? I'm guessing some of you responded 'Of course it does.' For the rest, I'll first make the case that being able to elicit an emotional response in your target audience is good for business. Then I'd like to explore how we can make that happen and avoid some common pitfalls.

The role of language

Marketing in multiple languages offers its own set of challenges. To help you manage, let's start by looking at the role that language plays in marketing promotion. First off, language conveys factual information – a vital function of communication that most eight-year-olds have mastered. Of course, this is important to marketing because facts are the fuel of rational decision making. There's just one catch: most decisions are heavily influenced by non-rational drivers. In fact, as Harvard professor Gerald Zaltman has noted, up to 95 per cent of what drives purchase decisions is not rational.[2] This research suggests that clear, concise, logical arguments can satisfy your buyer's rational sensibilities. But, you could be far more effective if you state your case in a way that satisfies their emotional sensibilities as well. Good marketing communication does this because it conveys more than facts. It also engages, motivates and inspires on an emotional level. It does that with skilled copywriting and art direction.

This creates three challenges for the international marketer:

1 Ensure the accuracy of the facts being communicated in the foreign language. This can usually be accomplished with a back-translation of the foreign text into your native language.
2 Ensure the right spelling, grammar and syntax are used in the foreign language relative to the target. This is not always straightforward, since the way a language is used day-to-day can vary from the official rules, and may also vary from one target segment to the next.

3 Ensure that the tone and manner of the text strikes the right chord with the reader on an emotional level. This is all but impossible for a non-native speaker to assess on their own. It puts a great deal of responsibility and trust on the person who is actually writing your copy in the foreign market, even with guidance from the source text you provide.

Whether they call themselves a translator, adapter or transcreator, the person working with your target text should be a skilled writer in the target language. A competent expository writer can convey information in a clear and compelling manner. A good copywriter, like a good novelist or poet, can do even more with language. They can use language, both explicitly and implicitly, to convey and elicit emotion that can have a very specific effect on the reader. In that sense, good marketing promotion functions more like creative writing than expository writing. This emotional component is useful to foster interest, trust, belief, affinity and advocacy among a brand's stakeholders.

How language is used also conveys contextual information about the sender in terms of how similar they are to the receiver and how aspirational or trustworthy they may be. For instance, I was once counselled by one of our younger consultants to stop using 'LOL' to indicate amusement when texting. She said it made me seem out of touch with her peer group, since the new norm at that time was to use 'HaHaHa'. Both phrases express amusement, but one also communicates how socially tuned-in the sender is – at least to her demographic. How we interpret information can be coloured by the context of our language as well as culture, socioeconomics, age, gender and belief system. This list is not exhaustive, but the point is that the writer needs to understand these contexts and reflect them in the text.

So it would seem that language can do more than simply convey factual information. In the hands of a skilled copywriter it also can accurately reflect the reader's context, convey implicit information and elicit specific emotions. All this can change the way the recipient thinks, feels and buys. Using skilled writers also costs more and takes more time. Can we justify the cost and time associated with getting the writing right?

The link to sales

Dr Zaltman is not alone in his conclusion that positive emotions equate to sales. A quick online search will reveal a trove of research from neurology, sociology, economics, and marketing that links the emotions a brand evokes to the money a business earns. For example, a 1991 study by the Advertising Research Foundation[3] compared 35 different advertising pre-testing methodologies to see which was the best metric for predicting product purchases. While all metrics had some merit, only one surpassed all others: likability. This basic emotion has since been linked to brand persuasion, memorability and loyalty. The likability of ads and other promotional materials, in turn, has been tied to storytelling that amplifies feelings, visual descriptions, empathy, use of metaphor and simile, as well as humour. These are all the hallmarks of good creative communication as practised by accomplished copywriters and art directors.

Researchers have established a credible correlation between the creative quality of a brand's promotion (ie the specific words and images that marketers use) to sales and market share. For instance, a study by Neilson in 2017 quantified the impact of advertising on sales.[4] The study looked at five variables to determine their relative importance to sales. Those variables were:

- Reach: The percentage of the target segment that is exposed to the message.
- Targeting: How well the message reaches the actual buyers
- Recency: The timing of the message so the target sees it immediately prior to the purchase decision.
- Creative: The communication concept and the words and visuals used to express it.
- Context: The content and media context in which the message appears.

All of these factors would seem pretty important to help your promotion drive sales. But the study found that one of these factors is more important than all the others combined: creative. That is, the concepts, words and images you use to convey your message. One take-away from studies like this is that if the quality of the creative is not up to scratch then the money you spend on media (which is often the largest part of a promotion budget) will be largely wasted.

What's more, the study found that the importance of creative quality in driving sales results is over 50 per cent higher for online video, display and mobile advertising compared to TV. That means that getting the words and images right is even more important for brands that rely on digital advertising. The study asserts that, 'In the case of digital campaigns… the quality of the creative is paramount. Even the best media plan won't save a campaign with poor creative'.

It seems safe to conclude that the conceptual ideas and words we use in our promotion are important to our sales in any given market.

Working with multiple languages

Some marketing communication will be market-specific. At other times you will have similar communication needs across multiple markets, as in the case of advertising campaigns. On those occasions you'll have to decide if you will create different campaigns in each market, create one campaign for all markets, or something in between. If you have equally skilled communication agencies in each market, then creating individual market-specific campaigns may provide the best return on objective, but will probably fare less well with regard to return on investment. That's because the cost and time required to create and manage campaigns in that manner can be prohibitive.

Even if you are running a highly decentralized marketing programme, there will be occasions when you may benefit from creating one campaign and then adapting it to local markets. This approach provides more centralized control and is somewhat less expensive, but creates the thorny problem of getting one concept to work across multiple languages and cultures. Google Translate to the rescue? Probably not, and to explain why let's break the problem down a bit.

Any advertisement typically has three working parts: the creative concept (the idea), and the words and images used to convey that concept. The concept and the words are inextricably linked to language, which is inextricably linked to culture. One of your biggest challenges as an international marketer is taking concepts and words that are interwoven into the fabric of one culture and seamlessly transplanting them into the fabric of a different culture.

Marketers are not the only ones with this problem. The world of literature has been grappling with this same problem for ages and there is plenty we can learn from them. In both cases we are talking about situations where more than factual information is being conveyed and where getting it right is crucial, at least to the project sponsors.

The point here is that translating creative text is not just matching up words with a dictionary. The denotative part, finding equivalent words, is just the beginning. The real work is in capturing the connotative part expressed through the original author's syntax, flow, diction, pace, rhythm, register, intensity and effect on the reader. This applies as much to the translation of well-written promotional text as it does to classic literature because both must evoke emotion to work.

How to translate promotional material

So, then, how do you translate promotional copy? In most cases you don't. You adapt it instead. Translation is the transposing of individual words and grammatical structure from one language to another. Sounds easy enough. And if marketing communication were simply stating facts it would be easy to get your message across in foreign countries. Unfortunately, that's not the case.

As with literature, promotional copy does more than communicate factual information. It has a much broader role in marketing. It must earn the reader's trust and convince them that the voice behind the words is honest and understands their unique situation. It should sound fresh and authentic. It should inspire and motivate prospects. This is hard enough to do when you are marketing a domestic brand and much harder when you approach your target as a foreign brand. To establish this credibility you'll need more than facts clearly stated in perfect grammar. You'll need both the denotative and connotative elements mentioned above. These elements of persuasive writing are not mere options or 'nice to haves'. They are essential to the effectiveness of the copy, and they rarely survive conventional translation.

Writing for the translator

It's worth noting here that the knee-jerk reaction of most marketing managers who lack international experience is to veto any promotional concept that includes words or cultural references that can't be literally translated. In its place, they ask for simplified text that will make it easy for the translator. I've often been asked to write in 'simple translatable English', 'culturally-neutral English' or, my favourite, 'mid-Atlantic English'. What they mean is English that is void of any colloquial expressions or cultural references – a sort of synthetic English that comes from nowhere and speaks to no one in particular. That way it can be translated by anyone.

This is a natural reaction for people who only know translation. They do it because they think it will provide them with greater quality control over the process. However, requiring that the writing be stripped of all cultural nuances is not a good idea if you want your promotion to connect with people. This is called 'writing for the translator' and is a classic case of the tail wagging the dog.

Fortunately, there is another way to get your message into other languages. It's called adaptation. Adaptation is the transposing of concepts and ideas (not just words and grammar) from one culture to another. It is better to hire competent people who can adapt well-written promotional copy into the local culture than to create weak, dumbed-down promotion to ensure goof-proof translation.

The art of adaptation

You invest in professional copy for its ability to inspire and motivate. Those are the first two qualities that can be lost in translation. To protect your investment and maintain the effectiveness of your original idea, it must resonate and motivate in another culture. That's why adapters exist.

One of my favourite examples of adaptation is an ad for SAAB automobiles I worked on as a creative director for the Lowe Group in Stockholm (now MullenLowe Group). My colleague Christine Björner headed up the adaptation work. Before joining an ad agency, Christine had taught English literature at Stockholm University. Not a typical career path for an advertising executive, but one that uniquely prepared her for her role. Teaching literature, she understands the craft of writing in all its thematic beauty, dramatic power and implicit subtlety. More importantly, she understands writers and the creative process that's required to produce great work. This, combined with her positive management style, is what makes her the best at what she does and a master at managing the adaptation process.

With this SAAB campaign the plan was to use the same visuals globally for all ads and collateral and to adapt the headlines and body copy per market. It was the global launch of the SAAB 9-3 cabriolet and one of the creative teams had come up with an ad that, in essence, suggested the car as an antidote to oxygen bars. At the time, oxygen bars were trending in the US. They were bars where instead of getting a cocktail you would get a canister of pure oxygen to inhale. The headline read 'SAAB vs oxygen bars'. The copy in the ad made the point that if you feel the need for more oxygen, you should be driving this car, not sniffing air from a can.

The ad fitted into the campaign nicely but was originally sidelined because someone made the observation that it could not be translated for use outside the US. They were correct. But Christine argued that it was OK because we were not translating these ads, we were adapting them. The challenge of copy adaptation is to get ideas from the source language into the target language in a way that:

- makes sense linguistically
- gets the point across conceptually
- resonates culturally

- has the same effect on the reader
- reinforces the personality and values of the brand.

Sometimes the writer can do that by sticking pretty close to the wording of the source material. Other times, as in this case, they can't – and that's OK. For instance, in Sweden, Christine turned to a skilled writer named Björn Hjalmar. He was the copywriter for SAAB Sweden and knew the brand inside and out. He understood what the US ad was getting at and adapted it from 'SAAB vs oxygen bars' to 'SAAB vs *klaustrofobi*'. You don't need to be fluent in Swedish to see that his headline positioned the car as the antidote for claustrophobia. Björn focused on the idea being conveyed in the US ad and forgot about the words. There is no way you can translate 'oxygen bar' into '*klaustrofobi*', no matter what dictionary you use. Björn's version used completely different words to create exactly the same effect for his reader. That's how adaptation lets your promotional copy be as persuasive as it can be in every market you enter.

Localization

Although I've worked extensively in Europe, I've never been asked by a European to help them launch their brand in Europe. They always specify the countries. This is rarely the case with requests we receive from outside Europe. Non-Europeans will ask for help 'creating a brand in the European market'. Not to be pedantic, but for all practical purposes there is no 'European' market. Europe consists of 50 sovereign states and almost 750 million people divided among 87 distinct ethnic groups speaking over 100 different languages.[5] While the formation of the European Union created some economic and legal standardization, it has not changed the underlying diversity of the region and the numerous markets that comprise it. From the other side of the Atlantic, the differences between European markets may be easy to gloss over, but from a European perspective these differences can be profound. The same goes for Asia, Africa, the Middle East, South America, Scandinavia, etc.

As I discuss in Chapter 2, strategies and materials designed for targets in one country may not readily transfer to the same demographic in another country. Likewise, strategies and materials developed for one market cannot be adapted for an entire region like Europe. They must be adapted for each country and, in some cases, different parts of the same country.

This becomes critical for companies who depend on the internet for sales or promotion. Should you have one global Facebook page run by someone in your office or, on the other end of the spectrum, have local Facebook pages run by people in the local markets? Should your brand have one global website (perhaps with a menu of language versions) or is it worth developing local sites with market-specific content? There is no easy answer, but the questions should be considered carefully because it can make a difference to your buyers. Some product categories are far more susceptible to market differences on a national and even sub-national level than others. I recall back in 2009 there was a bakery in San Francisco that would tweet to let people in the neighbourhood know when their cookies came out of the oven so locals could run down and get them while they were still hot.

When companies first set up their global web presence, the knee jerk reaction is to have it mirror their sales regions. So they will typically have a national site for their home market then use regional sites to handle the rest of the world. Creating web assets in this way is not advisable. It's better to figure out which are your priority countries and then set up assets to cater to those national markets in the way that the target will relate to and self-identify with. That means striving for an architecture that makes sense to your target and makes them feel they are important to you. For instance, if a Brazilian brand had a robust national site but a poorly translated bare-bones rest-of-the-world (ROW) site, it is understandable that the visitor from Paris might get the impression that the brand caters primarily to its home market and that serving customers in France is not a priority.

One common type of site set up in this manner is the Europe, Middle East and Africa (EMEA) site, or its cousin the EMEAI site, which tosses in India for good measure. How many people do you know that consider themselves proud Emeans? How much do buyers from these markets have in common with each other? Using Table 5.1

TABLE 5.1 Various levels of localization

Targeting level	For ...	Effectiveness
Global	Everyone	Acceptable
Regional	EMEAns	Avoid
Sub-regional	Northern Europeans	Avoid
National	Germans	Preferred
Provincial	Berliners	Preferred
Municipal	Berliners	Preferred
Neighborhood	Alexanderplatz	Preferred
Individual	Lieschen Müller	PERFECTION

as your guide, your web architecture should strive to ensure that your priority markets feel like they are a priority with content that is relevant to them. For some companies this may be a global site, for others it may require greater localization. If you can't afford the level of localization your brand needs today, then make priorities, define the ideal localization plan for your brand, and work at achieving it in a phased approach over time.

Once you have set up your architecture you need to think about how localized the content you publish will be. A story that is of great interest in Mumbai may be far less relevant in Moscow or Manila. Then there is the matter of how closely you will reflect the culture and how deftly you will use the local language. All of these considerations have a cost component that cannot be overlooked.

With 1.3 billion English speakers worldwide, it may be tempting to communicate in your native language to your home market and then use English for your other markets. This is often raised as a cost-cutting measure especially for countries like the Netherlands, Finland or Denmark where English is broadly spoken as a second language. This can work but it is not optimal. If the cost of localizing your brand's communication is a concern, consider the cost of not localizing. All the investment you make in strategy, message development and content production is for naught if no one sees it.

To help you make a business case in this regard, localization expert Nataly Kelly has compiled some facts that you may find useful. In her Born to Be Global blog, Kelly cites research that makes the connection between local language content and local revenue.[6] For instance, 72 per cent of consumers spend most or all of their time online browsing in their native language and 90 per cent of EU web users have a clear preference for websites in their own language. As someone who lives in a trilingual household, I can relate. Kelly takes this point one step further. She also points out that that 72 per cent of consumers say they are more likely to make a purchase from sites in their own language while 42 per cent say they simply won't buy from sites that are not in their native language. Even more compelling is the finding that more than half (56 per cent) of the 13,752 respondents interviewed in one EU study[7] said they would be willing to pay a higher price to companies that provided information in their native language.

Conclusion

Words matter. That's because language does more than convey facts. In marketing promotion, it is used to elicit a specific emotional response. It's this emotional component of marketing communication, when combined with facts, that drives purchase decisions. In fact, there is a positive correlation between the quality of the creative (the agility with which it uses and elicits emotion) and a brand's sales. It seems that the importance of how promotional material is written runs deeper than aesthetics. Artful use of language is, perhaps, the most important factor in driving sales. But great writing is nuanced and fragile. It can easily be ruined in translation. Most people think of translation in terms of the denotative task of matching words from the source language to their corresponding word in the target language. This ignores the greater connotative task of finding like associations to elicit the same emotional response in the reader. This requires a different process called adaptation.

An important decision for any brand today is the degree to which you will localize your web presence. The overarching rule of thumb here is make the content and language as localized as possible for priority markets. Research has confirmed that the locals will be more likely to buy, and pay more, if you do.

In the next chapter I take a closer look at the pros and cons of translation. I provide some practical advice on how to adapt copy and when other options, including translation, may make more sense for your project.

Notes

1. D Ogilvy, David Ogilvy quotes, BrainyQuote, undated. www.brainyquote.com/quotes/david_ogilvy_103081 (archived at https://perma.cc/5936-VUC4)
2. G Zaltman, *How Customers Think: Essential insights into the mind of the markets*, Harvard Business School Press, Boston, 2003.
3. R I Haley and A L Baldinger, The ARF copy research validity project, *Journal of Advertising Research*, 40 (6), pp 114–35, 1991.
4. Five keys to advertising effectiveness: Quantifying the impact of advertising on sales, 3rd edn, Nielsen Catalina Solutions, August 2017. www.ncsolutions.com/wp-content/uploads/2017/09/NCS_Five-Keys-to-Advertising-Effectiveness.pdf (archived at https://perma.cc/ASJ5-3PHP)
5. Europe: Demographics, Wikipedia, undated. https://en.wikipedia.org/wiki/Europe#Demographics (archived at https://perma.cc/66JN-SKU5)
6. N Kelly, 8 reasons to translate website content, Born To Be Global, 10 July 2020. https://borntobeglobal.com/2020/07/10/translate-website/ (archived at https://perma.cc/HF99-U8NR)
7. Directorate-General Communication, User language preferences online, Directorate-General Information Society and Media, May 2011. https://ec.europa.eu/commfrontoffice/publicopinion/flash/fl_313_en.pdf (archived at https://perma.cc/9NGT-F9DG)

06

Alternatives to translation

How to manage language barriers fluently

There are plenty of funny examples of what can go wrong when translating marketing material. I've mentioned a few of them in the preface, but my favourite is a story from the book *Another One Bites the Grass* by Simon Anholt.[1]

The director of marketing for a UK airline asked its advertising agency in London to create an ad to run in Saudi Arabia. The ad was for a flight promotion between Riyadh and London. To avoid any problems with translation from English to Arabic, the director of marketing told his ad agency to make the ad very simple so it could be translated easily. The headline of the ad read 'Fly to London this autumn and save up to 20 per cent on the normal return fare'. The ad was translated and ran in Saudi Arabia. It was a big success. The marketing manager for the Middle East was so pleased that he thanked the director of marketing for the zany and creative ad he had created. The director of marketing was confused because the ad was not zany at all. He immediately found someone to translate the Arabic ad back into English. The headline of the ad read 'Fly to London this autumn and save up to 20 per cent on the normal return fare. AND, while you're there, don't forget to eat at Ahmed's famous Kebab Oasis at 526 Edgware Road, where you will be treated like a prince'.[2] As it turned out, Ahmed was the translator's brother-in-law who owned two Kebab Oases on the Edgware Road.

I received my first lesson in the art of adaption sitting across the desk of Simon Anholt in 1991. My colleague Christine and I came to the London office of World Writers to see if Simon and his team could translate a campaign we'd been working on for Scandinavian Airlines (SAS) into a dozen or so languages. After relating the story above, Simon asked what we needed to be done. No sooner had the 'T-word' (as in translate) crossed my lips than he leaped up from behind his desk, obviously perturbed. With a remarkable combination of fury and eloquence, he schooled me in the difference between adaptation and translation, and how understanding these differences can make or break global campaigns. Being a copywriter himself, Simon understood the role that good writing plays in marketing and the conditions required for its creation. He spoke with evangelical zeal, and by the end of our meeting he was preaching to the choir. Over the ensuing years I have applied his advice daily and used the T-word sparingly.

The right name for the right job

A television screen only has three primary colours – red, green and blue – yet it combines those three colours in different ways to produce the range of hues you see onscreen. I'm reminded of this chromatic phenomenon every time I search for the right word to describe moving an idea from one language to another. There are three methods to do that, which I cover in this chapter: translation, adaptation and creation. Like your TV, these three methods can be combined in different ways to produce a spectrum of terms like transcreation, transadaptation, localization, transculturation, recreation, as well as word-for-word, literal, faithful, semantic, free, idiomatic, adaptive, communicative and marketing translation. In use, some of these terms seem to be separated by shades of meaning so subtle that they cannot be discerned by the naked eye. Typically, I'm grateful for a more refined vocabulary where it adds clarity and allows for greater disambiguation. But since practitioners themselves seem to be in disagreement over how these words should be used, I will do us both a favour and state my case in primary colours.

The right resource for the right job

The services required to produce marketing materials in a foreign language can be categorized in three functional buckets: translation, adaptation and creation. Broadly defined, translation focuses on getting the words from the source text into the target language, adaptation focuses on getting the concept from the source text into the target language and culture, and creation focuses on interpreting the creative brief to create materials for the local market without working from a source text. Which do you really need?

Once you decide what you need, you can decide which resources you want to use. There is a range of services you can use to get marketing communication from one language to another. There's Google Translate, professional translation firms, local ad agencies, freelance copywriters and bilingual friends and colleagues. In Table 6.1 I have identified the seven options I most often use and categorized them under the three functional buckets where I feel they offer the most value.

Each option has different prices, core skill sets, time requirements, etc – all of which will play into your choice of resource. When trying to get text from one language to another, be sure first to define exactly which of the three jobs you need to be done, then match the right skills to the right writing job. Always assess your options on a case-by-case basis. As a general rule of thumb, I avoid translation services for promotional text intended for mass communication. I use translation services for non-promotional texts and, in some cases, as the first step before adaptation or for back-translations afterward.

My personal preference not to use translation services for creative campaigns is not in any way meant to slight their ability or contribution. The lion's share of a company's cross-cultural language needs will be well served by one of the translation resources. My point is that there is a difference between 'translation' as most people know it and 'adaption'. It's important that marketers can make this distinction, to pair the right resources with the requirements of the communication job at hand.

TABLE 6.1 Options for translating text from one language to another

	TRANSLATION			ADAPTATION	CREATION	
TYPE	Translation app	Translator (non-professional)	Translator (professional)	Adaptation copywriter (transcreator)	Copywriter (local freelance)	Copywriter (local agency)	Copywriter (multinational agency)
COST	$$$$$	$$$$$	$$$$$	$$$$$	$$$$$	$$$$$	$$$$$
USE	Inbound	Inbound	Inbound & outbound	Outbound	Outbound	Outbound	Outbound

So, if not translators, who can you count on to adapt your promotional material? A lot of marketers who have failed with translators have turned to advertising copywriters. Copywriters are a natural choice, as they have excellent writing and advertising skills. They understand how to work with brands, briefs, and concepts. In ad agencies they are referred to as 'creatives' – and that's the problem.

Copywriters make their living creating concepts, tonality and style, not adapting other people's concepts, tonality and style. More often than not, they do this in one language. When you give them a piece of copy to adapt, they do what comes naturally: They recreate everything right down to the core concept and visual. Often you can barely recognize what you get back. Once I received copy back from an Italian copywriter that was nothing like the ad he was asked to adapt. 'Was there that much of a problem with the ad I gave you'? I asked. 'No,' the copywriter replied, 'but you have to admit, this is a lot better.' Perhaps, but at that stage in the campaign development process, reinventing the wheel for Italy or elsewhere was not an option. If the idea is really that good, then I would suggest that the writer and their art director be involved in concept development next time around, but not in adaptation. Trying to rein in such writers can be a time-consuming and costly challenge. Further, if they are not working in multiple languages on a regular basis, then you never really know how well their understanding of the source language is, or how adept they are at interpreting it into their own language.

Of course, these characterizations do not apply to all copywriters. Björn, the copywriter who adapted the 'SAAB vs oxygen bars' ad discussed in the previous chapter, was an exception to this rule. He was a very skilled Swedish copywriter who understood adaptation and took to it well. The fact that we worked in the same office also helped. Similarly, copywriters who are fluent in, and work with, multiple languages on a daily basis are often excellent at adaptation work. For instance, I've found Belgian copywriters to excel at adaptation because many are used to producing promotional material in three languages: Dutch, French, and German. Acknowledging such exceptions, I'd still suggest as a rule of thumb that your average copywriter may not be the ideal choice to adapt your promotional campaign. Having eliminated translators and copywriters, this leaves us with adaptation experts.

Adaptation: The best of both worlds

A good translator is proficient in the source language and a native in the target language. They are experienced in multilingual work and derive satisfaction from successfully bridging the two languages. A good copywriter understands the use of nuance and emotion to achieve the objectives of the brand. They derive satisfaction from delivering original text that can inspire and motivate in their market. Global brands need a blend of both translation and copywriting skills in one person, someone who can apply their copywriting skills to the unique needs of multilingual marketing. This individual must be someone who derives their primary work satisfaction not from creating original concepts, but from adapting concepts creatively from one language to another. This is a professional adapter.

These experts have enough of the linguistic skills of a translator to ensure the copy is clear and grammatically correct. They also have enough of the writing and advertising skills to ensure that the copy still performs its primary marketing function. Best of all, they specialize in adaptation. They have learned the tricks of the trade, and they know how far they can change the original copy without going outside the bounds of the brief.

Good adaptors are a lot harder to find than translators or copywriters. They range in price but adaptation houses usually wind up charging the same or slightly less than what you'd pay for an agency copywriter. Since the terminology can get a bit fuzzy, you'll have to do a little digging to ensure that the service with which you are dealing is actually an adaptation house and not an over-priced translation shop. I have experience with four adaptation agencies globally that I would trust adapting promotional material. Even among those four, I find that some are more skilled than others with certain subject matter, copy styles or target audiences. When setting up an adaptation process for large campaigns, I usually choose one adaptation agency but may supplement them where needed with my team's own global network of adaptation resources.

Adaptation isn't cheap. Adapting a campaign can cost almost as much as it costs to have it written in the first place, so it's not surprising that many clients are shocked at the price to professionally adapt copy for foreign markets. It seems expensive because they are comparing it to the price of translation. But think about the flip side. At the point when you need adaptation services, you have made a significant investment in research, communication strategy, account planning and concept development. Beyond that, you have also invested in professionally written copy for its ability to relate to the target, change their perception and motivate them to action. If the writer you choose to adapt it into the foreign language is not at least as proficient a writer as the person who developed the source text, then that investment could be wasted. The real question to ask when you receive the estimate for adaptation is: How much it is worth for you to ensure that the promotion you are investing in increases sales, maintains your premium price integrity and builds brand equity? We can be fairly confident that a traditional translation is likely to achieve none of those objectives. In that context, the fees most adapters charge will seem like a bargain.

Translators have often told me that they can adapt copy rather than just translate it. I believe many can, but it is difficult to assess. I always find it reassuring if the person working with the text has received formal training in adapting marketing materials or, at least, has worked as a copywriter for a decent ad agency. That implies some proficiency in their ability to interpret creative briefs, understand the nuances of brand and target markets, evoke emotional response in the target and motivate that audience to answer the call to action. This background makes it easier for them to understand and adapt another copywriter's work. Not possessing these skills leaves the translator ill equipped if a judgement call has to be made, of which there are many. In my experience, translators are linguistic experts who understand tone, manner and cultural nuance but do not wield them as deftly as a trained adapter in the focused pursuit of a marketing objective. If a translator can do that, then I would suggest they reposition themselves as a writer specialized in adaptation and increase their hourly rate.

A global client commissioned my team to do a study for their global campaign. They wanted us to compare the cost-effectiveness of translating vs adapting vs using local bilingual copywriters in a multi-national agency network. Several ads were sent through the three channels and tracked for quality, cost and time. The upfront cost of adaptation was relatively high compared to translation fees and about the same as using local copywriters. However, the overall value delivered by adaptation was far greater when the end quality, time to get it right and time to brief and manage the resources were factored in.

The use of traditional translation houses for advertising copy frequently showed that they were too faithful to the words on the page, often at the expense of a brand concept, nuance and personality. On the other hand, hiring bilingual copywriters who were not specialized in adaptation generally showed that they understood how to use nuance and personality, but often went off-course in trying to reinvent the creative rather than adapt it. Professional adapters were able to offer the best of both worlds, and we were able to secure all our adapters though one service, saving additional time and hassle.

Adaptation checklist

Below are my top ten questions to help improve the outcome of your adaptation.

- **Is the adapter living in the target market?**
  A good adapter will not only have complete mastery of the language, but they will also have complete mastery of the culture as well. Both are required to craft a convincing adaptation. The likelihood of finding someone who excels in both respects is much greater if you are looking

within the target culture. The closer the adapter is to your target market, the better. One reason is that both language and culture are constantly changing in subtle ways that are often difficult to perceive unless you are immersed in it.

- **Is the target language the adapter's native language?**
People typically translate in one direction. That is, from their second or third language into their native tongue, but not the other way. They may be competent in two or more source languages, but typically will only create in one target language.

- **Is the adapter qualified to adapt?**
Fluency in another language is not a sufficient qualification to translate or adapt text. One of the best interpreters I've ever worked with lives in Beijing. Her fluency in Chinese and comprehension of English are beyond question. I was so impressed after the first time I worked with her that I asked if she could help me with some written translations. She laughed and said, 'I'm an interpreter, not a translator,' as if I should have known that. I should have. Those two jobs require different skill sets, and neither are automatically inherited with fluency. Make sure your writer is experienced in the specific type of work you require.

- **Will the adapter work with a partner?**
When selecting an adapter, be sure to enquire about the process they use to adapt copy. I've found that the adapters that provide the best results always work in teams. That is, the adapter works from the source text and adapts it into the target language. The second writer doesn't even need to be bilingual. They are never shown the source text, only the adaptation, and are asked to critique it purely as a local writer who is proficient in the target language and culture. This way, the second writer reads the copy at face value as the target will. Even the best adapter can get caught in the trap of being too faithful to the original language at the expense of the cadence and vernacular of their own tongue. The second writer, acting as an editor, removes these impurities.

- **Have you accounted for text expansion/contraction?**
The length of the text can have big implications for print layout or TV commercials where the space and timing of the text are critical. Some languages require more or longer words than others to convey the same

idea. For instance, English to French can expand the character count by 25 per cent and as much as 35 per cent for German. Conversely, Chinese, Korean or Japanese will often contract an adaptation from English. Exact ratios for expansion or contraction are difficult to predict based on the language pairing alone. That's because the difference in length is also affected by the type of text. For instance, heavily conceptual texts like literature or promotional copy will usually expand more in any language pair compared to legal or technical texts. The writing style of the source text also affects the length of the adaption. Although there is no simple formula, the person adapting the text should be able to review the source text and give you a ballpark estimate of the target character count at the outset.

- **Is the writer adequately briefed?**
  Be sure to provide an adequate brief to the adapter. This should contain most of the information from the original creative brief plus any extra information the adapter may need, like word count restrictions to ensure the text fits the layout. It is critical that they understand the context in which their words will appear. So be sure to include any layouts and let them know where the promotion will be running.

- **Will you be allowed direct access to the adapter?**
  This will not please the adaptation service but I'd request direct access to the adapter who is working on your project during the process. This way, when snags occur, you can resolve them quickly and effectively by having the source writer speak to the adapter directly. The alternative is to have each side raise and resolve their concerns through project leaders, account managers and other intermediaries.

- **Have you developed your own network of resources?**
  You may have found a good adaptation service, but it helps also to develop a strong and diversified network of people to help you communicate with foreign markets from translators, to adapters, to local writers. You'll also need a network of non-marketing people in the local market on whom you can call for an objective second opinion when assessing texts. Understand each of your resources' strengths, weaknesses and pricing policies upfront.

- **Do you speak the target language?**
  If so, you may wind up being your own worst enemy. Clients with a second language often like to insert themselves into the process. I

understand the urge to do so. After all, when you have a second or third language, it's nice to take them out and use them once in a while. The problem is that, even if you believe you are fluent, you are probably not qualified to create the adaptation for the reasons outlined in this chapter. You may also be over-confident when you assess the work of the adapter. When you hire an adapter in the local market, defer to their judgement. I once used my high-school Spanish to provide feedback to an adaptation done by an eminently skilled adapter in Barcelona. My efforts wasted everyone's time and provided more amusement than insight.

- **Have you arranged for back-translations?**
  The story that started this chapter of the British airline flying from Saudi Arabia should be reason enough to back-translate. Unless you are completely bi-cultural and bilingual, it will be difficult to know what the adapted text says and if it's any good. When you get back the adapted copy, you may want to consider having a 'back translation' done by a professional translator. This is a down and dirty literal translation back into your language. This is good for ensuring that the copy is on topic and the main points were made, but it doesn't tell you much about how authentic the message sounded. Be mindful that the silent killer of many cross-cultural campaigns is an adaptation that looks fine in a back-translation, but sounds lifeless and utterly forgettable or foreign to a native. I often use a trusted local acquaintance for a second opinion. I usually back-translate and get a second opinion on everything when starting a relationship with an adapter. If my confidence increases over time, I start using a translation app for a quick check.

Conclusion

Language is one of the most potent marketing tools you will have in a foreign market. Make every word count. The translation, adaptation and creation of marketing communication are three separate jobs that require three different skill sets. No one of the seven resources listed in Table 6.1 is right for every job. To ensure the best result at the right price, it's important to decide at the outset what job you need to be done, then pair that job with the right resource. Knowing that the jobs and expertise required to succeed at them differ, resist the temptation to compare the prices between resource categories. For instance, comparing prices for adaption and translation is really comparing apples and oranges and could lead you to a poor decision. If you are producing communication that incorporates an emotional component (eg any branded promotion), consider either adapting it with a professional adapter or creating it from scratch with a local copywriter.

Your brand's foreign language skills will play an important role in your efforts to grow sales, maintain a premium price, and build brand equity. In the next chapter I look beyond language and explore other variables you can work with in foreign markets to build success. I start by exploring how strategy can help brands gain and, more importantly, retain leadership when entering new markets or categories.

Notes

1 S Anholt, *Another One Bites the Grass*, John Wiley, New York, 2000.
2 S Anholt, *Another One Bites the Grass*, John Wiley, New York, 2000.

07

Planning for departure

Bon voyage

As with Target, sometimes the biggest threat to succeeding in foreign markets is your own company, not your competitors. A few years after I founded Duffy Agency, the CEO of a successful medical-device company approached us to help grow his business globally. We followed an approach similar to that outlined in Chapter 3 to build a coherent global brand identity and marketing strategy.

The company had a medical division that sold a range of products to hospitals and medical clinics. Its products were well regarded by the medical community, where they were seen as the 'gold standard' in their categories. It also had a fledgling consumer division that sold a few of the company's muscle-toning products as fitness aids through a network of independent distributors across Europe.

As part of the framing exercise, we did store checks in several countries, the last of which was France. After visiting the last store in Paris, the CEO and I agreed to rendezvous at Place de la Madeleine and we recapped over a coffee. I gave him my appraisal. The medical division showed great promise. His products had clear advantages that could be leveraged against competitors to both increase his share of existing markets and grow the market overall. The consumer division also had potential. Since his company was the only consumer player with a medical background and the only one with results supported by research, we could use that credibility to support a price premium.

There was just one thing we needed to do first. After conducting over a dozen store checks around Europe, it seemed the consumer division was operating under one brand name but with several vastly different brand identities and marketing strategies. In some markets his product was the most expensive, positioned and sold as a premium product. In other markets it was the least expensive, advertised on late-night television as a bargain-basement offer. No two markets shared the same value proposition or brand values. Even the graphic profile varied wildly from market to market. None of the markets resembled the brand portrayed on the official website, which was controlled centrally. In many cases the local distributors had put up their own web pages. It was a mess. Worse still, the consumer division advertising was clearly visible to the medical division clients.

The remedy was straightforward. We would create a common brand identity and marketing strategy for the consumer division, tweak the marketing mix for each country, and then coordinate the European marketing activities with localized annual marketing plans based on a common template. As I explained this, the CEO looked pained. 'You don't think that's a good idea?' I asked. 'I love the idea,' he said, 'but the distributors will be the problem.'

The CEO had a different distributor in each country with contracts that gave each of them complete autonomy over sales and marketing in their region. That also included the ability to treat the brand as they saw fit. And they all saw fit to treat it differently. The distributors had no interest in developing brand equity. They were entirely focused on short-term sales and each had a different idea about how best to achieve that.

Remember the multi-domestic market approach discussed in Chapter 4? That can work to build a global brand, but there must be conditions on the autonomy and leverage over the local team to ensure compliance. This CEO had neither. The distributors ruled their dominions. This wasn't a multi-domestic approach as much as a feudal approach. The distributor agreements precluded the possibility of creating a global brand or even building brand equity on a national level. This is how operational decisions can not only hinder marketing but, in this case, prevent it from happening altogether.

When using local distributors or resellers, ensure that the agreement does not in any way hinder your ability to control your own brand and build brand equity in those markets or elsewhere. It was a rookie mistake on my part not to check the distributor agreements at the outset of the assignment. This is one of several items that you should be sure to nail down as you plan your international expansion. The rest I've included in the checklist below, to serve as a quick summary of the main points covered in Part One.

Planning checklist

The checklist is meant to highlight the main points raised in Part One and ensure you haven't missed anything obvious as you prepare to market outside your home market. You'll know you are prepared for departure when you have an answer you believe in for each of the questions below. For each topic, I've suggested whether it should be answered for each local market or globally. In the box that follows this checklist, I've also included a simple model to help you adapt your marketing mix to foreign markets. It defines the eight factors that shape the marketing mix, and how they tie into the workflow process defined in Chapter 3, Figure 3.1.

- **What management approach will you use in the foreign market?**
  Localization recommended – You need to decide where specific types of marketing decisions are made with regard to shaping the marketing mix either to suit their local business needs or to adapt to local buyers, competitors and market conditions. How much autonomy will you provide to local employees or partners in foreign markets? If you adopt a transnational approach, you also have to consider what type of decision, for which type of product, and in what market.

Centralized decision making provides greater operational control to those in the home office, but risks being out of touch with foreign markets. Decentralized control can keep a brand more in sync with the local market, but runs the risk of working against the larger goals of the organization as a whole. Is the sweet spot for any given function in any given market on one side vs the other, or somewhere in between?

- **How will the marketing mix be managed in the foreign market?**
  Localization recommended – Marketing mix adaptation refers to changes to the product, price, place and/or promotion. I've included a model in the box below to identify the eight elements that shape the marketing mix. Again, in this situation, the true transnational MNC would not make a blanket decision, but would instead consider each aspect of the marketing mix and their related functions. For example it might make sense to centralize some aspects of product development but not others. With regard to promotion, in some markets it might make sense to centralize media buying but to have completely autonomous campaign development, or, in the case of an online campaign, perhaps it makes more sense to go with a global online campaign concept. Certain organizations may allow some aspects of the marketing mix to be adapted but not others. Which makes sense for your business?

    o *How will the product be adapted to the foreign market?*
    Product changes can be made to core features, value-add features, or value-add associations (explained in Chapter 13). They can be done before launch and/or as part of an ongoing R&D initiative to further refine the product to the local market over time. How will R&D functions adapt to the addition of the new market?

    o *How will the cost be adapted to the foreign market?*
    The monetary price will typically vary between markets, but the pricing models used to arrive at the prices are often consistent. Will you look to adapt friction and associative costs (explained in Chapter 13) as well? For example, United Airlines maintained its ticket prices but reduced the friction factor for Chinese customers in 2010 when it replaced its English-language online booking engine with a Mandarin version. For customers in China this lowered the total cost of flying with United, even though the ticket price hadn't changed. Within a few months United saw a 300 per cent increase in online sales from China.[1]

- *How will place be adapted to the foreign market?*
  'Place' refers to how and where the product is distributed and sold. This is often overlooked, but it can be adjusted creatively to add value and differentiate to suit local-market conditions. For example, in 2018 the Japanese fashion brand Uniqlo receive a lot of publicity for selling down vests from a vending machine at San Francisco airport. The machine was said to ring up USD $10,000 a month in sales.[2]

- *How will the promotion be adapted to the foreign market?*
  Promotion is one part of the marketing mix that is usually not only tailored to the local language but often altered conceptually to adapt to the local culture and market conditions as well. Look for efficiency gains where possible. For example, online media buying, web development and production are good places to consider consolidation, while you may want to keep conceptual development and traditional media planning localized.

- **How will the brand identity be adapted to the foreign market?**
  Global approach recommended – Localized brand identity adaptation refers to selectively changing the core brand identity in some markets but not others. Local changes to brand identity run the risk of confusing buyers and eroding brand equity. In some cases, however, they may be unavoidable. For example, trademark conflicts resulted in the US fuel company Standard Oil being banned from using the brand name 'Esso' in several US states. To achieve one national brand it changed its name in 1973 to 'Exxon' for the US but continued to use Esso outside the US.[3]

  The Swiss humanitarian organization, the International Federation of Red Cross and Red Crescent Societies, has had a bumpy ride in this regard. It was founded in 1863 as the International Committee of the Red Cross in Geneva with a logo that was the inverse of the Swiss flag.[4] As the organization grew globally, it faced objections from the Ottoman Empire concerning the historical connotations of its logo relating to the medieval Crusades. As a result, in 1906 a parallel brand called Red Crescent was launched with a logo that was an inverse version of the Ottoman Empire flag featuring a crescent.[5] Although the parent organization emphasizes that the logos are not religious symbols, the public may make those associations on their own. In 2005 yet a third logo was introduced as a compromise to allow Israel to join. Defined by the BBC as 'the new non-religious symbol',[6] it is a red diamond on a white field. Having three different logos is not optimal since, in this case, immediate logo recognition can be a matter of life and death.

Changing the core brand identity may be required in some circumstances, but should be avoided if possible. Managing variants of the same brand globally requires more time and budget than managing one unified brand. Today, stakeholders from one market are likely to be exposed to the brand as it is presented in other markets. Is there a compelling reason to alter your brand identity in any given market you serve?

The brand's identity is the anchor. Strive to make it the same in every market, allowing you to fine-tune your marketing mix to local conditions along with your position without appearing schizophrenic. Just make sure that the local position supports your brand identity and never contradicts it. If adjustments to the marketing mix and position have made it impossible to reconcile with the brand identity, then perhaps the brand is not suited for the market. Instead of diluting the brand to make it fit, consider this as an indication that creating a second brand may be in order.

- **How will you adapt your value proposition so it is suitable for global use?**
  Global approach recommended – Try to develop a universal value proposition that can compete in the markets you are entering and planning to enter in the foreseeable future. This will make it easier to manage the brand across multiple markets. However, not all value propositions travel well. If that applies to the value proposition you are using domestically, consider an update.

  Companies and their products provide value in many ways. The value proposition highlights and communicates the one aspect of value with which the brand can differentiate, build a reputation around and compete. In Chapter 13 I describe the different aspects of value that brands compete with. All of those aspects defined should be assessed and modified on a market-by-market basis to match local conditions, not just the value highlighted in the value proposition.

- **How will you position the brand in the foreign market?**
  Localization recommended – Given the country's unique market environment, how do you want local buyers to compare your brand to their other options, and what can you do to encourage a positive perception?

The position you choose does not need to be identical from one market to the next. This is often a sticking point with domestic brand managers, since they are trained in the doctrine of absolute consistency for brands. Nationally, your brand should be consistent, but some tweaking is often required to position brands from one market to the next. As long as the tweaks are, in fact, just tweaks and don't violate the brand values, you should be OK. Having a strong global brand identity and value proposition can help smooth over differences in positioning and other local-market-specific activity.

- **How will you ensure you get regular input from the market?**
  Localization recommended – When you enter a foreign market, you will often be competing with a mix of local and other expat brands. The locals have the advantage of being part of the fabric of that society. It will be difficult to be as in-tune to the market as they are, even if you are living there. This can put your brand at a significant disadvantage for which you have to compensate. How will you keep your finger on the pulse of developments in the market with regard to buyer perceptions and attitudes, competitor activity, and market outlook? It helps to approach this in a structured manner, since a lot can fall through the cracks when you treat it casually. For instance, a quarterly customer survey and competitor analysis would be better than a quarterly conversation with the local sales manager.

- **Have you documented core marketing strategies and processes?**
  Global approach recommended – The best weapon you have to combat the chaos that comes with increased complexity is documentation that is clear and easily accessible globally. One solution developed by Duffy Agency is to create a secure 'Guiding Star' web portal. Like its namesake, this site is intended to provide a fixed point of reference to guide and direct those working with the brand no matter where on Earth they are. This password-protected site holds the most recent versions of all key marketing documents in a user-friendly, searchable format that is updated regularly. This ensures that the key information is centralized, up to date and readily accessible globally. No matter how you provide access, it helps to have your go-to strategies and processes documented somewhere where your team(s) can easily access them. Here are a few suggestions to get you started:

- *Global brand identity*
  This would include things like brand values, purpose, architecture, personality, backstory, narrative and visual profile.
- *Global copy and graphic guidelines*
  Hands-on guidelines to help those who are creating communication assets for the brand.
- *Global digital strategy*
  It helps to understand the master plan for things like global website and social media architecture and URL/naming conventions as well as how the brand uses online publishing, networking, advertising, SEO, as well as plans for specific platforms.
- *Local marketing strategy*
  Include things like localized target segmentation and profiling, category, value proposition and support, and position, as well as strategic direction for media, advertising, PR and online activities.
- *Local web presence plan*
  This gets into the nitty-gritty of how web presence will be used in the local market, including asset plans and playbooks.
- *Local 12-month marketing plan*
  This is a detailed, calendared, and budgeted breakdown of all marketing activities over the year.
- *Global marketing glossary*
  This defines all key terms, concepts and tools used by the marketing department.
- *Local marketing standard operation procedures (SOPs)*
  This addresses the details of how the local marketing programme will be run, like: How are ads adapted for local use? How is communication that is created locally approved? How do we purchase online media? How do we conduct a target survey?
- *Local communication protocols*
  When working at a distance, you become much more reliant on technology for communication and sharing. I have no fewer than 18 different communication apps on my phone and almost

as many file-sharing platforms. While many of the apps for messaging, file transfer, video conferencing, etc, are global, their popularity can vary from one market to the next. It's best to establish what apps and platforms will be used for what type of communication.

- **Have you documented the steps you will follow to enter the market?**
Global approach recommended – Presumably this will not be the last market your company enters. Launching in a new country can be a very disruptive and time-consuming process. It would serve your company well to have a repeatable process documented that you can use to make market entry more efficient globally. This way, you or your predecessors will not have to reinvent the process with each new market. By having a process, you can also capture the lessons learned with each new market entry and use that information to continually improve your process and thus the effectiveness of your market entry.

THE EIGHT INPUTS REQUIRED TO LOCALIZE YOUR MARKETING MIX

When entering a new market, your vehicle to deliver value is the marketing mix: product, place, price and promotion. There are many variations of Kotler's classic 4Ps Model – any will apply here. For simplicity's sake I will stick with the original.

In the Eight Inputs Model you see that the marketing mix is in the middle, shaped by the eight factors that surround it. Defining and documenting these eight elements will make managing your brand a lot easier, especially if you are dealing with multiple markets. In that case, these eight items should be defined for each market. There are strong interdependencies between the items, so they should not be viewed in isolation.

PLANNING FOR DEPARTURE   113

The eight inputs required to localize your marketing mix are:

Buyer wants & needs	Buyer options	Internal strengths & weaknesses
Buyer beliefs & perceptions	Marketing mix: product place price promotion	Brand identity
External opportunities & threats	Marketing strategy	Corporate goals & priorities

When framing the project we define:

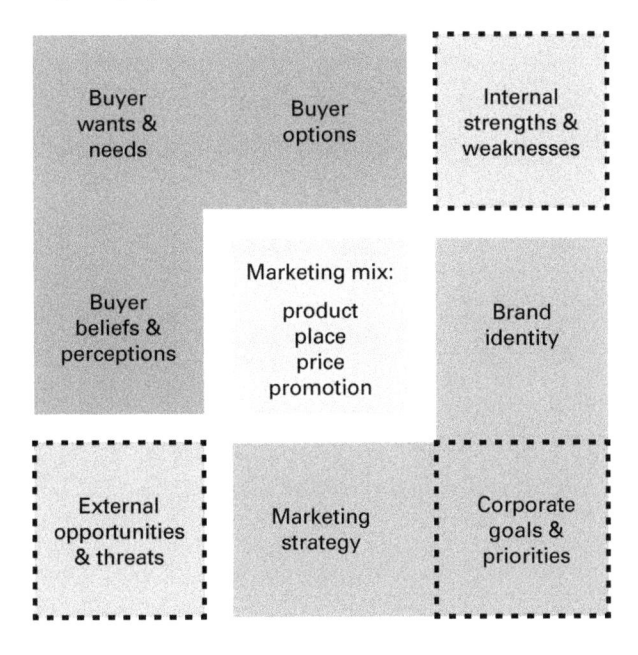

Buyer wants & needs	Buyer options	*Internal strengths & weaknesses*
Buyer beliefs & perceptions	Marketing mix: product place price promotion	Brand identity
External opportunities & threats	Marketing strategy	*Corporate goals & priorities*

To validate assumptions and provide input for our strategy we define:

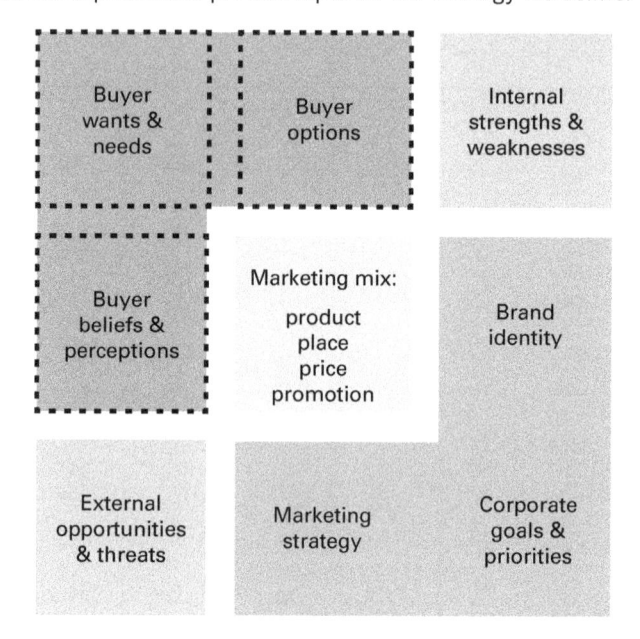

Buyer wants & needs	Buyer options	Internal strengths & weaknesses
Buyer beliefs & perceptions	Marketing mix: product place price promotion	Brand identity
External opportunities & threats	Marketing strategy	Corporate goals & priorities

We define these last two items before defining the marketing mix:

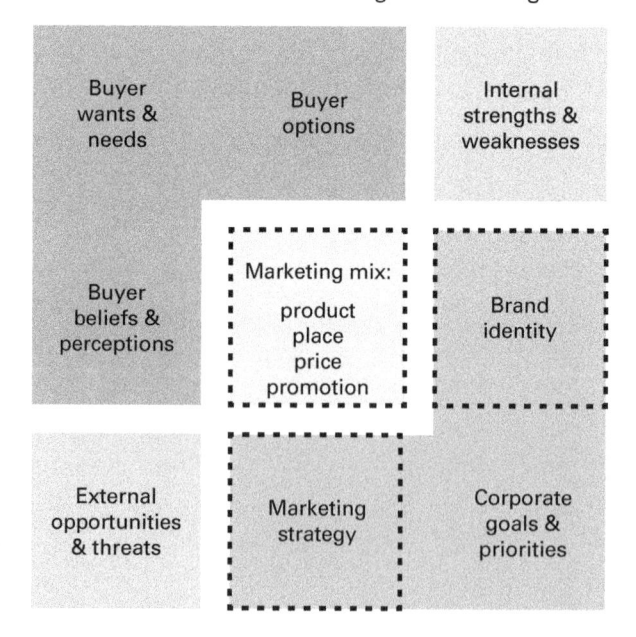

Buyer wants & needs	Buyer options	Internal strengths & weaknesses
Buyer beliefs & perceptions	Marketing mix: product place price promotion	Brand identity
External opportunities & threats	Marketing strategy	Corporate goals & priorities

PLANNING FOR DEPARTURE 115

Management: Once the brand is launched, we monitor these five things:

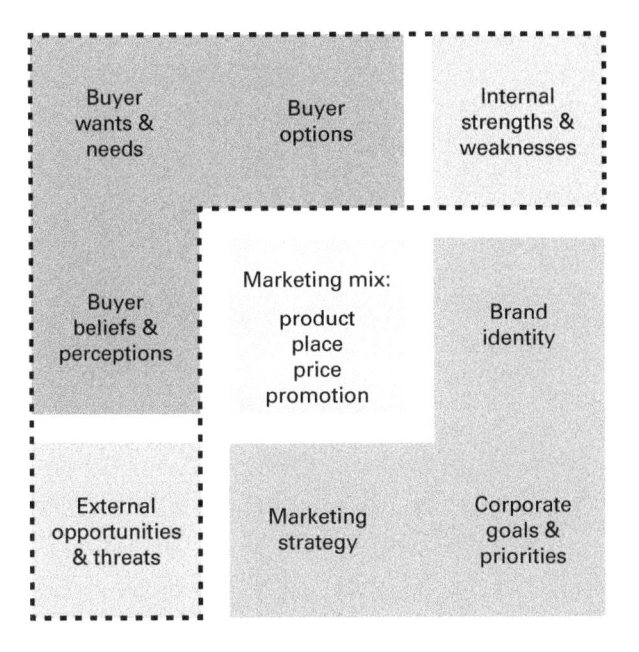

Buyer wants & needs	Buyer options	Internal strengths & weaknesses
Buyer beliefs & perceptions	Marketing mix: product place price promotion	Brand identity
External opportunities & threats	Marketing strategy	Corporate goals & priorities

...and we adapt with these four things:

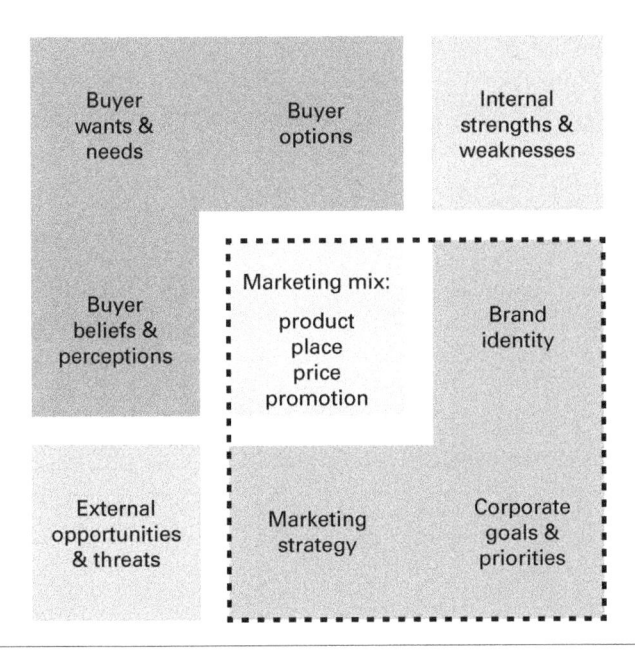

Buyer wants & needs	Buyer options	Internal strengths & weaknesses
Buyer beliefs & perceptions	Marketing mix: product place price promotion	Brand identity
External opportunities & threats	Marketing strategy	Corporate goals & priorities

Conclusion

Marketing internationally is more complex than marketing domestically. That shouldn't put you off. Chess is more complex than checkers, but that doesn't mean it can't be mastered or enjoyed. The part that is not at all enjoyable is when you are blindsided by the complexity because you didn't see it coming. Now you know better. The best way to manage the complexity that comes with marketing outside your home market is to be prepared for it. Most marketers are not. As a result, they find themselves taxed with trying to sort out many of the topics above while they are in the middle of the launch. That's enough to sour anyone on marketing abroad. Save yourself the headache and try to check off as many of these boxes as you can well before launch.

These first seven chapters have looked at what you can do to prepare for entering a foreign market with your brand. In Part Two, I take a deeper dive into how you can build value in that market once you are there.

Notes

1 N Kelly and J Zetzsche, *Found in Translation: How language shapes our lives and transforms the world,* Perigee, New York, 2012.
2 M Woodrow, SFO's vest vending machine creating a buzz, ABC7 News, 31 July 2018. https://abc7news.com/sfo-san-francisco-international-airport-uniqlo-vending-machine-machines/3851468/ (archived at https://perma.cc/8FUJ-KGJW)
3 Our history, Exxon, undated. www.exxon.com/en/history (archived at https://perma.cc/A5UT-SJ72)
4 International Federation of Red Cross and Red Crescent Societies, History, IFRC, undated. www.ifrc.org/en/who-we-are/history/ (archived at https://perma.cc/9EYH-C388)
5 International Red Cross and Red Crescent Movement, Wikipedia, undated. https://en.wikipedia.org/wiki/International_Red_Cross_and_Red_Crescent_Movement#The_Red_Crescent (archived at https://perma.cc/R3M8-4HEL)
6 Red crystal gets official status, BBC News, 14 January 2007. http://news.bbc.co.uk/2/hi/europe/6260353.stm (archived at https://perma.cc/H8ET-E9HB)

PART TWO: CREATING AND DELIVERING VALUE

Introduction

The problem with quality

The email read: 'Herr Duffy, we will no longer be requiring the services of Duffy Agency.'

Being a good marketing consultant means you are often put in the position of helping company leadership interpret what the market is trying to tell them. Sometimes that message is not what company leadership want to hear. At that point, leadership either acts on the insight or shoots the messenger. The latter was the reaction of a northern European photonics company whose CEO had hired my team one year earlier to solve a riddle.

The company was a remarkable success story that began with an incredibly talented engineer – we'll call him Hans (not his real name). Hans discovered a new way to use lasers to test components for imperfections as they rolled off the assembly line. Hans started a company to commercialize his invention that, in turn, spawned an entire industry in laser-based quality-assurance testing. For the first few years, he had very light competition. His company grew quickly and eventually went public. At the outset, the company seemed to have it made. Producers loved it. The stock market loved it. Employees loved it.

At that time, Hans' company had over 80 per cent market share. To ensure it remained in the lead, he and his team worked hard to push the boundaries of the technology ever further. With each new model release came amazing innovations. The number of parameters measured steadily increased, and astounding new levels of sensitivity were achieved. The strategy seemed to work. No competitors entering the market could match the technical performance of Hans' tester. To capitalize on this advantage, the sales team promoted its product as the 'Rolls-Royce of testers'.

The power structure inside the company was dominated by engineers. There was a sales department and sales support but no real marketing function. To his credit, Hans had the good sense to step aside as CEO and hire a professional manager so he could focus on his passion: research and development. The new CEO – we'll call her Alex (not her real name) – was not an engineer and had no experience in photonics, but she was an accomplished CFO and a skilled manager.

A few months after Alex joined the company she invited me to her office. She said she had a nagging question that she was hoping my team could help her answer. She explained that, although the sales growth was strong, the rate of growth was slowing and not keeping pace with the growth in industry demand. Some of this could be attributed to other European competitors, but not all of it. She wanted to figure out what was going on.

I didn't know why her company was losing market share or to whom. But I knew some people who did: her customers. I proposed a study design where my team would speak with buyers in different markets to see what we could learn. Shortly after accepting the assignment I was representing Sweden as part of a trade delegation to China. Coincidentally, Asia Pacific was the biggest region for the company's testers, so I used my visit to make some enquiries with component producers there.

It took just a few days in China to piece together the mystery. When production of the components started, the producers didn't have enough experience to know what could go wrong. But they did know that if their components were flawed then they would lose original equipment manufacturer (OEM) contracts worth millions, so purchasing a highly sophisticated and expensive tester made sense.

Over the years, however, their production techniques improved considerably and the number of flaws in their product fell. Now there were only a few parameters that the producers felt they needed to monitor. The producers felt that our client's tester was overkill. It tested parameters they didn't care about, at a sensitivity level that exceeded their needs. Also, because of its complexity, when new component standards came out it took months for our client to produce an upgrade that could test for them. These frustrations had been building for years before Alex had arrived. Complaints had gone unheeded. Customers felt ignored.

One enterprising engineer in China took notice and saw an opportunity. He spent a lot of his time talking to managers on the production lines. He got to understand their issues from their perspective. He then went and built his own tester that fitted their testing needs like a glove. It was certainly not the Rolls-Royce of testers – it was more like the VW Beetle of testers: a practical, plain-looking metal box that tested far fewer parameters at much lower sensitivity. It was a fraction of the cost compared to our client's tester and could be adapted to suit new standards in a matter of weeks, not months. This new tester was under the radar because it was much more basic, not from a recognized brand and did not have a big advertising budget. But it offered greater value and was gaining in popularity.

Right after I returned from China my team finished our investigation and assembled our findings in a report to show the leadership team. At this point, we had conducted in-depth interviews with buyers from Asia Pacific, North America and Europe. All buyers shared the same frustrations about cost and time to market that we had heard in China. A significant number of buyers also felt that our client's testers exceeded their day-to-day production testing needs.

We concluded that the new category of mini-testers we had seen in China was gaining momentum in Asia Pacific, taking market share, and contributing to the decreased rate of growth our client was experiencing. Based on what we had learned from buyers in North America and Europe, it was reasonable to assume that producers there would eventually pick up on the mini-tester trend as well. Our recommendation was that our client take this threat seriously and develop a mini-tester of its own before this small competitor gained any more traction in the market. This would also require changes to its brand architecture and updating the brand identity and marketing strategies. To put it in perspective, we calculated that, if the threat did materialize as we defined it and if they did not respond, then they could be forced out of the market within five years.

The leadership team knew the category was growing and would eventually attract lower-priced Asian competition, so they did not consider our discovery of the mini-testers notable. The engineers argued that the mini-tester was a poorly engineered, inferior product that was not even worthy of comparison to their testers. I argued that it was not that the rival engineers could not produce a more sophisticated tester – it was that the market didn't want one. Hans felt that the notion that this crude tester from an unknown company posed a serious threat was absurd. He told me that if I were an engineer, that would be obvious to me.

He was right. Had I been an engineer, I too would have seen nothing of significance in my team's findings. But I am not an engineer; I'm a marketer. As a marketer, I saw a company pursuing a differentiation strategy based on technical features that were not valued by buyers. I saw a market category with priorities that were evolving in a predictable fashion away from my client's offer. I saw new, underserved needs emerging, and growing disenchantment with the traditional solutions. I saw an ambitious competitor spending time with my client's customers. I saw a company that did not listen to buyers or respect their opinions. If Hans or his engineering colleagues could see that, I reasoned, then perhaps the threat from the mini-tester would be obvious to them.

That didn't happen, but it was not for lack of trying. My team and I explained all of these factors at length. At the end of our presentation, Hans said that we had forgotten one thing in our analysis. 'What's that?' I asked. 'Quality,' he replied. His engineering colleagues all nodded. 'No matter what you may have heard, the fact is that the engineers who produced that mini-tester will never achieve our quality and certainly not in five years,' he said.

'They don't have to achieve your quality to take your sales,' I replied. 'Quality is completely subjective. Markets never respond to quality, only value.' At this point, he had heard enough. He stood up. 'We invented this industry,' he barked. 'We make the world's best testers. Our engineers decide what quality is in this industry, not the factory managers and certainly not the marketing people.' Ouch. I could only agree to disagree as he stormed out of the room. Alex stayed behind and thanked my team for a job well done.

Over the following months the market for testing continued to expand, but the rate of sales growth for the client continued to slow until it flattened and eventually went into decline. This did not deter Hans from his position, but I suspect it did give pause to Alex. One afternoon, she called to thank me for the work we had done together and to inform me she was resigning as CEO to join another company. She warned me that once she was gone, we would likely be fired. I wished her well and waited for the email mentioned earlier from her successor. It arrived a few weeks after her departure.

My former client was surpassed in global sales within the next year but fervently maintained they were the market leader. When challenged with his declining sales figures, he would say his company led on the technical superiority of its product. This bolstered his team's confidence and blinded them from taking their situation seriously. Once sales were in a free fall, the company finally went against its principles and came out with a less sensitive, lower-priced tester. But its brand identity and architecture couldn't accommodate this type of product. It had not built any equity in the corporate brand and was only known for its 'Rolls-Royce' product offering. What's more, the sales team had done such a fantastic job positioning the original product line that no one wanted to buy a VW from a Rolls-Royce dealer. Strategically, the company had painted itself into a corner.

Ultimately, however, I was proven wrong in one regard. On the day we presented, I had warned that if they did not act, then the company would be forced out of the market within five years. On the fifth anniversary of that presentation, my former client was still in business. It wasn't until five days later that it filed for bankruptcy.

What can we learn from this?

The example above is the case of a company that had everything going for it. In the end, it wound up creating a lucrative category and then handing it over to its competitors. When presenting a case like this, I always feel it is necessary to remind the reader that these were not foolish people. Condensing several years of missteps into several paragraphs can make anyone appear foolish. Hans and his colleagues were some of the smartest people I've worked with – in their respective fields. They felt that if they made the best product they could engineer, then the marketing would take care of itself. It didn't. They pursued a deeply flawed strategy. Hindsight is always 20/20 but many of the mistakes made by Hans and his team were pretty obvious at the time to anyone who was looking for them. To help you as you enter new markets, use the lessons learned from cases like the one above.

Don't mistake ruling the category for leading the category

Rulers don't invite criticism or input. They send down edicts from on high and expect compliance from the masses. Think Darth Vader of *Star Wars* fame. Leadership is a completely different thing. It's about listening and service. A leader will motivate people to follow even when they don't have to. Think Princess Leia. Hans thought it was his responsibility to rule the category he created instead of leading it.

Don't mistake a head start for a competitive advantage

Hans created the proverbial blue ocean by launching his own thriving category, where he enjoyed incredible demand with minimal competition – for a while. Being in that position makes you feel like you've won the race. In reality, it's only a head start and a slim one at that. When you have the type of lead Hans had, you need to take advantage of that time to build barriers to protect the market share you have gained from would-be rivals. Hans tried to do that with technology alone and ignored his customers. One of the strongest barriers you can build is the loyalty of your customers to your brand.

Brand loyalty may develop on its own, to a point, but you should not take that for granted as Hans did. To really create a bond with customers, you need to work at it.

Don't mistake quality for value

When I told Hans that markets do not respond to quality, only value, he flat out rejected the idea. You may feel the same, because it does sound counterintuitive. There is a business maxim: 'Build a better mousetrap and the world will beat a path to your door.' When we talk about building a better mousetrap, one must ask, 'Better for whom?' The seller, the buyer, the mouse? They will all have different perspectives. If the mousetrap manufacturer uses imported teak instead of pine for the base and titanium instead of aluminium for the mechanics then, arguably, you have increased the quality of the mousetrap, but if it is no more effective at catching mice in your basement, have you increased its value?

Building value in foreign markets

In Part One of this book, we focused on preparing your company to build sales, maintain premium pricing, and develop brand equity in foreign markets. Part Two focuses on what you can do to achieve those objectives once you arrive.

A theme that runs through Part Two is value: how to define, develop, and deliver it to buyers. I start that discussion with defensive moves your company can make to hinder competition and protect market share. These tactics can slow the progress of competitors and create some welcome breathing room in which to operate. The most powerful way to keep competitors at bay, however, is to offer more value to buyers than they can. At the end of the day, value is all that matters to buyers and all you have to compete with.

When marketers discuss value it's often in the context of how we can provide more of it to our target buyers. This second half of the book will explore that topic at length. But value is a two-way street.

People who buy products provide revenue in exchange, but they also provide another type of value back to the organization: brand equity. In this section I argue that while every company has found ways to capture and manage revenue, far fewer are as effective at capturing and managing brand equity – if they capture it at all. This isn't simply a feel-good factor; brand equity is bankable and has cash value that can be significant in terms of both the financial valuation of the brand and its mid- to long-term revenue.

Part Two overview

Arrival in a new market is often accompanied by expectations of ramping up sales. As the new kid on the block, will sales tactics alone be enough to get your sales going? Is your intention to milk the market for sales, or to invest in building a brand? Chapter 8 will help you find the balance every marketer has to achieve between short-term sales, long-term-sales and profit. We pay particular attention to B-to-B brands, which often have the most to gain from brand development.

No doubt you anticipate success in your new market, but do you have a plan for what will happen if your brand is a hit? Chapter 9 will emphasize the role that strategy will play once you arrive and offers advice on how to make the most of initial success in the market to avoid the consequences that Hans encountered. It will touch on the need to factor competitors into your strategy and develop methods to slow their progress.

The results of your sales efforts are captured in revenue, but how will you capture brand equity in your new market? The brand provides value to its stakeholders. Stakeholders, in turn, provide value back to the brand in terms of revenue and brand equity. The brand becomes the store of that value increasing its worth. In Chapter 11 I introduce the Duffy Brand Equity Model to illustrate how the market creates value in your business and how you can manage and facilitate that flow of value to capture as much as possible.

How will the buyers in the markets you are entering decide whether to go with your brand or your competitor's? Understanding that would give you an edge. Chapter 12 introduces the concept of Net Perceived Value. The chapter defines how consumers assess value and gives you a simple model to help visualize the process.

The sales function converts the value of the brand's offer into currency through transactions, but sales cannot create value for buyers. How will you accomplish that in your markets? In Chapter 13 we discuss six measures you can take to increase the net perceived value of your offer with the 3-D Product Model and the 3-D Cost Model.

Could the concepts in this book related to international brands also work in the case of commodities where there are no product brands? In Chapter 14 I answer this question with an emphatic YES! This last chapter addresses the case of companies that sell commodities. Even if that does not apply to your company, you may find the examples in this last chapter provide some clarity on the application of key principles discussed in this book.

One last note on the word 'value'. This term has different meanings in different business contexts. The finance professional may see it monetarily as in 'New Present Value'. The human resources director may use the word to talk about the core beliefs and principles shared by employees. For an engineer, the word may trigger associations to value engineering. A retailer may see it as synonymous with sales price. In Section Two I often use the term 'Net Perceived Value' and refer to creating value for buyers. In this context, I am referring to increasing the relative worth of your offer as judged by your buyers so they choose your product over your competitors'. Section Two will explore this idea in detail, but for now, I want to resolve any ambiguity.

08

Balancing short- and long-term growth

Building sales vs building a brand

There is a constant and, for the most part, healthy tension in every marketing department. It exists between the drive for sales to secure short-term revenue and the drive for brand equity to secure long-term revenue. It's like a tug-of-war, with the sales folks on the left and those responsible for the brand's development on the right. The flag in the centre of the rope tends to move off-centre to the left when times are tough, only for the brand side to gain ground when the business is doing well. In recent years, however, I've noticed a steady, insipid creep to the left, with more brand development budget being consumed by short-term sales activity.

The contest between these two forces has been framed as a choice between 'performance marketing' and 'brand marketing'. I share the admiration expressed by Charles Vallance who said, 'I take my hat off to the person who coined the phrase "performance marketing" and then fiendishly restricted its definition to the narrow end of the marketing funnel: to search, programmatic, retargeting and affiliates.'[1] It is a master stroke in positioning on many levels, not least for its suggestion that 'brand marketing' simply doesn't perform.

I was speaking about this with Jeff Jackett, who helped me understand it from the client perspective. After 25 years in senior marketing positions with Unilever, PepsiCo and McDonald's, Jackett is no stranger to this tug-of-war contest. He sees the emphasis on 'performance marketing' growing as brands settle for rational selling propositions to gain immediate sales results at the expense of emotional reasons, which build brand equity when executed properly. The steady migration of budget from building brand equity to driving short-term sales is something he feels poses a real threat to brands. 'The only brands that grow from performance marketing are the Googles and Facebooks of the world, not the brands they claim to serve.' He says that multinationals with direct-to-customer retail are particularly vulnerable. 'The local market managers feel the pressure to deliver positive numbers on a time horizon that stretches no further than the end of the next quarter.' The safest bet under those conditions would seem to be the option labelled 'performance' that comes with reams of numbers to support its claims. When the problems being created at the top of the funnel show up at the bottom, well then, even more performance is needed. 'A better balance is needed,' said Jackett, 'but this balance is hard to find when local officers are incentivized to deliver short term.' Equally vulnerable to the siren song of 'performance marketing' are the management teams of smaller companies who don't yet know that there is more to marketing than driving quarterly sales.

If you recall the Marketing Contribution Model from Chapter 2 (Figure 2.1), it states that the objective of any marketing department is to maintain the balance between increasing sales today, maintaining healthy margins and increasing brand equity to ensure future sales. The pursuit of sales today has a tendency to consume the other two if it's not kept in check. The challenge for marketers is maintaining balance. Unfortunately, the brand equity side of the equation does not have an army of salespeople meeting with marketers every week to promote the research supporting brand development and the long-term benefits it provides. It does have advocates, however. Two of the most persuasive are Les Binet and Peter Field, the authors of *The Long and the Short of It*,[2] which was published in 2013. Drawing on 30 years of data from the IPA Effectiveness Databank, they conclude that while short-term tactics do trigger short-term sales, it is the investment in long-term strategies that drive long-term revenues as well as market share and profit. The preface to their research features a quote from management consultant Peter Drucker, who summed up the gist of their findings 20 years earlier: 'Long-term results cannot be achieved by piling short-term results on short-term results.'[3]

Binet and Field argue that too much emphasis on either short- or long-term results will have a detrimental effect on the other, but 'the trend is strongly towards pursuing short-term results and short-term metrics, so the balance of the resulting threat is to the long-term success and profitability of brands.' They recommend that business-to-consumer (B-to-C) brands invest about 60 per cent of spend in long-term brand building and 40 per cent in short-term activation. Their initial research in 2013 was followed up with additional research in 2017[4] and 2018[5] supporting their original claims about the importance of investing in brand equity development to achieve long-term business results.

In 2019 Binet and Field released additional research, this time focused on B-to-B. They conclude that the differences between these two marketing factions have been grossly exaggerated, and that building brand equity benefits B-to-B brands as much as it does B-to-C. The differences they did find were reflected in their suggestion that the sweet spot for B-to-B brands is about 46 per cent of spend towards long-term brand building and 54 per cent towards short-term activation. Other conclusions from their research include the following:

1 **Invest in share of voice:** The strong relationship that exists between share of voice and share of market (discussed in Chapter 2) applies as much to B-to-B as it does to B-to-C.

2 **Strike a balance between brand and activation activities:** The ideal mix being about 45 per cent brand development and 55 per cent sales activation.

3 **Focus on customer acquisition category-wide:** Companies that constantly strive to broaden their base as opposed to selling more to existing customers grow more.

4 **Make your brand top of mind:** Research supports the availability heuristic (also known as the availability bias) that says: when given options, people have a preference for the one that comes to mind most easily.

5 **Use emotion to build B-to-B brands:** Rational triggers work best for short-term sales activation, but engaging on an emotional level is more effective for long-term growth.

Binet and Field hope that their research will help restore balance in B-to-C marketing and create it in B-to-B. The problem, as I see it, is that there is no tension in most B-to-B marketing departments, because in that tug-of-war match there is no one pulling on the right side of the rope.

The case for B-to-B brands

Binet and Field notwithstanding, there is a persistent myth circulating among people who sell their products to other businesses that the benefits of strategic marketing and brand management simply do not apply to them. The supporting narrative is that B-to-B buyers are rational buyers, and since brand development is all about emotions, it would be a waste.

This belief stems in part from a misunderstanding about the role of brand management and perhaps previous experience with brand-related projects that just seemed like a lot of useless fluff. If you work in B-to-B, I can't blame you if you feel this way. Over the past three decades, many companies have been burned by brand development programmes that turned out to be glorified graphic design projects with a lot of smoke and mirrors but no positive impact on the business. That's a shame. When properly developed and managed as part of a broader marketing strategy, brand image can help companies accelerate growth, decrease risk and increase profits, regardless of whether they sell to consumers or other businesses.

One example of this was Gardner Denver, a manufacturer of commercial pumps. Before merging with Ingersoll Rand in 2020, Gardener had carefully cultivated an exceptional reputation for its brand. This not only helped sales but also helped them to maintain price integrity and build brand equity. As a team of consultants from McKinsey & Company put it, 'As Mercedes is to cars, Gardner

Denver is to pumps.'[6] McKinsey reported in 2013, when a private equity firm bid USD $3.74 billion to purchase Gardner Denver, that the pump manufacturer's brand accounted for 43 per cent of the company's value based on the previous year's annual report. For comparison, B-to-C giant Proctor & Gamble's brand accounted for 40 per cent of its asset value at the time.

A study by McKinsey & Company went as far as to suggest that brand matters even more in B-to-B purchase decisions, simply because there is so much on the line. 'Buy the wrong toothpaste, and you can always change brands when the tube runs out. Buy the wrong turbine, and you could hurt your company's earnings for years.'[7]

Other findings include:

- Strong brand image correlated with a higher earnings before interest and taxes (EBIT) margin. All else being equal, companies with a strong brand image outperformed companies with a weaker brand image by 20 per cent.
- Decision-makers were willing to pay a premium for companies with a strong brand image, partly because they perceive them as being less risky – per the old adage, 'no one was ever fired for buying IBM' – and partly because they felt the choice helped build their own personal brand, or that of their company, by association.
- Just like consumers, professional buyers also used the brand image as a short cut to reduce risk and simplify evaluation.
- In a survey of 700 executives, brand image was a central criterion in the selection process in B-to-B purchases for all respondents. How central was dependent upon the country. In the US, for example, brand image influenced the purchase decision more than the salesperson. In all countries, the brand image influenced the purchase decision more than factual information about the product.
- The survey also revealed a mismatch between the issues that corporations most often talk about and what business buyers really want to know. The top five topics found in corporate brand communication were: 1) corporate social responsibility, 2)

sustainability, 3) global reach, 4) market influence, and 5) innovation. However, the top five topics that business buyers cared about most with regard to these brands were: 1) honesty and open dialogue, 2) responsibility across the supply chain, 3) specialized expertise, 4) a good fit to the buyers' values and beliefs, and 5) leadership in the company's field.

The idea that B-to-B brands are underutilized corporate assets is not new but has gained renewed attention, especially among small and mid-sized companies. The findings of Binet and Field have been reinforced by research from Google and CEB that concluded B2B customers are 'significantly more emotionally connected to their vendors and service providers than consumers',[8] the implication being that B-to-B brands have even more to gain from emotionally based communication than B-to-C brands. A 2019 survey of 600 B-to-B marketers revealed that those B-to-B companies that invested in long-term, brand-developing promotion were twice as likely to outperform their competitors who did not.[9]

Blurring the lines

A few years after its publication in 2006, I was invited to debate ideas raised in Yoram Wind's paper, 'Blurring the lines: Is there a need to rethink industrial marketing?'[10] In this paper, Professor Wind suggests that the emergence of new business models and technologies like the internet has made the dichotomous classification of a business as either business-to-business (B-to-B) or business-to-consumer (B-to-C) less relevant.

I agree with Professor Wind that the traditional boundaries between B-to-B and B-to-C marketing can be hard to distinguish. I also agree with his point that the internet integrates audiences that have traditionally been siloed. And I, too, join the author in celebrating the demise of the conceptual wall that has separated B-to-B and B-to-C marketing. Obviously, there are very real differences between the way a satellite propulsion system and a stick of chewing gum are sold, but the importance of brand identity and the marketing principles that are fundamental to closing sales while maintaining price integrity and building brand equity apply equally to both. Tactics may change, but not the underlying principles upon which the tactics should be based but often are not.

My only issue with this paper is: What took the *Journal of Business & Industrial Marketing* so long to arrive at this conclusion? I disagree that the blurred lines between B-to-B and B-to-C marketing are a new development ushered in by the internet era. The blurring of which Wind speaks went mainstream at least 45 years ago when, in 1973, FedEx launched a national consumer-style television campaign in the US for its B-to-B overnight delivery service[11] and in 1989 when chip manufacturer Intel began to develop brand awareness among the general public for a product only OEMs could buy.[12] So, yes, the traditional boundaries between B-to-B and B-to-C marketing can be hard to distinguish, but this isn't new. These artificial constructs have been ignored by smart marketers for decades and should never have been erected in the first place.

Honeywell is another good example. The USD $42 billion conglomerate is involved in a number of B-to-B segments from aerospace and building controls to advanced materials and safety solutions. The company can trace its origins back to 1885, when its only product was a thermostat. One challenge the young company faced was that manufacturers and installers of stoves and furnaces were not incorporating the thermostat into their designs. In 1893 WR Sweatt took control of the struggling company. He was unable to convince manufacturers to use his thermostat. That's when he introduced a radical idea: brand building with consumer advertising. Sweatt advertised in trade publications but put the majority of his budget on consumer advertising. The advertising worked, as consumers began asking the manufacturers for the thermostat by name. This approach of amplifying its message to OEMs with emotionally resonating consumer advertising set the foundation for Honeywell's marketing approach that lasted for over a century. In fact, the very first campaign I worked on as a copywriter at BBDO in the 1980s was a consumer radio campaign for the Honeywell corporate brand.[13]

In 1961, James H Binger became President of Honeywell and wanted to make the business more international.[14] He redefined the company's sales approach, putting an emphasis on profit rather than volume.[15] One strategy he employed to help defend price integrity and gain traction in new markets was to further strengthen the brand. He started by changing the company's corporate name from 'Minneapolis-Honeywell Regulator Co.' to 'Honeywell' in 1963.[16] Under Binger's leadership, Honeywell continued to embraced Sweatt's strategic marketing (what B-to-B managers often refer to as B-to-C marketing) and build brand awareness and image through advertising.

Although Honeywell had always sold primarily to businesses, it had been running corporate campaigns in consumer media since the 1900s when it launched its first thermostat. In 1964, the company was vying for the number two spot behind IBM in the corporate mainframe computer market. To help, BBDO created a campaign featuring cute animals fashioned from Honeywell computer parts and ran the ads in mainstream media as opposed to restricting them to trade publications or even business magazines. It became so popular with children that they would write to the company suggesting which animals they would like to see in future ads. The campaign was a hit in the US, and the animal sculptures were equally well received as Honeywell expanded into Europe and Asia. Because the images were so well recognized and adored, Honeywell was able to leverage the print campaign's popularity with outdoor advertising and direct mail. The animals were used at trade shows and for corporate gifts like playing cards, calendars and sculptures. The demand was so great that Honeywell began selling to the public reprints of the animals suitable for framing.[17]

You may be asking, 'Why on Earth would a company selling mainframes to governments, manufacturers and financial institutions create such a consumer-friendly campaign?' That was the first question I had when I began working on the Honeywell account. The answer is because, for 16 hours of every workday when the decision-makers in those huge organizations are not in the office, they are simply men and women living their lives like the rest of us. And like the rest of us, they are, at their essence, emotional beings. To quote

Carl W Buehner, 'They may forget what you said, but they will never forget how you made them feel.'[18] I've found this to be as true for brands as for people. Morrie Dettman, the director of advertising for Honeywell Information Systems, who started the animal campaign, knew that. He said, 'The animals have helped us structure a personality for Honeywell. We've introduced lightness to a serious industry.'[19]

The legacy of WR Sweatt could still be felt as late as 1999 when Honeywell was acquired by AlliedSignal. AlliedSignal had an equally long corporate history and was much larger than Honeywell with almost twice the annual revenue. One would have expected the merged entity to assume the larger company's name. However, AlliedSignal retired its brand and adopted the Honeywell name instead, citing its greater brand recognition and value.[20]

For B-to-B companies like Honeywell, there was no blurred line between marketing for B-to-C and B-to-B. It was clear as far back as 1893 – there was no line. The real driver that causes B-to-B companies to behave like B-to-C marketers is not the existence of the internet but the adoption of strategic marketing principles and practices. The internet has simply made it easier for more B-to-B brands to experiment with marketing.

Look at BlendTec. The company was a sleepy producer of commercial blenders that had been in business since 1975. It saw itself as a B-to-B brand and played the role accordingly. Blendtec relied on salespeople armed with traditional sales support material to bring in revenue. All that changed in January 2006 when they hired a new marketing director named George Wright. Speaking at a conference in 2008, Wright said that after 31 years of business as usual, Blendtec had a strong product but a weak brand which, in turn, delivered weak sales.[21]

In October 2006, Wright asked for a budget to run a brand awareness campaign. The fact that he was given 50 bucks for his campaign may provide some insight into how much brand awareness was valued in the company at that time.[22] Wright learned that owner Tom Dickson, an engineer by trade, often stress-tested the blenders himself in the basement. Wright asked if he could film Dickson in action. When he got the thumbs up, he used his budget to buy the domain willitblend.com along with a handful of marbles, a rake, a McDonald's Value meal, and a rotisserie chicken soaked in Coca-Cola. The next day, Dickson was filmed putting the various objects in the blender and flipping the switch. Wright uploaded the four videos to YouTube with the title, 'Will it Blend?' Within a week, they had topped six million views and Dickson was a minor celebrity, not only on YouTube but also with appearances and stories on NBC, CBS, Fox, BBC, Food Network, History Channel, Discovery Channel, *Wall Street Journal*, *Harvard Business Review*, *Scientific American* and *Business Week*, not to mention the usual trade publications. The videos were to BlendTec what the animals were to Honeywell: an effective vehicle to gain awareness and engage people emotionally with a pleasant and differentiating personality.

Today this former B-to-B brand offers a range of premium-priced blenders for both home and professional use. Its consumer models start at about US $300 with the top-of-the-line commercial blender selling for USD $2,700. BlendTec is a privately held company and does not publish its financials, but in a 2011 interview Dickson said, 'When the "Will It Blend?" videos hit, our sales went up 1,000 per cent in week one.'[23] Interest among commercial buyers spiked, but BlendTec also attracted an entirely new market of people buying their blenders for home use. Over the next three years, average sales were up 700 per cent compared to when they relied on traditional B-to-B sales tactics.[24] To date, BlendTec has published over 180 'Will it Blend?' videos, the most popular of which garnered 18 million views. With most of the videos costing around USD $20 to shoot, BlendTec shows us that a little emotion can go a long way for B-to-B brands.

Conclusion

If your company and all your competitors are relying entirely on sales tactics to generate revenue, then investing in strategic marketing and brand management can seem an unnecessary expense. But there are limits to how far sales tactics alone can take you. These limits become more apparent over time, particularly if one of your competitors commits to building their brand first. Taking the time and budget required to develop a brand that connects with people is an investment that provides lasting returns to any business. The idea that B-to-B brands are exempt from these benefits is a persistent, unsubstantiated myth. It is not for lack of YouTube that B-to-B companies have been slow to adopt strategic marketing and brand management over the past century. It's for lack of trying. Internet or no internet, companies that sell to other companies have always been able to benefit from a more disciplined application of strategic marketing principles, but relatively few have tried when compared to consumer-oriented companies. The notion that B-to-B companies cannot benefit from strategies designed to increase sales while protecting margins and building brand equity is unfounded. If anything, B-to-B companies have the most to gain. One reason these companies struggle to embrace good marketing practices is precisely because of the artificial limitations they place on themselves with the B-to-B label. This enables the traditional B-to-B mindset and marketing straitjacket that comes with it.

If you are prepared to succeed with your new market entry, then you need to be prepared for what follows: increased competition. In Chapter 9 I focus on strategies to develop your competitive advantage as you enter new markets.

Notes

1. C Vallance, It's all performance, Campaign, 10 February 2020. www.campaignlive.co.uk/article/its-performance/1673130 (archived at https://perma.cc/G3CK-WPQW)
2. L Binet and P Field, *The Long and the Short of It: Balancing short and long-term marketing strategies*, IPA, London, 2013.
3. P F Drucker, *Post-Capitalist Society*, Harper Business, New York, 1993.
4. P Field and L Binet, Media in focus, Effworks, 11 October 2017. https://effworks.co.uk/download-media-in-focus/ (archived at https://perma.cc/3SSJ-RZTN)
5. P Field and L Binet, Effectiveness in context, Effworks, 8 October 2018. https://effworks.co.uk/effectiveness-in-context/ (archived at https://perma.cc/BKU4-ZBAW)

6   A Claye, B Crawford, S Lehman and T Meyer, Why B-to-B branding matters more than you think, Forbes, 24 June 2013. www.forbes.com/sites/mckinsey/2013/06/24/why-b-to-b-branding-matters-more-than-you-think/ (archived at https://perma.cc/JCY6-SFKL)

7   A Claye, B Crawford, T Freundt, S Lehmann and T Meyer, B2B business branding, McKinsey & Company, 1 March 2013. www.mckinsey.com/business-functions/marketing-and-sales/our-insights/b2b-business-branding (archived at https://perma.cc/6FJ3-CFZM)

8   S Nathan and K Schmidt, From promotion to emotion: Connecting B2B customers to brands, Think with Google, October 2013. https://www.thinkwithgoogle.com/consumer-insights/consumer-trends/promotion-emotion-b2b/ (archived at https://perma.cc/87TC-6HVV)

9   Think long and learn fast, The Marketing Practice, undated. https://themarketingpractice.com/wp-content/uploads/2020/02/TMP-MW-research-report-Digital.pdf (archived at https://perma.cc/ZE52-KYF7)

10   Y Wind, Blurring the lines: Is there a need to rethink industrial marketing? *Journal of Business & Industrial Marketing*, 21 (7), 1 December 2006. https://doi.org/10.1108/08858620610708975 (archived at https://perma.cc/NSM7-AC47)

11   FedEx at 40: 'Absolutely, positively' built on advertising, *Advertising Age*, 29 April 2013. brandedcontent.adage.com/pdf/FedEx-online.pdf (archived at https://perma.cc/5S3A-BF88)

12   Intel: Marketing, Wikipedia, undated. https://en.wikipedia.org/wiki/Intel#Marketing (archived at https://perma.cc/4Y6A-SFU6)

13   J L Rodengen, *The Legend of Honeywell*, Write Stuff Syndicate, Ft Lauderdale, FL, 1995.

14   J L Rodengen, *The Legend of Honeywell*, Write Stuff Syndicate, Ft Lauderdale, FL, 1995.

15   Honeywell, Wikipedia, undated. https://en.wikipedia.org/wiki/Honeywell#1950–1970s (archived at https://perma.cc/75VD-5L9X)

16   About us, Honeywell Home, undated. https://heatingcontrols.honeywellhome.com/footer/about-us/ (archived at https://perma.cc/DK7S-74SW)

17   BBDO Newsletter, 'Morrie's Menagerie' is what they call it at 'The Other Computer Company', March 1972. https://computerhistory.org/wp-content/uploads/2019/08/honeywell_bbdo_sm.pdf (archived at https://perma.cc/EKJ3-KZ5B)

18   C W Buehner, Quote Investigator, undated. https://quoteinvestigator.com/2014/04/06/they-feel/ (archived at https://perma.cc/HKJ3-SK7L)

19   BBDO Newsletter, 'Morrie's Menagerie' is what they call it at 'The Other Computer Company', March 1972. https://computerhistory.org/wp-content/uploads/2019/08/honeywell_bbdo_sm.pdf (archived at https://perma.cc/GE6K-9ZRS)

20   Allied, Honeywell tie knot, CNN Money, 7 June 1999. https://money.cnn.com/1999/06/07/deals/allied/ (archived at https://perma.cc/G6YM-QC8R)
21   T Weinberg, Keynote address by George Wright of Blendtec, Search Engine Roundtable, 12 November 2008. www.seroundtable.com/archives/018700.html (archived at https://perma.cc/5S79-DRA3); R Salazar, Will it blend? A short story of how Blendtec started, Krig Krafts, 16 June 2018. www.krigkrafts.com/blogs/businesscraft/will-it-blend-a-short-story-of-how-blendtec-started (archived at https://perma.cc/E66E-VQLC)
22   R Scoble, The accidental innovator: Blendtec's Tom Dickson, YouTube, 25 March 2011. www.youtube.com/watch?v=L0a_phNb-bs (archived at https://perma.cc/UXS7-MBGD)
23   T Dickson, Will It Blend viral video star Tom Dickson has turned an everyday product into a global YouTube sensation, Small Business Big Marketing, 31 October 2017. https://smallbusinessbigmarketing.com/will-it-blend-viral-video-star-tom-dickson-has-turned-an-everyday-product-into-a-global-youtube-sensation/ (archived at https://perma.cc/NF9N-4GJ8)
24   Notebooks, BlendTec CEO says sales up 700 per cent since launching 'Will It Blend', YouTube, 14 January 2009. www.youtube.com/watch?v=u6t92m1gwTY (archived at https://perma.cc/RN5P-L58J)

09

Developing a competitive advantage

The case of EMCO

In 2010 I had a startling revelation while working with one of the world's largest medical technology companies. We'll call them EMCO (not their real name). Their new CMO had hired my team to help sharpen their global strategic marketing capabilities. We set up an internal education programme where every three months all EMCO's regional marketing managers would meet in Lisbon for three days of classes and workshops centred around different aspects of strategic marketing. One of the objectives of the training programme was to help them develop a common conceptual framework and template for their annual strategic marketing plans.

We had received a brief backgrounder on each participant from the CMO and had reviewed their LinkedIn profiles. Many had started their careers in sales, but all had been in a marketing role for at least four years. We also reviewed all the training materials with the CMO in advance and tailored them to his needs. 27 marketers flew in to participate. They were a great group: enthusiastic about the programme and eager to learn. About 90 minutes into our first session, I felt something was off. The group was engaged and asking lots of questions, but all their queries were rooted in tactics. These were not the types of questions I had anticipated from a room full of strategic marketers.

After the first break, I said, 'Before we start up again, I'd like to get a better idea of what you do day-to-day in your roles as heads of marketing at EMCO.' Using the classic marketing mix as my framework, I asked, 'How many of you participate in product development for your region?' No hands. 'How about pricing? Do you help determine prices for your region?' No hands. 'How many of you work with sales channels to influence how the products are sold in your markets?' Still no hands. This wasn't surprising. Many companies narrowly define marketing in terms of promotion only. 'Okay,' I said, 'then I guess you spend most of your time developing promotional strategies and campaigns?' I still had no takers. One of the marketing managers spoke up, 'No, we don't do any of those things.' I was puzzled. 'Then what do you do?' I asked. 'Mostly, we get requests from the sales teams to provide information or develop tools to help them sell better.'

They were all working on sales support with marketing job titles. The notion that there was any marketing activity in the company was simply a mirage. I was filled with both fascination and horror – like discovering how Mike the headless chicken lived for 18 months after his head was severed with an axe (you can Google him). I knew the business was having issues, but I would not have thought that it was possible to survive as long as they had on sales alone. How could a company grow so large with virtually no marketing? We spent the rest of that session exploring this question.

During the 1960s, EMCO had made a series of disruptive innovations that helped them build and dominate a segment of the medical industry that today is still growing and valued at around USD 100 billion annually. In the early days, the superior performance of its technology was easily quantified with standard treatment metrics and patient outcomes. Existing technologies at the time couldn't compare. In this type of 'blue ocean' market environment, the value of EMCO's product offer was so novel and demonstrable that winning market share was largely a matter of scaling production and hiring enough sales representatives. As it turns out, that formula for success stuck. It wound up defining the company's approach to the market from then on. Strategic marketing and brand equity were not part of this formula because, in the company's formative years, they were irrelevant to its success. EMCO's approach remained unchanged for decades.

What did change, however, was the category. New players arrived with rival technologies that severely eroded EMCO's perceived performance advantage. By the 1990s, all players in the category had duplicated EMCO's technology. What was once a breakthrough innovation was now perceived as a commodity product. EMCO was no longer able to command a price premium and found itself in a race to the bottom, competing solely on price. This made EMCO increasingly dependent on revenue from the sale of the disposables used to run the machine, but even those low-tech items were under intense price pressure from rival brands and generic offerings. Growth came only through acquisition, which increased EMCO's size each year but had created an onerous debt burden in the company. The explanation from EMCO's marketing managers gave me a clearer understanding as well as an excellent case study to use for the rest of that training programme.

Around the same time that EMCO was founded, psychologist Abraham Maslow said, 'I suppose it is tempting, if the only tool you have is a hammer, to treat everything as if it were a nail.'[1] EMCO's only tools for growth were the same ones it had used at its inception: production and sales. Through that lens, the only alternatives for growth they could see were expanding production though acquisition and pushing products though sales tactics.

EMCO milked the head start it had over its competitors but never used it strategically to consolidate its leadership position, build brand equity or create other meaningful barriers to entry for competitors. It had everything it needed to do just that. EMCO and its products were celebrated as game-changers in the industry. It had well-defined, easily targeted buyers with clear needs. The EMCO brand had a compelling back-story and was universally known and even respected among healthcare professionals. People also understood the types of products it sold. All this would be a huge advantage for any brand. Initially, it was able to attract the best and brightest talent in its field. Yet EMCO was not able to leverage any of these advantages because leadership did not see brand equity, or even marketing strategy, as a tool that could be used to grow. They only saw production and sales capacity. Those strengths did little to help the company develop buyer loyalty, attain category dominance, command a price premium or create barriers to entry for competitors. In Chapter 11 I explore in depth the mechanics of developing brand equity to achieve these ends, but before that I address the more fundamental issue of how you can use marketing strategy and brand management to compete in foreign markets – especially when it seems like you don't need them.

How to avoid mirage marketing

When you launch in your new market, all the preparation covered in Part One of this book will put you on a sound footing to compete. It's at this moment that your plans will encounter reality. No matter how well you prepared, there will be twists, turns and surprises you could not have anticipated. Some will be opportunities, others will be obstacles. Successfully dealing with both will require skills in strategic marketing and brand management. You will need a marketing department that is up to both tasks.

Any company can get so focused on sales tactics that they neglect marketing strategy and brand equity development. Companies that sell B-to-B are particularly inclined to discount the value of strategic marketing for their business. Marketers who try to change that perception are faced with a daunting challenge. As François M Jacques pointed out in his *Harvard Business Review* article, 'Even commodities have customers', 'It isn't easy to establish a marketing function in a company that doesn't think it needs one.'[2] However, it is possible. In 2001, Jacques was the newly appointed CMO of Lafarge, which was founded in Paris in 1833 and grew to become one of the world's largest producers of concrete. In 2015 it merged with Swiss concrete giant Holcim to become LafargeHolcim, with 80,000 employees operating in over 80 countries. In 2001 Jacques embarked on a five-year programme to introduce the function of marketing into Lafarge. It wasn't long after he began his stint as CMO that he too made a shocking revelation: 'Like Lafarge in 2001, many companies have a marketing function in name only.' He is referring to the fact that the company had a robust sales department but no strategic marketing function. The marketing department was, in essence, a glorified sales support team. It could be mislabelled 'marketing' because no real definition or understanding of that function existed in the company. Jacques initiated a carefully planned and well-executed process. He used profit margin as the main metric to monitor the results of his efforts. After five years of steady progress, marketing was credited with increasing profit margins by 1 per cent. If that seems like a modest increase for five years' work, consider that Lafarge's annual sales are USD $28 billion in a low-margin industry.

Remember, the primary function of marketing is not communication. As defined in Chapter 2, it is rather to generate sustainable sales demand, price integrity and brand equity among specific market segments. What is the primary responsibility of your marketing department? Faux marketing departments are typically charged with producing promotional materials based on skills in communication and print/digital production. This can provide a convincing illusion of marketing for those who equate marketing with communication. However, for most companies, promotional materials on their own will not produce sustained, defendable growth or profits. In markets where there are competitors, profitable growth requires a tightly coordinated effort between product, price, place and promotion (product and price are defined in Chapter 13). Only then can the company generate superior perceived value in the market. If your marketing department exists to provide the sales department with updated websites, brochures, and trade show booths then you do not have a marketing department. You have a sales support department. If your marketing department serves primarily to produce communication for stakeholders, then you do not have a marketing department. You have a corporate communications department. If your marketing department is charged with promotion but is not also directly involved with gaining buyer insights and using them to adapt product, price and place, then you do not have a marketing department. You have a promotion department. Sales support, corporate communications and promotion are all vital to a healthy company – but they are not a substitute for a marketing programme since communication alone cannot sustainably drive sales while maintaining price integrity and growing brand equity.

Building an advantage from strength to strength

If companies like EMCO teach us anything, it is that if you do manage to build a truly better mousetrap and buyers find out about it, and they trust you, then the world will beat a path to your door with no marketing strategy required. There is a catch, though: The day that someone else finds another way to control vermin that is reasonably as effective as your mousetrap and you still don't have a marketing strategy, well, then you're toast.

The list of 'mousetrap builders' who learned this lesson the hard way is long. Take, for example, the first commercially successful MP3 player. The broader category of portable music players was launched in 1979 with the Sony Walkman cassette player. MPMan was introduced in 1998 by the South Korean company SaeHan Information Systems. It was the first solid-state, mass-produced digital audio player.[3] It offered up to 64 MB of flash storage and was apparently named to trigger associations with the Sony Walkman line that had dominated portable music for almost two decades prior to MPMan's release. Unlike its namesake, however, the MPMan found itself losing market share a few months after launch to a number of new entrants into its category, most notably the Rio PMP300 MP3 player from Diamond Multimedia. In many respects, the MPMan was a better mousetrap that did launch a new category in portable music, but it and all the other early entrants that followed its lead into the category left much room for improvement and failed to establish barriers to discourage future competitors from entering the category. Singapore-based Creative Technologies took note of this. In 2000, Creative released its 6GB hard-drive-based NOMAD Jukebox portable music player.[4] This was over a year before Apple entered the market with a very similar 5GB hard-drive-based device. In fact, it wasn't until February of 2001 that Steve Jobs even entertained the idea of creating a music player.[5] The first iPod was developed in only nine months, largely from technology that would have been available to any player in the market, including SaeHan and Diamond.

On 23 October 2001 Steve Jobs introduced the iPod as 'a breakthrough digital device'. But the breakthrough was not the device.

Apple was a late entry in the MP3 player category. The real breakthrough for the category was that Jobs launched his device in the context of a broader strategy that included the technology, along with a way to build market share and defend it from competitors. The iPod was released upon an impressive foundation of interconnected attributes that added to its value and would have been prohibitively expensive, complicated and risky to replicate. These included a number of hardware patents and software copyrights, strong brand equity, tacit knowledge and skills inside Apple, ease of compatibility with a growing network of entrenched proprietary technology, and let's not forget about iTunes, the online music library and device management utility Apple had launched nine months earlier. The iTunes app would be followed by the iTunes Store that, among other things, allowed for the legal purchase and download of audio files. It would have been easy to create an MP3 player that was technically superior to the iPod; in fact, Creative Technologies had done so a year earlier. However, the iPod itself was just one part of a much greater value-added platform offer. Duplicating the resources Apple had created behind the iPod would have been a heavy lift for even the mightiest of competitors. Apple's gradual shift from a product to a platform strategy has created a powerful competitive advantage.[6]

One of the more counter-intuitive aspects of the way Steve Jobs built the iPod business is that it wasn't necessarily planned out years in advance, nor did he try to push the market in a particular direction. Apple had tried that with the Newton personal digital assistant (PDA) under John Scully's leadership and failed miserably.[7] Job's primary skill seems to have been more patience and preparedness than predicting and planning. He didn't instigate market trends so much as he was able to recognize which ones were duds and which would provide the most value for Apple. That required him to have a very real sense of what his company's strengths and weaknesses were relative to consumer trends as well as potential competitors. Then he would wait for a groundswell in the market. If he felt it was a trend a) that would fit with the Apple brand, b) where Apple had a competitive advantage, and c) that would augment that advantage further, then he moved swiftly and decisively, as was the case with the iPod.

Those three criteria are the formula for moving fluidly from strength to strength. Waiting for the market to provide a general direction, recognizing which of those directions provide the maximum competitive advantage, then being able to capitalize on it more swiftly and with demonstrably more value than competitors, has made Apple a formidable competitor. Using Jobs' three criteria to assess opportunities and being at the ready to respond decisively to them can make your brand a formidable competitor in the markets you are entering as well.

The success of iPod was a breakthrough not only for Apple, but for the music industry and music lovers globally as well. At its peak, the iPod held over 90 per cent market share for all MP3 players with disk drives[8] and 78 per cent for the portable music player market overall.[9] By 2015 most people were listening to music on their phones, and Apple stopped reporting iPod sales. By that time, Apple had sold over 400 million iPods in 13 years.[10] To put that number in context, according to Apple CEO Tim Cook, 'it took Sony 30 years to sell 230k Walkman cassette players'.[11]

As the fathers of product positioning, Al Reis and Jack Trout, point out in *The 22 Immutable Laws of Marketing*,[12] it is not uncommon that the innovators' initial success simply paves the way for their more strategic successors like Apple vs Creative in the MP3 player category. Trout and Reis cite such profound innovations as the first commercially successful US automobile, washing machine, television, personal computer and word processor. It seems hard to believe that any company with a first-mover advantage in such massive categories could lose the plot, but who's ever heard of Duryea automobiles, Thor washing machines, Du Mont televisions, Mits computers, or Wang word processors? In their day, all these brands were the proverbial 'better mousetrap'. Each enjoyed a period of very light competition at the outset when their owners focused on sales and production to keep up with demand. In that environment they did well. As soon as someone showed up with a comparable offer backed by a coherent marketing strategy built around a defendable competitive advantage, they were forced out of the market.

For companies that attain initial success, these halcyon days can last several months or go on for years, depending upon how difficult it is to equal the incumbent's innovation. Ultimately, however, competitors will show up creating problems that cannot be solved by a larger, more incentivized sales force or greater production capacity. Caught unprepared without an effective marketing strategy to compete, companies that launch in new markets and/or new categories often find themselves overtaken by rivals that are less innovative but more strategically inclined.

Preparing for competition

All competitive advantage is temporary. It may not feel that way when you pull ahead of the pack, but the pack will catch up. Some advantages can last longer than others, but eventually your company's own entropy and inertia, and the market's innovation and evolution, will pull you back into the throng. By the time that happens, you need to have used your previous advantage to have moved on to your next advantage.

Strategist Rita Gunther McGrath has expounded on this idea in *The End of Competitive Advantage: How to keep your strategy moving as fast as your business*.[13] She believes that the days of cultivating one sustainable competitive advantage are over. She argues that companies today need to focus on swiftly ramping up a never-ending series of short-term 'transient advantages'. In a sense, this is what Steve Jobs did in the Apple iPod example above. I wholeheartedly agree that decisively moving from strength to strength based on market input is the way to go. But I'm not completely sold on the demise of the sustainable advantage. I think companies can have both. Apple has used design and simplicity as a competitive advantage for over four decades as it also pursued multiple transient advantages during that period. The ability and discipline to successfully pursue a transient advantage strategy would be difficult to achieve for most companies – so much so, in fact, that the ability in itself could provide a sustainable competitive advantage.

When your product is a hit, it can seem as if the entire market is conspiring against it, and indeed it is. Therefore, if you plan for sales success in your new market, then you should also plan for the reaction of incumbent brands and/or the torrent of new competition that inevitably follows. If you have started a new category of product like ENCO or SaeHan, then you'll want to use your head start to build barriers to entry to thwart the progress of new competitors when they arrive. If you are in a crowded category already then this strategy should also develop your competitive advantage and how it will be sustained against known rivals. You should consider how you can produce your product more efficiently than competitors to increase margins (comparative advantage) and how you can increase the unique value that buyers see in your product (differential advantage).

Discussions about 'barrier to entry' and 'competitive advantage' – with the former aimed at mitigating the threat posed by new entrants and the latter aimed at others already in the category – can get confusing. This is because the terms have multiple definitions, many people use the terms interchangeably, and many measures a business can take to protect its market share from new entrants are equally effective on existing rivals. This was eloquently explained by Eric Jorgenson on his blog Evergreen.[14] He likened competition to a car race where barriers of entry refer to what it takes to get to the race, like building the car, finding a driver, getting sponsors, registering, qualifying and getting your car to the starting line with the other cars until the green light flashes. In this analogy, competitive advantage would then be what it takes to beat the other cars in the race.

When you are taking about either class of competitors – existing vs future – in isolation, then the terms are useful but when you are taking about defending against both types of competitors it gets cumbersome. For that reason, I'll use the term 'economic moat' that Warren Buffett uses to describe factors that make it more difficult for current and would-be rivals to steal market share.[15] This refers to the water-filled moats that surrounded medieval castles. A wide economic moat is one that is difficult for competitors to cross and gain market share at your brand's expense. One way in which competitors cross the moat is by imitating your offer outright. Strong patents may prevent that for a while, if you have the resources to enforce them, but competitors will often circumvent these protections by using different means to deliver the same or similar result as your offer. Internally, your ability to deliver superior value may be diminished over time by attrition of key employees, by your inability to maintain quality as you scale, or by actions or accusations that tarnish your brand's reputation. Alternatively, the market environment may change in ways that make your advantage less relevant over time, as was the case with the iPod when portable music players became less relevant as their functions were consolidated into smartphones. Being one step ahead (again), Apple drove that consolidation, cannibalizing its own product line to boost the next big thing: the ubiquitous iPhone.

Widening the moat is all about making it so difficult, costly and risky to cross the moat that most competitors will feel it's not worth the effort to try, while at the same time staying on the right side of antitrust legislation. One effective way to widen your economic moat is to develop superior brand equity and value, which I discuss in Chapters 12 and 13. There are several other advantages that can be exploited or created to help prolong your brand's success. Some are inherent to your product category, such as large capital investment requirements to get started, or high legal, regulatory or licensing requirements. Other advantages can be directly influenced by companies, such as ownership, exclusive rights, or favourable pricing on key technology, resources or raw materials, or loyalty schemes that provide customers with incentives not to switch brands.

For example, when EMCO's technical innovation created a new category of medical device, it was given about a five-year head start. Following the advice above it could have used the time to develop:

- the next big thing to move on to once the current innovation had run its course
- economies of scale so that when competitors arrived it could drop prices and maintain profits
- a platform effect by linking its devices to other proprietary devices and accessories, which would have also made it more difficult for customers to switch

- strong brand equity, as defined in Chapter 11
- value-add features and value-add associations while reducing friction costs and associative costs, as defined in Chapter 13

The point here is that when you succeed in your new market, don't rest on your laurels. Get busy finding ways to cultivate the advantages you have over current and future rivals to offer even greater value and sustain your winning streak as long as possible. Whether you are building moats or barriers, I'd offer one word of caution: don't forget about the buyer's perspective. I've found that their perspective is not always factored in when companies deliberate over the best initiatives to protect and build market share. Whatever tools or methodologies you employ to define, develop and leverage your competitive advantage, the aim should be the same: to offer greater value to buyers while imposing excessive costs, complexity and risk upon any brand that chooses to compete with you.

In his book *Good Strategy, Bad Strategy*,[16] Richard Rumelt explores the nature of competitive advantage and how companies can build strategies around them. He says that advantage lies in the differences that exist between competitors. Since these asymmetries are numerous, a company must decide which are critical and will be turned into competitive advantages. Rumelt believes this is one of the essential responsibilities of leading any business. He credits military strategists with shifting the perspective on competitive advantage from focusing purely on the strength of the offer to focusing on ways to 'impose asymmetric costs on an opponent'. This is the type of advantage that will discourage competitors by making it unprofitable for them to match the value your brand provides. Rumelt cites examples of this type of competitive advantage with companies like Walmart.

Over the past three decades, Walmart's secret to success has been dissected in so many case studies that it no longer has secrets to yield. Still, no other retailer has been able to duplicate its success. Why is that? Any retailer could open a store in smaller population centres like Walmart and offer the same products and prices. To be profitable, however, they would also need many such stores and be able to duplicate a very intricate supply chain formula, along with a proprietary

IT and logistic infrastructure, to say nothing of achieving the same level of brand awareness, interest and trust that Walmart enjoys. Likewise, a furniture producer could not replicate IKEA's value simply by copying its product range, then producing a catalogue. An online retailer could not successfully take on Amazon simply by copying its website. Nor, in the case of Apple, could an MP3 player in 2001 have taken on the iPod and won. The value that each of these businesses offers to their customers has been built over time by methodically moving from strength to strength while exploiting a number of interdependent factors. This makes it very complicated to profitably duplicate the value they offer to buyers and limit the number of companies that want to try.

Conclusion

New companies, like EMCO, often start out with lots of trial and error until they find an approach to the market that works for them. When success hits, the company rapidly ascends along a steep growth curve that is often seen as irrefutable market validation for the product, the leadership team and every decision they made up to that point. The market approach that was in use at the time of this positive inflection point becomes imprinted into the corporate DNA and serves as a model for future success. With many B-to-B brands, that initial growth spurt was driven by a combination of innovative R&D and a rapidly scalable production and sales function to keep up with demand. On their own, the combination of these three strengths is enough to yield impressive growth – at least, initially. As categories mature, the rules of the game change. The strategies and tactics that lead to initial success often do not serve these companies well later in their lifecycle. Companies that create sales plans without marketing plans are not planning for success. That's because success brings competition whose mission it is to erode your competitive advantage and take your market share. Any strategy that fails to address this is actually a prelude to failure.

The missing links for companies like EMCO are strategic marketing and brand management. This leaves them vulnerable to existing competitors and new entrants alike. In Chapter 10 I present the three strategies you can adopt to compete.

Notes

1 A H Maslow, *The Psychology of Science: A reconnaissance*, Harper & Row, New York, 1966.
2 F M Jacques, Even commodities have customers, *Harvard Business Review*, May 2007. https://hbr.org/2007/05/even-commodities-have-customers (archived at https://perma.cc/7RG2-ML4M)
3 E V Buskirk, Bragging rights to the world's first MP3 player, CNET, 25 January 2005. www.cnet.com/news/bragging-rights-to-the-worlds-first-mp3-player/ (archived at https://perma.cc/3JPB-S6KK)
4 R Menta, We test drive the Creative Nomad Jukebox, MP3 Newswire, 21 November 2000. web.archive.org/web/20200224100028/http://www.mp3newswire.net/stories/2000/nomadreview.html (archived at https://perma.cc/G2SF-7H8Q)
5 L Kahney, Straight dope on the iPod's birth, Wired, 17 October 2006. www.wired.com/2006/10/straight-dope-on-the-ipods-birth/ (archived at https://perma.cc/S4KS-QM5L)
6 S Lohr, The power of the platform at Apple, *The New York Times*, 29 January 2011. www.nytimes.com/2011/01/30/business/30unbox.html (archived at https://perma.cc/S5CC-KB9B)
7 M Honan, Remembering the Apple Newton's prophetic failure and lasting impact, Wired, 8 May 2013. https://web.archive.org/web/20200312011705/www.wired.com/2013/08/remembering-the-apple-newtons-prophetic-failure-and-lasting-ideals/ (archived at https://perma.cc/Z3YC-BPJ8)
8 A Ries, Why being first matters so much, AdAge, 20 June 2005. https://adage.com/article/viewpoint/matters/46026 (archived at https://perma.cc/8PDD-EDXD)
9 S Macale, Apple has sold 300m iPods, currently holds 78 per cent of the music player market, TNW, 4 October 2011. https://thenextweb.com/apple/2011/10/04/apple-has-sold-300m-ipods-currently-holds-78-of-the-music-player-market/ (archived at https://perma.cc/3WEM-BX94)
10 S Costello, This is the number of iPods sold all-time, Lifewire, 23 December 2019. www.lifewire.com/number-of-ipods-sold-all-time-1999515 (archived at https://perma.cc/E4ND-UQ3B)

11 S Macale, Apple has sold 300m iPods, currently holds 78 per cent of the music player market, TNW, 4 October 2011. https://thenextweb.com/apple/2011/10/04/apple-has-sold-300m-ipods-currently-holds-78-of-the-music-player-market/ (archived at https://perma.cc/H7GQ-8Q48)

12 A Ries and J Trout, *The 22 Immutable Laws of Marketing: Violate them at your own risk*, Harper Business, New York, 1993.

13 R G McGrath, *The End of Competitive Advantage: How to keep your strategy moving as fast as your business*, Harvard Business Review Press, 2013.

14 E Jorgenson, How barriers to entry confused me terribly, and what I figured out so far, Evergreen, 29 February 2016. https://medium.com/evergreen-business-weekly/how-barriers-to-entry-confused-me-terribly-and-what-i-figured-out-so-far-75df799b2559 (archived at https://perma.cc/LJ5D-4L27)

15 A Hayes, Wide economic moat, Investopedia, 2 July 2019. www.investopedia.com/terms/w/wide-economic-moat.asp (archived at https://perma.cc/GBB7-4KWN)

16 R P Rumelt, *Good Strategy, Bad Strategy: The difference and why it matters*, Crown Business, New York, 2011.

10

Defining a strategy to compete

Home-field advantage

At this point in the book, I hope you are starting to see a pattern: When marketers enter new markets with their guard down, they usually pay a dear price. Home-field advantage applies as well to marketing as it does to sports. It certainly will not decide the game but it will give the local brand an advantage in some respects. The most devastating application of this advantage is if the local brand is able to influence legislation or regulations that make it difficult or unprofitable for you to do business in that market.

Barring that, you can level the playing field with a local brand simply by adopting the right mindset. The best advantage you can have over local competitors is to enter the market assuming the role of the underdog. This isn't about how you position your brand; it's an internal management tactic to keep complacency from creeping into the process. You assume you are at a disadvantage and therefore are more vigilant, more strategic and more disciplined than the incumbent brands. Do your homework and leverage every competitive advantage you can find. It's difficult to fight a strategy with tactics and win. As shown in Figure 10.1, if local brands are strategic, then you are prepared. If they are not, and many are not, then they will need to develop these skills to compete with you successfully. That does not happen overnight. While they are figuring that out, you can use the time advantage to build your business. That starts with deciding how you will compete.

FIGURE 10.1 Likely outcomes when pitting your strategic skills against those of local competing brands

	How strategic are local competitors? LOW	How strategic are local competitors? HIGH
How strategic are you? HIGH	**QUICK GAINS** — Caught off-guard the locals will struggle to catch up, providing you with even more time to fortify your position and make it even more difficult for rivals to overtake you.	**TEST OF EQUALS** — You will slug it out with the locals on a strategic level. Unlike fighting with tactics, this contest will force you to sharpen your strategy and will eventually yield a clear winner.
How strategic are you? LOW	**LONG SLOG** — You will slug it out with the locals on a tactical level, giving and taking market share like a perpetual tug-of-war contest that never produces a clear winner.	**QUICK DEFEAT** — Caught off guard, you will struggle to catch up, providing rivals with even more time to fortify their position. This makes it even more difficult for you to rally.

Before deciding on a competitive strategy, it's a good idea to take stock of your company's strengths and weaknesses in relation to the brands with whom you will be competing and the buyers to whom you will be selling in the foreign market.

In his seminal book *Competitive Strategy*,[1] Michael Porter of Harvard Business School introduced the three basic strategic options with which to compete:

- **Price:** How price sensitive are buyers in this category? Does your company have lower production costs than other companies with similar offers in the market? Could you sustain that advantage? If that is the main strength of your business, then you should consider a cost minimization strategy where you compete across the category with a lower cost structure allowing you to offer lower prices.

- **Differentiation:** Do buyers in this category have underserved needs that your brand could address? Does your company have a product offer that is truly unique in a way that is valued by those buyers and difficult for rivals to copy? Could you sustain that advantage? If that is your company's main strength, then you should consider a product differentiation strategy where you compete across the category with your value offer.
- **Niche:** Is there a distinct segment of buyers in this category that have underserved needs and is large enough to support your business? Does your company possess a unique product or particular credentials that, although not of great interest to the broader category, is highly valued by this segment of buyers? Could you sustain that advantage? If that is your company's main strength, then you should consider a market focus strategy where you will dominate a category niche with either price or differentiation.

Porter's Three Generic Competitive Strategies were based on an analysis of over 1,000 different companies. As an economist, Porter is less interested in the size of a business as a measure of success than in its profitability. The goal of a competitive strategy is to create a sustainable competitive advantage that will yield the company above-average profitability for its industry.

When entering a foreign market, choosing the best competitive strategy for your business requires assessing the competitive environment and your company's own strengths and weaknesses. Having done that, you will have two decisions to make.

First, how will you compete? In Porter's model there are only two options here. Companies can compete by offering a comparable (not identical) product at a lower price. Alternatively, they can offer a differentiated product that provides additional value and therefore can command a higher price.

Second, on what scope will you compete? A broad scope would mean that you would target buyers across the entire category and therefore compete with other companies doing the same. Alternatively, you could have a narrow scope where you choose one or more niches and try to dominate them with either a lower price or product differentiation.

The latter is more common, where the company adapts its offer to meet the specific needs of the niche and thereby commands a premium price. The premium price, in turn, helps offset the fact that the market niche may offer less room for growth.

The ideal niche buyer has a specific need that is not adequately addressed by the main offerings in the category because there is not enough volume in the niche to be of interest to the main players. To find a niche, first identify an underserved segment of the market that you could serve profitably. This buyer typically understands that a seller would need to develop a custom product for their special case and would, therefore, be willing to pay a premium for that.

A good example of a niche company is the US organic grocery chain Whole Foods. Most mainstream grocery stores today include a relatively small organic section with a limited selection and high prices. Whole Foods expanded that to an entire organic grocery store concept. Whole Foods still has the high prices associated with organic fare, but it offers a much wider selection. It does this at the exclusion of all the popular non-organic brands. Whole Foods went 'all in'. This was a big risk that paid off within a certain demographic. In fact, with regard to acquisitions, one of the main reasons Amazon acquired Whole Foods was to access its customers, specifically because of its brand loyalty and buying power. Amazon didn't just see a brand to acquire, so much as the customers that came with it.[2]

Planning for profit

The strategy you choose will influence how you compete with local brands in the foreign markets you enter, but competition is only one of several factors affecting profitability. Porter has condensed the factors that shape industry profits into a model known as Porter's Five Forces. This is important when entering new markets because, although some forces may apply to your industry globally, they often play out differently from one geographic market to the next. A good strategy will help you navigate the Five Forces below better than your competitors:

1. **Competition in the industry**
   The number of competitors and their relative strengths put limits on your ability to call the shots with regard to pricing and terms. This diminishes control over profitability.

2. **Potential of new entrants into the industry**
   New entrants can be very disruptive to business and profits. If the category is characterized by low barriers of entry and/or outmoded offers or business practices, then it is likely to attract new competition.

3. **Power of suppliers**
   If the suppliers and the inputs they provide are scarce and/or difficult to replace, then they will have more power to dictate their prices and terms, which has a direct effect on your profit.

4. **Power of customers**
   When a company has a small number of customers who are costly to replace, which is common for B-to-B companies, those customers have more power to negotiate lower prices and better terms. The more a company's revenue is generated from multiple customers and the less it costs to acquire those customers, then the less bargaining power any one customer has, which gives the company more leverage and helps it maximize profits.

5. **Threat of substitute products**
   A substitute is another option available to the buyer that could be substituted for your product to get the same result (or close enough). Your competitive stance is weakened in proportion to the number of such substitutes that exist in your market. When you offer a product for which there is no close substitute, you will have more power to dictate prices and terms to maximize profits.

As a rule, profits decrease as competitive pressure from these factors increases. As a corollary to that rule, competition generally increases over time. The company that is best able to manage the Five Forces to their advantage and adapt as competition increases will be the most profitable. Accepting those two facts will help inform which competitive strategy will best serve your company to achieve superior profitability compared to your competition.

'But we don't have any competitors'

A common trap for company leadership is the misguided notion that they have no competition. As in the case of Hans, when you press for more details, they typically explain how some aspect of their product offer is unlike anything else on the market today, thereby arriving at the faulty conclusion that they have no competitors. This flags a fundamental misunderstanding of competition that can cause irreparable harm to the company.

Having a unique product conveys no competitive advantage on its own. In marketing, as in nature, being unique is not unique. Every product, like every person, every company, and every grain of sand, is unique in one way or another. Defining your brand's competitors narrowly as only those companies that have exactly the same offer as you is self-defeating, if not self-deluding. The use of this narrow definition is widespread, which is unfortunate as it can cause miscommunication and friction as you develop your approach to the market.

For this reason, avoid using the word 'competitors' early in your strategy planning process. Instead, use the words 'options' or 'substitutes'. If options other than using your product exist to serve a given need in your market, including non-consumption, then you have competitors. If your target could substitute your product with another product in the market and arrive at a reasonably similar result, then you have competitors. The US retailer Toys-R-Us thought that it had no competitors as it expanded its presence to 40 countries around the word.[3] If that were true, then none of us would have been able to purchase another toy once it went bankrupt in 2018. Obviously, that was not the case. In fact, Toys-R-Us had a great deal of competition. A failure in company leadership to acknowledge that reality might go a long way in explaining what has been described as its '20-year decline into insolvency'.[4]

Think of Porter's Five Forces Model the next time you hear a colleague or company spokesperson proudly proclaim that their product has no competitors. For that to be true, then there could be no company nor product in the market that could reasonably address the same need as that product. Nor could there ever be such a product or company. I'm not saying that this is impossible to achieve, but I'd gladly wager my Toys-R-Us loyalty card that the person who makes such a claim has not taken a close enough look at the market or their prospective customers.

As we saw in cases like EMCO in Chapter 9, it is not uncommon for an innovative company that builds a better mousetrap to start with relatively little competitive pressure and succeed in that environment. However, markets do not sustain those conditions indefinitely. If a company is unprepared, unable or unwilling to adapt as competitive pressure increases then it will experience a steady erosion of profitability, often to the point where it is no longer viable.

Competing on price

Assuming a price leadership position in your market will require you to find and use all possible advantages; you have to lower your cost of production so you can offer the lowest price while still delivering adequate perceived value to buyers and maintaining profits for your company. Customers who are loyal to a low-price leader are usually focused on price. They are not swayed by the latest bells and whistles added to more expensive products. They are, however, very vulnerable to a lower-priced rival. The highly competitive airline industry offers several examples of this.

One of the first transatlantic airlines to adopt the low-price strategy was Laker Airways from the UK, which operated its no-frills 'Skytrain' service between London and New York City. The service was launched in 1977 and quickly developed a loyal following of international travellers. Skytrain was able to offer prices that were sometimes half of what competitors were charging, yet in its first year, it still generated a profit of around US $12 million in today's dollars.[5] But Laker was competing with much larger airlines with much deeper pockets. In October 1981 Pan Am, British Airways and TWA all slashed their transatlantic economy fares on routes where they competed with Skytrain.[6] Within days, Skytrain lost half its passengers. Four months later, Laker Airways was bankrupt.[7] Easy come, easy go. When you adopt a low-price strategy, it's worth remembering that customer loyalty, quite literally, comes at a price. You can't sustain that advantage if current or future entrants into your category can easily undercut your price.

Laker developed a cost structure that was hard for rivals to duplicate, but they didn't need to duplicate it. Pan Am, British Airways, and TWA were large enough to match Laker's price and take a loss on certain routes until Laker was driven out of the market. This isn't always the case. Many companies have succeeded at developing cost structures that resulted in a sustained advantage, including Germany's Aldi supermarkets, IKEA home furnishings from Sweden, South Korea's No Brand, Zara fashion from Spain, France's F1 hotels, Turkish retailer BIM and US brands like Walmart, Dell and Suave. Even healthcare has cost leadership brands such as Teva Pharmaceuticals from Israel, Sweden's Exavir HIV viral load monitoring, India's Ara-vind Eye Hospitals, and medical tourism destination Bumrungrad International Hospital in Bangkok, Thailand.

If you do find a way to offer a product that can serve as a lower cost substitution, don't stop there. Use that advantage and find ways to offer even greater value that will not increase your costs or the prices you charge. This helps develop deeper loyalties. Southwest Airlines was able to do this in the US low-cost airline segment. When it started in 1971, Southwest served only Texas with flights between Dallas, Houston and San Antonio. By the 1990s, it was flying coast to coast in the US.[8] As Southwest grew its route map, it steadily took market share from full-cost airlines but surrendered little. That was mostly because its prices were much lower than rival carriers. But Southwest found a way to add even more value without adding more cost. It did this with its brand. It developed a far more 'human' brand identity than any of its US rivals. This identity was internalized and expressed through its prices, policies and, most of all, its people. If you have flown on Southwest you will have noticed that while the cabin may be 'no frills', the service is anything but that. The crew are demonstrably more friendly than on other carriers and provide a much more welcoming atmosphere inside the plane. In fact, YouTube videos of their flight attendants doing their job routinely go viral (search YouTube for 'Southwest flight attendant'). This extra measure of brand personality won't protect them from other lower-cost competitors completely, but having a personality also doesn't cost much and can buffer the ill effects of challenges from lower-cost rivals. The first such challenge to Southwest came in 2000 when JetBlue entered the market with costs that were about 25 per cent lower than those of Southwest, allowing it to offer prices that were even lower. Southwest lost some business but held its own.[9] By 2018, Southwest had not only become the largest domestic carrier in the US based on passengers but had also been ranked by JD Power number one in customer satisfaction among low-cost carriers.[10]

Competing on differentiation

When Tesla launched its first car in 2008 it wasn't a little different – it was a lot different. That differentiation wasn't limited to the fact that its first release was the world's only high-performance electric luxury sports car. Everything the company did, for better or worse, veered away from auto industry convention, from Tesla's direct-to-customer showrooms and no-hassle pricing to its innovative battery and manufacturing technology to the antics of its CEO. There is nothing conventional about Tesla. That includes its performance. Just 12 years after releasing its first model, Tesla surpassed 83-year old Toyota on 1 July 2020 to become the world's most valuable automaker with a market capitalization of US $207 billion.[11]

If you choose not to compete on price, then you will be adopting a differentiation strategy. To provide a sustainable advantage, this differentiation should be pronounced and difficult for competitors to copy. One way to ensure that is to draw on your company's unique combination of strengths to differentiate your offer. Having a well-differentiated product can allow you to sell at a premium price. How much of a premium will depend upon how differentiated the product is perceived to be and how valued the points of perceived differentiation are among buyers.

Good strategy, like good business, is often about having clear priorities. At its core, that is how Porter's generic strategies can help you when competing in foreign markets. Keeping costs down and providing a superior product experience are often at odds with each other. Both are important, but Porter feels that companies need to decide which is more important to them and then act accordingly.

What you do not want is to be perceived as 'a little less expensive' or 'kind of different' in the middle ground between a well-executed price strategy and differentiation strategy. Trying to appease these two antagonistic forces at once means there are no clear priorities. This tends to draw companies into the strategic middle ground where they fail to create a value advantage, achieving neither price nor product differentiation. Competing here is a grind, with greater risk and lower returns. Porter's research showed that despite the fact that brands in the middle have lower profits, that is where the majority of companies ultimately wind up. It's worth pondering why that is and how close to the middle your brand sits.

Choosing a low-price strategy does not mean you can ignore your product offer. Likewise, working off the differentiation strategy does not mean you can ignore the price. It's just that when decisions need to be made where these two factors are in conflict, then either price or product will be prioritized depending on the strategy you have chosen. For instance, every company wants to keep its costs down, but the price-strategy company may want to invest in proprietary artificial intelligence (AI) and robotics to lower production costs and may be less concerned about gaining advantage over rivals by developing new proprietary features. Likewise, every company must maintain a certain standard for its products, but the differentiation-strategy company would want to invest in developing its product offer in ways that would be impossible for competitors to copy and may be less concerned about devoting that level of resources to lower production costs.

The remainder of this book will be dedicated to helping you find new ways to differentiate your brand in foreign markets in ways that will add value to your offer. That last part is the key. Differentiation for its own sake without adding value won't get you very far. In that sense, you don't really compete on differentiation as such. You only ever compete on value – which brings me back to Michael Porter.

A final note on strategy

Porter's book *Competitive Strategy* is over 40 years old now, and it remains required reading in many MBA programmes. That makes it a good departure point for discussing strategy. However, thinking on the subject has developed with other frameworks, such as the resource-based view popularized by Jay Barney.[12] Today, Porter's work is often criticized for not being able to keep up with the rapid pace of change, not taking buyers sufficiently into account, and not jibing with the new market realities ushered in with the internet and globalization. I wouldn't dispute these limitations, but I also wouldn't use them as a basis to invalidate his observations or conclusions. His models for assessing industries and making fundamental decisions about strategy are still some of the most useful and well-supported tools at your disposal. Unlike 40 years ago, more companies today work across several industries. Challenges and opportunities can come from outside your industry. For instance, today Domino's Pizza considers itself a tech company. It realized that its core product offer, pizza, could be copied by just about anybody. When the global pizza franchise went into decline in the early 2000s, Domino's staged an impressive comeback by improving its pizza recipe but also harnessing information technology related to ordering and delivery. This added value by making its pizzas easier to order. It no longer competes on its pizza alone, but increasingly on the technology that surrounds it.[13]

The glitch with Porter's work that I bump up against most often relates back to value and perspective. I would like to see the perceptions of buyers play more heavily into his work. His value chain model is ingenious for the way it methodically breaks down a company's primary value-producing activities (inbound logistics, operations, outbound logistics, marketing and sales, service) and support activities (company infrastructure, human resources management, technology development, procurement) to show how they all interact to add value to the company's offer. Porter acknowledges that a company's value chain exists in the context of a broader value system where it must feed into the buyer's value chain. All good.

FIGURE 10.2 The value loop

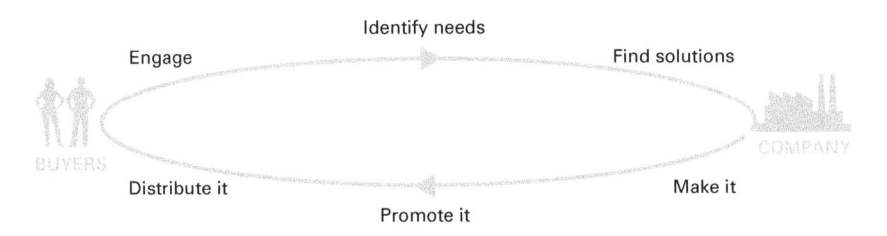

```
                    Identify needs
       Engage                           Find solutions
                    ─────────►
   ╭──────────────────────────────────────────────╮
   │                                              │
  BUYERS                                       COMPANY
   │                                              │
   ╰──────────────────────────────────────────────╯
                    ◄─────────
       Distribute it                         Make it
                      Promote it
```

The linear value chain concept does as Porter intended by providing a 'systematic way of examining all the activities a firm performs and how they interact' to produce value, margin and profit.[14] However, from a practitioner's perspective, I've found that it's more productive to think of value in terms of a loop rather than a chain.

In the value loop pictured in Figure 10.2, the process of creating value doesn't start with the seller. It starts with the buyer. More specifically, it starts with the buyer's needs, options, perceptions and value requirements. The company that understands these things better has an advantage if it uses these insights to focus on its value-producing activities. In this cyclical model, each iteration of the company's product is treated as a hypothesis of how best to satisfy the value requirements of buyers, and its introduction to the market is treated as an experiment. Once released, the company re-examines how well its product addressed the value requirements of the buyer relative to the buyer's other options. Since both the buyer's needs and competitors' offers are changing over time, there is no end-point to this process. It is a feedback loop that keeps the company's value-production mechanisms calibrated to the needs of the market it serves.

Conclusion

Most companies enter foreign markets because they spot an immediate sales opportunity. But what about the opportunity for sustainable profits and building brand equity over time? Ultimately, that is what separates the winners from the losers in a market. Adopting that focus suggests looking beyond tactics and developing a coherent strategy to manage the factors that influence profit and brand equity to prevail over local competition. Local brands may be prepared for your product's arrival but will likely not be prepared for a well-conceived strategy. This will require you to assess the competitive forces that drive profit in your industry and how they are shaped by the local market, competitors and buyers. It will also require you to make a frank assessment of your own company's strengths and weaknesses vis-à-vis local rivals.

In the next chapter, I take a closer look at what 'brand equity' actually means, defined in terms that relate to your day-to-day marketing activities. I share a model that can be used to assess and manage brand equity in markets both at home and abroad. I also revisit the idea of the value loop shown in Figure 10.2 to show how buyers deliver value back to the company.

Notes

1 M E Porter, *Competitive Strategy: Techniques for analyzing industries and competitors*, Free Press, New York, 1980, Republished with a new introduction, 1998.
2 G Petro, Amazon's acquisition of Whole Foods is about two things: Data and product, Forbes, 2 August 2017. www.forbes.com/sites/gregpetro/2017/08/02/amazons-acquisition-of-whole-foods-is-about-two-things-data-and-product/ (archived at https://perma.cc/V8VP-DV3B)
3 M Ruzicka, Toys R Us finds Sweden a really tough game, Joc, 1 August 1995. www.joc.com/toys-r-us-finds-sweden-really-tough-game_19950801.html (archived at https://perma.cc/T2WJ-78DE)
4 B Unglesbee, Inside the 20-year decline of Toys R Us, Retail Dive, 26 June 2018. www.retaildive.com/news/inside-the-20-year-decline-of-toys-r-us/526364/ (archived at https://perma.cc/QMF2-HVRV)
5 C Woodley, *Flying to the Sun: A history of Britain's holiday airlines*, The History Press, p. 154, 2016.
6 W Borders, Laker in bankruptcy owing $300 million; All flights canceled, *The New York Times*, 6 February 1982. www.nytimes.com/1982/02/06/business/laker-in-bankruptcy-owing-300-million-all-flights-canceled.html (archived at https://perma.cc/H2MM-CW2X)

7 C Woodley, *Flying to the Sun – A History of Britain's Holiday Airlines: 10. Transatlantic services – Laker Airways*, The History Press, Stroud, 2016, p 154.
8 J Singh, The history of Southwest Airlines, Simple Flying, 6 July 2020. https://simpleflying.com/southwest-airlines-history/ (archived at https://perma.cc/YHX5-F6ZW)
9 N Kumar, Strategies to fight low-cost rivals, *Harvard Business Review*, December 2006. https://hbr.org/2006/12/strategies-to-fight-low-cost-rivals (archived at https://perma.cc/T8B8-YZ7M)
10 Southwest Airlines ranks highest in customer satisfaction among low-cost carriers in North America according to JD Power, Southwest Airlines, 15 June 2018. http://investors.southwest.com/news-and-events/news-releases/2018/06-15-2018-155031252 (archived at https://perma.cc/3JX2-JEF4)
11 B Roberson, Tesla takes over top spot from Toyota as world's most valuable carmaker, Forbes, 1 July 2020. www.forbes.com/sites/billroberson/2020/07/01/tesla-takes-over-top-spot-from-toyota-as-worlds-most-valuable-carmaker/ (archived at https://perma.cc/XFW6-LE59)
12 J Barney, Firm resources and sustained competitive advantage, *Journal of Management,* 17 (1), March 1991.
13 J Beer, How Domino's became a tech company, Fast Company, 22 May 2014. www.fastcompany.com/3030869/how-dominos-became-a-tech-company (archived at https://perma.cc/FAW4-ZNPB)
14 ME Porter, *The Competitive Advantage: Creating and sustaining superiorperformance*, Free Press, New York, 1985, republished with a new introduction, 1998.

11

Building brand equity

The mechanics of building brand equity

Behind the Stockholm Concert House (Stockholms Konserthus) is a large cobblestone square called Hötorget. During the day, the square hosts an open-air market. My first office in Stockholm was near this square, and on sunny days I'd often sit on the steps of the concert house that overlooked Hötorget and eat my lunch.

One spring afternoon, two of the street vendors caught my eye. They were only two stalls apart, selling the exact same assortment of fruits, vegetables and flowers. The stalls were identical, as were the prices displayed. Even the proprietors of the two stalls were similar in appearance. There was one difference, however. The man who tended the stall on the left smiled more, engaged his visitors in conversation, seemed to know some by name and generally behaved in an open and friendly manner. The man in the stall on the right was certainly not unfriendly. He seemed pleasant and courteous but smiled less and was less engaging.

Over the course of about 20 minutes, I counted how many transactions each completed. In a purely rational market, the two should have done exactly the same amount of business. In fact, the vendor on the right should have done more business because he was situated on the corner, so he had more foot traffic, and since he didn't chit-chat he was capable of greater throughput. The friendly vendor on the left had fifteen transactions, and the other had eight. Many customers walked past the corner stall, literally going out of their way to do business with the friendly vendor.

Obviously, this was a casual observation, not a controlled experiment, but it got me thinking. That lunch break provided a simple metaphor that, for me, crystalized the research I'd read relating emotion and purchase decisions (see Chapters 5 and 8). It also helped me understand the advantage that positive brand equity can have in a crowded market.

The vendor on the left was the de facto brand for the products he sold, and he was very likable. That adds value to his offer. He alone differentiated his offer from others in the market. He wasn't just making sales. With each transaction, he was also increasing the probability of future transactions. He was building brand equity and, by doing so, creating a preference for his apples, green beans and daisies even though they were identical to those sold in dozens of other stalls around him.

Brand management and brand equity

The Oxford dictionary defines brand equity as: 'The commercial value that derives from consumer perception of the brand name of a particular product or service, rather than from the product or service itself.'[1] If we can agree that developing brand equity is a worthwhile investment for your company, then we have to ask exactly how do we create brand equity? What are its components? What are the management objectives associated with creating that value? These are the questions that practitioners deal with on an operational level.

When seeking to answer these questions, it's not as if there is a shortage of brand-equity models. A quick survey reveals a plethora of options. I've found that most of these models are too general, too theoretical or too complex for practical use. Even models by marketing luminaries like Kevin Keller, Jean-Noel Kapferer, and David Aaker help clarify what brand equity is but not necessarily how to create it.

That's why in 2000 I developed the Duffy Brand Equity Cycle[2] for my team. It takes a customer-centric view of brand equity that is inherently operational in nature, mapping the 10 marketing challenges that must be addressed to acquire and retain buyers. This model assumes the consumer's perspective following a sequential series of conditions that must be satisfied in the buyer's mind to increase the probability of trial, repeat purchase and advocacy. Our job as marketers is to facilitate this journey. That means looking at each of the 10 challenges, identifying potential barriers and figuring out ways to overcome them.

In biology, the Krebs cycle is what converts simple sugars to energy inside your cells. It can never produce more energy than the glucose available to it, but if the cycle is not running efficiently, it can produce less energy because it's not able to convert all the glucose your body produces. In marketing, the Duffy Brand Equity Cycle is how the value in your offer is converted to revenue. Managed well, it will ensure that your company derives the most revenue possible from the value it produces. It can also provide vital clues as to how your brand might produce more value. The model outlines 10 tollgates that the marketer must help the prospects pass through over time. They enter the cycle at the top, work through the different stages, and, if all goes well, are retained in the advocacy loop at the end. Each prospect adds equity to your brand at each tollgate.

The Duffy Brand Equity Cycle helps explain why the brands of companies that do not show an operating profit can still command high valuations. It requires time and investment to draw potential buyers into this cycle and move them through each tollgate. For instance, simply attaining the awareness and understanding of millions of people in a segment may not result in a single sale. It is, nonetheless, a very time consuming and costly endeavour with a moderately high risk of failure. There is value in a brand that has come that far, even if the company has not yet reached profitability.

This model has helped us explain to our clients how brand equity is built by customers over time. We have found that using the model provides a clear understanding of strategic marketing objectives, shows how those objectives relate back to both sales and strategy, gives practitioners an operational framework and provides a working vocabulary we can use on a day-to-day basis.

Adding insight to your net promoter score

Adopting your buyer's perspective is one of the most challenging aspects of entering a foreign market. It's also one of the most important, since it is the buyers who ultimately decide your brand's fate. This model is intended to provide you with a conceptual framework to ensure you stay in step with the markets you serve. It defines brand equity as the degree to which a brand has achieved relevance, awareness, understanding, interest, trust, trial, belief, affinity, loyalty and advocacy among a defined target group. The desired end state for every prospect is that of brand advocate, also known as brand promoter.

How can you tell if the cycle is running efficiently? Like any system, you can check the output. For the Krebs cycle, its output is energy measured in terms of adenosine triphosphate (ATP). For the Duffy Brand Equity Cycle, output is brand advocacy measured in terms of net promoter score (NPS).

Brand promoters are people who claim they would recommend a brand to a friend or colleague. This can be easily measured with a one-question survey: 'How likely is it that you would recommend our company/product/service to a friend or colleague?' The results of this survey are used to generate an NPS for the brand based on the proportion of promoters, detractors and passives. Research has demonstrated a correlation between this score and a company's growth in revenue. This has made it one of the most widely used business metrics adopted by more than two-thirds of Fortune 1,000 companies.

In his article on NPS, Reichheld concludes, 'This number is the one number you need to grow. It's that simple and that profound.' This may be true, but critics of NPS are quick to point out that NPS can be easily rigged by, for instance, incentivizing buyers to provide positive reviews. Like any metric, safeguards must be put in place to ensure the integrity of the measurement. The bigger issue with NPS is that it fails to tell us why our brand got the score it did, or what we could do to improve it.

What are the operational drivers that influence net promoter scores? If we knew, then we would be able to use them to improve our score and troubleshoot when problems arise. I'd argue that there are nine keys to increasing promoters and decreasing detractors. They are the nine tollgates that precede advocacy. In this way, the Duffy Brand Equity Cycle can be used as a diagnostic framework to increase and manage your NPS and the prospects for your brand's growth at home and abroad.

Brand equity in action: The CrayOffs example

I'd like to run through the model to show how the Brand Equity Cycle works (Figure 11.1). I'll use the example of a fictional brand of children's crayons called 'CrayOffs'. CrayOffs' value proposition is that these crayons wipe off any surface with a damp cloth. Our research tells us that, in the market we are entering, mothers tend to buy the crayons, so we decide to target them. To help demonstrate their point of view, I incorporate quotes that reflect the target's perspective at each point in the cycle.

In this model, prospects enter the cycle on top. The objective for marketing is to keep a flow of prospects and customers circulating, and retain as many people as possible in the advocacy loop. A description of each phase is presented below.

1 Relevance

Value does not exist in a vacuum, but rather in relation to a consumer's needs. An underserved need in the market is like a coiled spring, loaded with potential economic energy that is waiting to be released by the marketer. The Brand Equity Cycle starts with this need. Specifically, it starts with a sound market diagnosis that defines potential buyers, explores their habits and perceptions, identifies underserved needs in the market, and maps competitors' weaknesses. This is usually done with a combination of desktop and field research. It helps us to identify those segments of the market where the need for our solution, and therefore its relevance, is strongest relative to competing brands. In this case, the mothers of toddlers are targeted. Although we have identified them, they are not yet aware of our brand.

FIGURE 11.1 The Duffy Brand Equity Cycle, modelled from the consumer's perspective

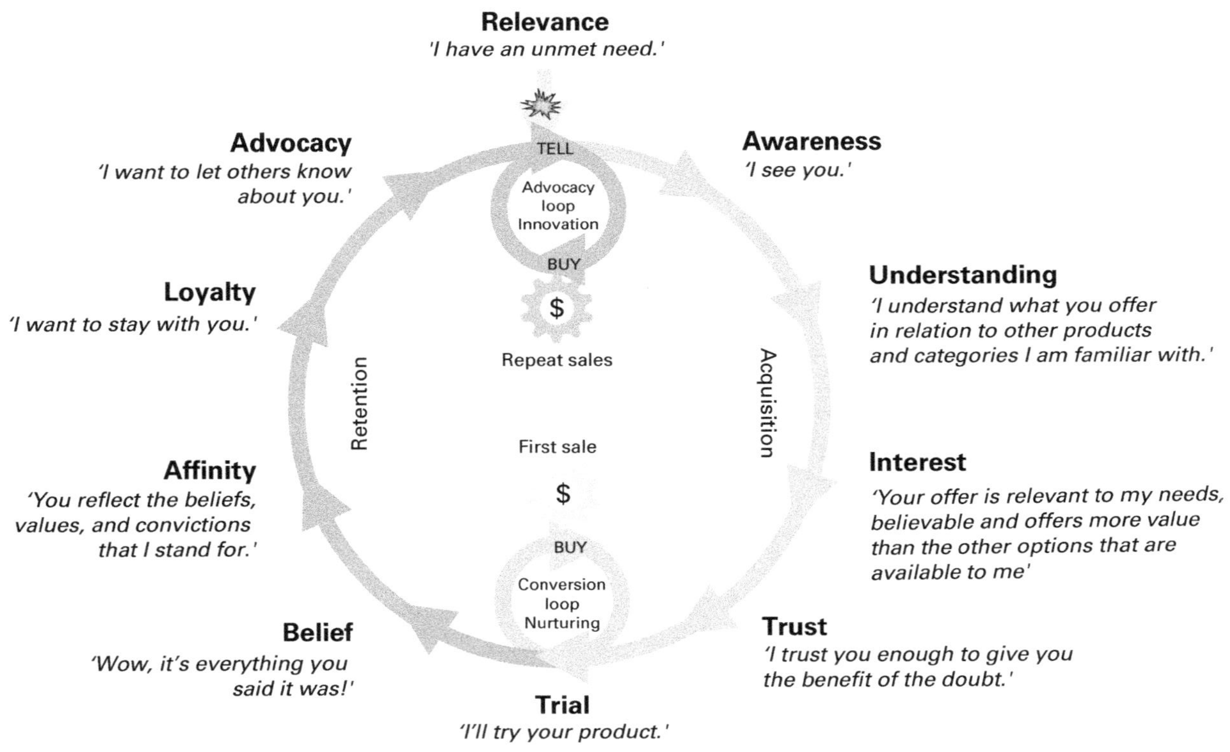

Relevance
'I have an unmet need.'

Awareness
'I see you.'

Understanding
'I understand what you offer in relation to other products and categories I am familiar with.'

Interest
'Your offer is relevant to my needs, believable and offers more value than the other options that are available to me'

Trust
'I trust you enough to give you the benefit of the doubt.'

Trial
'I'll try your product.'

Belief
'Wow, it's everything you said it was!'

Affinity
'You reflect the beliefs, values, and convictions that I stand for.'

Loyalty
'I want to stay with you.'

Advocacy
'I want to let others know about you.'

Acquisition

Retention

Advocacy loop
Innovation

Conversion loop
Nurturing

TELL

BUY

BUY

Repeat sales

First sale

To pass this tollgate, the prospect you have identified needs to have a relevant underserved need, as in: 'I want my little Jimmy to draw but my problem is that he scribbles all over the walls and it doesn't come off very easily.'

2 **Awareness**

Awareness simply means being seen in the crowd. This is not an easy task in today's media environment. It is best achieved through a coordinated effort between public relations and advertising programmes, attracting online search by publishing your own content, stimulating mentions through online networking, developing mailing lists, investing in sponsorships, product placement and/or cooperation with other brands. Awareness is one of the engines that power this whole cycle and keep it moving, along with its precursor, share of voice. That also makes it one of the most expensive points on the cycle to address.

The prospect passes this tollgate when they are exposed to the brand and it registers with them, as in: 'I remember seeing the CrayOffs logo in a banner ad but I don't know what it is. Something to do with kids' art, I think.'

3 **Understanding**

After you have the prospect's attention, the next hurdle is being understood. This requires the marketer to adopt the buyer's perspective. Clayton Christensen makes the case that consumers hire products to perform certain jobs they need to get done.[3] Understanding means the prospect is clear about what job your product can do for them and how your product fits with their existing product categories. This step appears deceptively simple but has been the downfall of many brands that were blessed with high awareness from the start, such as Segway, Apple Newton and Google+. People understand products in relation to the landscape of product categories that already exist in their minds. If they cannot fit your product into one of these existing categories, or at least understand it in relation to these categories, then they will move on. So whether you are entering an existing category or seeking to create a new category, understanding your target's current category landscape is essential. Other factors such as name, packaging, tone and manner, and visual profile also provide the prospect with vital cues to understanding.

To pass this tollgate, the prospect must understand to which category the brand belongs, as in: 'I get it, CrayOffs is a children's crayon brand like the Crayola® crayons I buy for little Jimmy.'

4 Interest

Okay, so let's say your target understands what your product does. Well done. Now you need to capture their interest. After all, there are other brands out there. To capture interest, your offer needs to be relevant to a job that the prospect needs to be done. It also needs to be likable, believable and different from other options that are available. You are competing with value here. Nailing this requires a genuine understanding of the target, their beliefs and perceptions. You have to know what other options they have at their disposal to address their need so you can be sure to favourably position your solution in relation to those other options. If you get all that right, then you're bound to capture interest.

A brand's value proposition, support points, personality and position help generate interest. Most products have at least a dozen valid points they could use to convince prospects of their value, but you can only say one thing first, so select carefully. In the CrayOffs example, the product has many selling points: They are the only 100 per cent sustainably produced crayons using beeswax from organic beehives, are water soluble, have more vibrant colour, are 100 per cent non-toxic, and provide income to indigenous tribes across South America as well as giving 1 per cent of sales to fund urban education and art initiatives. From all that, our fictional brand owners chose the value proposition 'washes off walls' based on the support point 'water-soluble'. Of all the attributes they could talk about, they felt that this would trigger the most interest before trial and the most belief after trial. Once that was decided, CrayOffs had to convey that proposition in a way that made the target both like the brand on a gut level and believe that its claims were at least plausible.

Getting the interest of the target is one of the toughest hurdles for many brands, often because the product has dozens of features and benefits, and companies have a hard time narrowing the focus of their offer. Here is a quick exercise you can use to focus:

a Make a list of all the features, benefits, and other value your product offers.

b Now ask yourself which of the items the competition is known to offer. Cross all those off your list. Now you have a list of your unique attractors.

c Which of these unique attractors does the target really want? Which do they value most? Keep those things and cross out the rest. These are your unique strong attractors. Remember, no matter how well you think you know your buyers, you are not qualified to answer this question. Only the buyers are, so ask them.

d Which of these unique strong attractors could you develop so that your brand could be best in category at it, or at least unsurpassed? Could you sustain that lead? These are your sustainable unique strong attractors.

The things that are left are things that your target values, that your competitors don't offer or are not perceived as offering, and that you could be best at. This is the place to defining your brand's value. Not all your sustainable unique strong attractors will be valued equally by your buyers. Not all will be strong enough to compete with the unique strong attractors of rival brands. Dig deep into your buyers' priorities and shape your strategy to what they value most and where your brand offers more value than competitors.

To pass this tollgate, the prospect should be able to differentiate your brand from others in the category, based on a value proposition that is relevant and believable to them, as in: 'That's interesting: CrayOffs crayons are water-soluble so they wash off easily, especially from walls. Other crayons can't do that.'

5 Trust

The target may be interested in the product, but can they trust it? Trust doesn't come easy but can be earned in several ways. Trust starts with the first impression the brand makes as part of its brand identity and profile. Any red flags at this point can cause the prospect to exit the cycle. On top of that, the brand should strive to be seen by the target as often as possible, both online and off. Familiarity alone can earn trust over time when combined with a convincing brand story and a well-managed reputation. But even if you win those battles, buyers don't want to simply take the seller's word for how good the product is; they want third-party validation. The best way to get that is by having people who the target already trusts to endorse your brand. The internet provides a wealth of opportunity in this regard in the form of recommendations from friends, influencers, rating sites, publications, etc. Marketers should manage their online recommendations with a proper online monitoring and networking strategy.

The prospect passes this tollgate when they trust the brand enough to give it the benefit of the doubt, as in: 'Little Jimmy chews on his crayons. I was wondering if they were safe but they are made from organic beeswax and I read some positive reviews on Working Moms Blog and saw that Jimmy's paediatrician recommended them on Facebook. I think CrayOffs crayons are okay.'

6 **Trial**
This is the moment of truth. The prospect is interested in buying, but is the product easily accessible and at a price that is consistent with the value promised? Your pricing strategy and distribution/place will answer those questions. It's worth noting that while we all know the dangers of pricing a product too high, pricing too low can also drive your target away if it seems out of sync with the value you claim to offer. The sales outlets you choose should provide easy access to your target but should also reinforce your brand identity.

Bottom line, your offer has to fit the target's value equation and expectations. That is, you have to strike the right balance between what they get and what they give. With regard to what the target gets, try to deliver value across all three dimensions of your product offer – the core offer, tangible value-add features and intangible value-add associations. On the other side of that equation is what the target has to give to acquire your product. Consider the overall cost of acquisition in addition to your pricing strategy. For instance, is it a hassle to order your product? Could you improve where or how the product can be purchased to eliminate any hassles? These topics will be covered in more detail in Chapter 13.

This tollgate is passed when the prospect purchases the product, as in: 'I saw them at Walmart and they cost about the same as normal crayons, so I bought a pack for little Jimmy.'

In many cases, a prospect may develop trust but, for a variety of reasons, may not be ready to make a purchase. In our CrayOffs example, it could be that the mom had recently bought another pack of crayons and wants to wait until those are used up before she buys more. These prospects who are not ready to buy yet are retained in the conversion loop. The idea here is to nurture them by maintaining brand awareness, keeping their interest alive and increasing familiarity until they are ready to buy. This can be done in a variety of ways. Prospects are often incentivized to provide their email address and then nurtured with 'drip' email campaigns.

7 Belief

Trying a product does not mean you like it. The real closure on a first sale comes when the buyer reaches a state of belief. Belief is based on the degree to which the product delivered on the expectations the seller created before the sale. This is why a focused value proposition and key claims are so important. You can deliver adequately on other areas, but you should try to knock the prospect's socks off with regard to your value proposition. If you win them over on that, you open the door for a lasting and profitable relationship. Generating enthusiastic belief will require an ongoing dialog with product development and would benefit from regular user testing. In our example, CrayOffs has a very demonstrable value proposition. The first time the buyer cleans the crayon marks easily from the wall, they believe in the brand – even if the product has other shortcomings. This solidifies trust and has a halo effect on all other claims made by the brand. This opens the door to further the relationship.

This tollgate is passed when, based on their experience with the product, the prospect concludes that the brand delivered on its value proposition, as in: 'Wow, CrayOffs really work as promised! They wiped right off the wall.'

8 **Affinity**

Buyers don't want to go through the hassle of evaluating a range of brands every time they make a purchase. In most cases, they prefer to select a brand for a given category and be done with it until they are given reason to reconsider. That's why, if you get past belief, then there is a very good chance the prospect is looking for other reasons to like your brand. For instance, they may take a look at the brand's website to see what the brand is all about. Don't disappoint them. This is where all the softer parts of a brand identity come into play. Ideally your brand will reflect the beliefs, values and convictions that the target identifies with or aspires towards. It's important to make sure your brand identity is in order with clear brand values, relevant causes and consistent behaviour to help solidify the relationship and create an affinity with the customer.

A mistake that lots of companies make when developing their go-to-market strategy is to lead with their values and social responsibilities. In many categories today this no longer differentiates. On top of that is the problem that emphasizing this too early in the cycle (eg in your value proposition or position) can get in the way of understanding and interest. This overshadows your brand's relevance and the more immediate needs the potential buyer is trying to satisfy.

At this point, the prospect is looking for reasons to like the brand. They pass this tollgate when they feel that the brand shares their beliefs, values and convictions, as in: 'This brand really understands me. They are into education, the arts and supporting indigenous people – just like me. We have a lot in common.'

9 **Loyalty**

At the loyalty stage, the prospect is a customer. They have decided to stop spending energy searching for solutions and are now willing to remain in a buying cycle as long as you don't let them down. Maintaining loyalty has a lot to do with ensuring that the reasons the person chose the brand in the first place are maintained. This involves all aspects of the buyer's experience, both during and after purchase, such as quality control, distribution (easy availability), customer support and value reinforcement.

To ensure loyalty, look for friction points in the buyer's experience when acquiring your product and when using it. Friction erodes loyalty. Friction can be something subtle that is easily overlooked – for example, slow-loading pages on your website, packaging that's difficult to open, or inconvenient customer service hours. On their own, these are typically not deal-breakers but over time they can erode loyalty and make your buyer more receptive to competitive offers.

The prospect passes this tollgate when they stop actively looking for other solutions because they are satisfied that your brand delivers sufficient value, ideally best-in-category, as in: 'From now on, CrayOffs are the only crayons for me and little Jimmy.'

10 Advocacy

Before the internet, loyalty via word of mouth was the highest form of advocacy a customer could provide for a business. Today we can take it one step further. Advocacy is the desire to publicly identify with the brand and recommend it to others. Now, word of mouth is nothing new, but with the average adult today having hundreds of people in their online networks, a few good words online can deliver immense value to your marketing programme. In this sense, your customers are a powerful media channel for your brand. Not only because they provide your brand with awareness, but also because they can dial their friends all the way from inertia to trust with a single post.

In fact, advocacy alone has been found to be the single most reliable predictive indicator of growth for most businesses. In his 2003 landmark paper 'The one number you need to grow',[4] Frederick F Reichheld from Bain & Company quantified the importance of advocates with research involving over 4,000 Bain clients. His work established a close correlation between the number of advocates a brand can cultivate and their sales growth. You probably know the output of this research as net promoter score. The NPS is, in essence, a measure of how well your brand is performing on advocacy. Reichheld acknowledges that there are other factors, beyond the buyer's willingness to recommend a brand, that influence growth. However, his research into brand advocacy led him to conclude, 'While it doesn't guarantee growth, in general profitable growth can't be achieved without it.'

Some brand advocates may spread the word in person or across their digital networks all on their own, but even if they don't, their willingness to recommend your brand (even if they don't act on it) is what the NPS measures. This is why it is a more accurate measure of advocacy than actual online 'mentions' and should be used as the definitive measure of advocacy.

Having said that, it is generally beneficial to the brand if its advocates actually step up and vouch for the brand to family, friends and followers, as in 'I am so happy I discovered CrayOffs. They are the perfect crayon for toddlers.' There are also plenty of ways marketers can encourage this behaviour online with campaigns, buzz monitoring, rapid response programmes and a solid social media networking strategy. These tactics can coax a public endorsement out of those who are already predisposed to do so, as in, 'I'm posting little Jimmy's wall drawings on the CrayOffs art contest site and sharing them with my friends on Pinterest and Facebook so they can vote for Jimmy's drawing.'

A prerequisite of such a public display of affection is that the brand is one with which people are comfortable associating themselves online. This comes back to brand identity and image. We refer to this as the brand's social currency. That is, the degree to which the target wants to be publicly associated with the brand. Usually this is because they feel the brand says something positive about them.

We can see this with many luxury brands, like Lamborghini, that are advocated online by people who never have purchased the product, and most likely never will. In the same sense, you might expect significantly fewer buyers to advocate their favourite brand of haemorrhoid medication online, although they may do so to close friends or family.

The customer passes the advocacy tollgate when they want to be associated with the brand, as evidenced by their willingness to tell others about the brand.

The final destination in this cycle is the advocacy loop, where the company collects and nurtures a growing audience of brand advocates who buy and tell, buy and tell, ad infinitum. The more they advocate, the more new buyers they attract into the cycle. Of course, it is best to keep communicating with them while they are in the advocacy cycle. But the real key to keeping them there is product innovation.

Companies that are best at this adhere to a regular schedule of innovation, constantly listening to their market and then delivering constant improvement to their products and services. Perhaps the best example of this is Apple, who has amassed one of the largest and most engaged group of brand advocates the world has ever known.

Buyers and other stakeholders contribute revenue to the company but also brand equity, as shown in Figure 11.2. This is an important but often overlooked aspect of value transfer. The brand is the store of that value but it must be set up and managed to capture it. If brand equity were electricity, the brand acts as the battery. It needs to be properly set up and managed to accept and retain the charge. Companies that are not set up to do this can lose this value, or never capture it in the first place.

The Duffy Brand Equity Cycle is intended to illustrate the ways that consumers create brand equity for companies over time, as they transition from potential customers to brand advocates. The activity of strategic marketing is to identify potential buyers and then simply facilitate their journey from relevance to advocacy, maximizing the effectiveness of each step along the way. All marketing activities should contribute directly to the flow from one step to the next with one caveat: Anything you do to get people through one tollgate can't cause a

FIGURE 11.2 Companies receive two types of value from markets, and should manage both

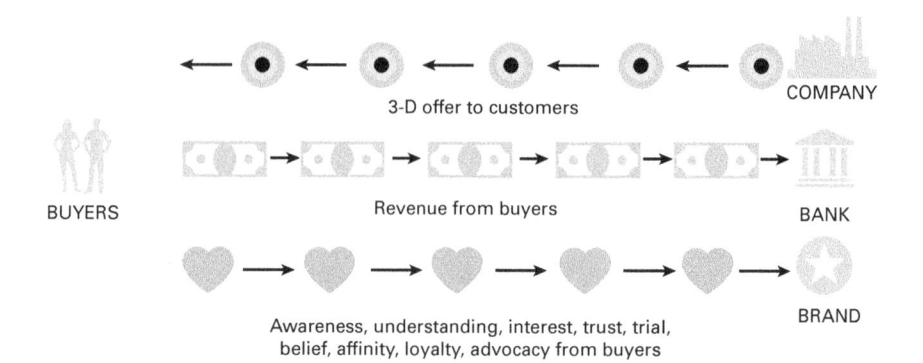

BUYERS

3-D offer to customers → COMPANY

Revenue from buyers → BANK

Awareness, understanding, interest, trust, trial, belief, affinity, loyalty, advocacy from buyers → BRAND

blockage (ie make it more difficult for people to pass through) or leakage (ie the target exits) at any other tollgate. For instance, using a bizarre image in your launch ad may increase awareness dramatically but detract from the brand in terms of interest, trust, affinity and advocacy later on.

Conclusion

Like a vendor in a crowded market, your brand doesn't need to smile at customers in order for you to sell products in foreign markets, but you are likely to capture more value from being there if you do. Sales-focused organizations look at new markets and asses them in terms of their ability to sell there. Strategic marketers take a different approach. They look for markets where they can sell while also maintaining a price premium and build brand equity to ensure future sales with each transaction. If your company could benefit from this approach, then the Duffy Brand Equity Cycle provides a pragmatic model you can use as a framework to plan, manage and diagnose your marketing programme. By measuring various aspects of brand equity cycle we can assess the impact of the marketing on brand equity. For instance, measuring advocacy with NPS will give you a readout on your brand's growth prospects in the markets you serve. Measuring other aspects of the cycle can provide insight on how to improve it.

Managed well, your brand functions not only as a differentiating trademark but also as a receptacle to capture the associations and value you work so hard to create. In the next chapter I explore the value equation that potential buyers in foreign markets will use to assess your offer and suggest ways you can tip the balance in your brand's favour.

Notes

1 Brand equity, Lexico, undated. www.lexico.com/definition/brand_equity (archived at https://perma.cc/P4NQ-MRK8)
2 J Bertilsson, and V Tarnovskaya, *Brand Theories: Perspectives on brands and branding,* 1st edn, Studentlitteratur, Lund, Sweden, 2017.

3 C Christensen, S Cook and T Hall, Marketing malpractice: The cause and the cure, *Harvard Business Review,* December 2005. https://hbr.org/2005/12/marketing-malpractice-the-cause-and-the-cure (archived at https://perma.cc/RZ4G-FHWU)

4 F Reichheld, The one number you need to grow, *Harvard Business Review,* December 2003. https://hbr.org/2003/12/the-one-number-you-need-to-grow (archived at https://perma.cc/N2H7-YMT7)

12

Net perceived value

Planning for profit

In the previous four chapters I have made several arguments in favour of building a strong brand in your new market despite the cost and time implications. Not least among these reasons is profitability. In his book *Positioning for Professionals*, business consultant Tim Williams points out that the ability to command a higher price is the most direct way to ensure profit. He makes the case eloquently that 'Profit is driven mostly by price. Price is driven mostly by brand perception. That makes brand-building an activity central to business success.'[1] He reasons that although investments in building brand equity may not boost sales in the short term, these activities create the conditions that allow the brand to charge higher prices over the long run. Or, to paraphrase Philip Kotler, if you are not a brand, you are a commodity – then you can only compete on price.

In the final analysis, profit will define the success or failure of your marketing efforts in foreign markets. Knowing that, local competitors will often lower their prices to keep your brand from gaining traction if they perceive you as a threat. In this environment, how can you ensure a healthy margin without losing customers to lower-priced rivals? Moreover, how can you charge a higher price than your competitors while taking their market share? In this chapter, we will take a look at the factors that underlie operating profit and how your marketing activities can have a direct effect on them.

Profit margin is the percentage of sales revenue we are able to keep once all other financial costs are subtracted. To increase that percentage we can increase sales and/or decrease costs. That's easy to understand because it's tangible: money in, money out. But there is a third variable at play: value.

From the perspective of the seller, value usually equates to money. Product quality (the costs the producer put into the product) and price are the seller's go-to metrics for value. That's the disconnect. From the buyer's perspective, it's a lot more nuanced and essential to understand. The dictionary defines value simply as 'relative worth'.[2] The keyword for marketers is 'relative'. It does not rest in the product nor in the price tag. Value is a judgement call made by the people you want to buy your product. Given that, I'd encourage you to understand it even if initially it seems to defy quantification. Since buyers can have very different value requirements from one market to the next, I'd also advise that you think about value anew in each market you enter.

When executives adopt a strictly cash-centric view of the business, it's easy to be blind to value. That's risky because value is the one thing that is responsible for every sale and the most important contributor to profit.

It can be sobering, if not disheartening, to realize that every time someone buys your competitor's product it's because they felt it offered superior value to your offer. Not better quality, not a better price – better value. That's how markets work. Value is the gravity of commerce, and money flows to it like water to a puddle. Like the force of gravity, value can also be hard to see and define, but that doesn't make it any less real.

Value in action

Even if we can't see value, we can easily see its effects. The ability to sustain small increases in price can yield far more profit than moderate gains in volume or reductions in cost. In their book *The Price Advantage*, the authors state, 'Pricing is far and away the most sensitive profit lever that managers can influence. Very small changes in average price translate into huge changes in operating profit.'[3]

These results have been replicated several times and are compelling. A Harvard Business School study of 2,463 companies found that an increase in unit sales volume of 1 per cent, assuming no decrease in price, yields an average 3.3 per cent increase in operating profit. But a 1 per cent increase in price, assuming no decrease in sales volume, yields an average 11.1 per cent increase in operating profit. This study found that the 1 per cent price increase also yielded more profit than 1 per cent decreases in both variable and fixed costs combined. The authors cite examples of a consumer durable goods company that increased operating profit by nearly 30 per cent with a 2.5 per cent increase in price, and an industrial equipment manufacturer that increased operating profits by 35 per cent with a 3 per cent increase in price.[4] A McKinsey study that used the S&P Composite 1500 Index found a 1 per cent increase in price produced an average 8 per cent increase in operating profits for these companies. This result was 50 per cent greater than a 1 per cent drop in variable costs and more than three times greater than a 1 per cent increase in sales volume.[5] A study published in *Business Strategy Review* shows the effects a 2 per cent increase in price would have on ten different types of companies (see Figure 12.1).[6]

FIGURE 12.1 Percentage increase in operating profit based on a 2 per cent increase in price

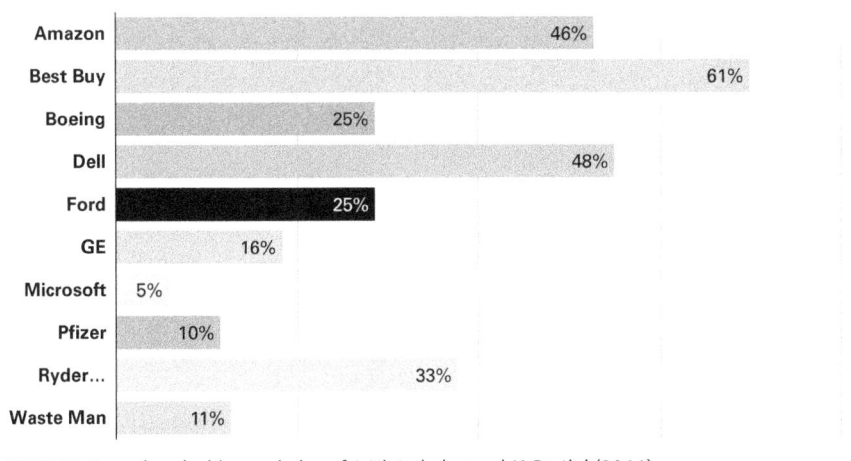

Company	%
Amazon	46%
Best Buy	61%
Boeing	25%
Dell	48%
Ford	25%
GE	16%
Microsoft	5%
Pfizer	10%
Ryder...	33%
Waste Man	11%

SOURCE Reproduced with permission of A Hinterhuber and M Bertini (2011)

Companies with the thinnest margins saw increases in operating profit of up to 61 per cent. The authors say the aim of pricing based on value is 'to align price with real, unique value – the "stuff" that customers care about and competitors currently do not provide'. Applying this approach to a yoghurt brand, they were able to increase profits six-fold over plan.[7]

The challenge here is to increase the brand's perceived value so the company can charge higher prices without losing customers to lower-priced competitors. The ability to charge a premium price and grow market share simultaneously is the formula for wealth creation. This ability is called 'pricing power' and is the force of value in action. Pricing power is based entirely on the value of the product or brand as perceived in the market. Speaking at a US Congressional hearing, investor Warren Buffett said,

> The single-most important decision in evaluating a business is pricing power. If you've got the power to raise prices without losing business to a competitor, you've got a very good business. And if you have to have a prayer session before raising the price by a tenth of a cent, then you've got a terrible business.[8]

In theory, everyone in the company adds value to the company's offer. But adding value isn't the same as creating it. Where does value come from in an organization? It's not from the CFO, even though they deal with money. The CFO manages the aftermath of value by tracking revenue, keeping costs in line, and dealing with the surplus cash the company earns because of the value it offers. It's not the sales team, although they deal with customers. The sales team help convert the demand created by value into cash through transactions.

Value creation comes from buyer insight. That is the realm of strategic marketing and the responsibility of the CMO, but the CMO can't do it alone. As noted above, value is created by everyone in the company and expressed to the market through a combination of product, price, place and promotion. The only person in charge of all those things is the CEO. By understanding prospective buyers, competitors and market conditions, the CMO can define what value the company needs to create to satisfy buyers and compete with the value being offered by rivals. Then, the CEO, along with the rest of the C-suite, puts the company on the path to producing that value profitably.

Fewer than 20 per cent of companies report that they manage value in this way.[9] That set-up, or something like it, would only be found in a value-driven company where value management would be the CMO's primary focus. The CMO in such a company would see profit margin as the amount of value the company can create, minus the cost of creating that value. They would live and breathe value and weigh every choice the company made based on its potential value impact. The good news to anyone reading this is that over 80 per cent of your rivals are handicapped by a value blind spot that you can exploit.

To be clear, I'm not proposing that companies abandon financial management in place of value management. It's not an either/or choice. The importance of managing the finances of an organization cannot be overstated, but as the precursor to revenue and income, value is also important. Someone at the table must be representing the interests of the buyers with any decision that has the potential to affect the way they perceive the value of the company's offer. More often than not, in mid-sized firms, value isn't even acknowledged by senior management, let alone managed. In that environment, it's easy to make decisions based on financial, R&D, HR or other priorities that silently erode or even destroy value. Knowing how your offer's value ranks relative to competitors' can provide you with a more forward-looking indicator of where the business is heading than can sales.

Creating scarcity within a category

Pricing power and scarcity go hand in hand. The pricing power of most products can be enhanced with perceived scarcity. We all saw this in the spring of 2020 when the COVID-19 pandemic fuelled an acute interest in hand sanitizer, disinfectants and face masks. This temporarily boosted demand beyond production capacity. The resulting scarcity allowed some sellers to increase prices by over 200 per cent with no shortage of buyers who still saw value in the offer (how those sellers fared with buyers after the pandemic is another story).

But you don't need a crisis to trigger perceived scarcity. You can do it yourself by differentiating your offer to the point where buyers find it unique and will not settle for substitutes. We all have at least one or two brands that we feel this strongly about. It may be your favourite sneakers, wine, shampoo, restaurant, outboard motor, ballpoint pen or jeans brand. The point is that, when it comes to that particular category of goods, there is only one brand that meets your value requirements. That's scarcity. A category may have 28 competing brands in it, but in your eyes there is only one that is acceptable.

For example, several years ago I developed a fairly irrational loyalty to a Dutch confectionery company called Tony's Chocolonely. I first saw one of its chocolate bars at a grocery store in Brussels. Based on the packaging alone, I had to try it. The more I learned about the brand, the more I liked it. I'm not a chocolate fanatic, in fact, I'm generally indifferent to chocolate, but this brand got me interested and has helped cultivate my belief that it is unique. In a blind taste test, I'm certain I could not tell the difference between Tony's and any other premium chocolate. I suspect I'm actually consuming the brand more than the product itself, but the fact that it's twice the price of the mass-market bar next to it on the shelf doesn't factor into my purchase decision. In my mind, the two can't be compared – even though for all purposes the core products are identical.

Although the chocolate industry is highly competitive and dominated by a number of huge multinationals, the idea for this confectionery brand wasn't dreamt up by the marketing department at Nestlé or Lindt. It was a bootstrap operation born in 2005 out of necessity by a fair trade advocate with a compelling back story. Case in point, three years before he started making chocolate, company founder Teun van de Keuken filed criminal charges against himself in a Dutch court to demonstrate how governments were turning a blind eye to atrocities in the chocolate trade. Van de Keuken's bold convictions and eccentricity shine though the brand identity he created. By 2018 Tony's Chocolonely market share had reached 19 per cent, making it the largest chocolate brand in the Netherlands, topping huge multinationals like Verkade, Mars and Nestlé.[10]

The owners of Tony's Chocolonely seem to understand that the value it provide through its confections goes beyond the chocolate. They attend to this value and cultivate it with great care. At this time of writing, there is no shortage of chocolate, and there are at least 15 other brands of fair trade chocolate I can buy on Amazon, and yet Tony's is able to create a sense of a scarcity in the chocolate bar category that gives the brand pricing power because enough people feel there is nothing else quite like it.

At the company's annual meeting in November 2019, an arena-sized crowd of investors and enthusiasts packed Amsterdam's Westergasfabriek. They each paid €14 (USD $15) to be told that the company made 0 per cent net profit – and seemed to accept the news with enthusiasm. CEO Henk Jan Beltman also reported that he willingly pays up to 60 per cent over the industry average for the same cocoa as his competitors so farmers can make a living wage. Despite this, Tony's Chocolonely maintained a 40 per cent gross profit (Nestlé's gross profit was 49 per cent for the same period) and experienced a 26.5 per cent increase in sales from the previous year.[11] It would appear that even investors believe there is nothing else quite like it.

Understanding value

The reason executives give for not managing value is that they have a hard time understanding it or measuring it. If value is the precursor to profit, what's the precursor to value? What do your customers at home and abroad value? How can a company know what value it needs to produce in a given market, and how does it produce it? These questions are all worth considering. Let's start with the first one.

Value won't give you an edge if your competitors offer the same value. So what you are really trying to create is proprietary value that is unique to your brand. The precursor to that type of value is buyer insight. You can't have proprietary value without proprietary insight into the wants, needs, perceptions, beliefs and tolerances of buyers.

Some insights are obvious. For example, you don't need to conduct a research study to confirm that people want their jeans to fit. This is an essential insight to grasp if you want to sell jeans. The problem with these types of obvious insights is that your competitors can see them too, and create similar value around them by offering a range of sizes just like you. If you were on a mission to provide more value than that competitor to command a higher price, you would need to dig deeper. You would need to identify the needs that your competitors have missed. For example, you might seek to discover how the buyer likes their jeans to fit, what problems they have in finding the right fit today, how they perceive the fit of your jean brand vs rival brands, or what feelings and associations they attach to different jean brands.

To gain these insights, you need to be able to extract yourself from the company's top-down perspective on the market. You'll need to understand how things look from the outside-in, because that's the perspective of buyers. This is the most essential skill for a strategic marketer: the ability to put themselves in the shoes of the buyer and adopt their point of view. It requires more than demographic information and website analytics. That type of data provides knowledge about the buyer, most of which your rivals also possess. Buyer insight is different. It's not so much about knowledge as it is about understanding. Proprietary buyer insight comes from focused empathy: the ability to understand and share the feelings of others – in this case, the people you want to buy your product.

Albert Einstein is credited for saying 'Any fool can know. The point is to understand.'[12] But one of the most lucid explanations of the difference between knowledge and understanding was submitted by Michel Paul on Quora: 'Knowledge is awareness that something is the case. Understanding is awareness of why or how it is the case.'[13] This type of less-obvious insight does not come easy. That's why most mid-sized companies don't invest in acquiring it. But, if your company has established the priorities, people and processes that allow it to consistently get to the 'how and why' before your competitors, then you will have the insights required to continually create unique value, and the unique value to command a higher price, and the higher price to earn more profit.

This requires a different type of marketing department with a different type of budget than is often found today. Many CEOs define the marketing department in terms of its output of ads, online content and other forms of communication. It is then budgeted to serve that purpose. But just as critical is the department's ability to ensure a reliable flow of buyer insight into the company. Without that, much of the output will simply be 'happy talk' that helps maintain awareness but conveys little proprietary value. The investment required to gain meaningful insight consistently is rarely funded in the annual marketing budget. Lobbying senior management for episodic investments in market research is the best most marketing departments can do, but it is not the same thing. The gathering of proprietary buyer insight needs to be prioritized by leadership then hardwired into the mandate of the marketing department and budgeted accordingly.

Identifying value

When entering a foreign market you will have a lot to think about: different regulations, different languages, different cultures, different competitors, etc, but your guiding light through the entire process should be value as defined by your buyers in relation to their other options. Understanding the value requirements of your buyers is never easy, but it's even more challenging when competing in foreign markets, because the criteria that buyers there use to assess your offer may not even be on your radar.

Most people think of the price tag when they hear value, but the perceived value is not a number that buyers calculate in order to decide. It is a ratio. It consists of two opposing factors from the buyer's perspective: 'What I give' versus 'What I get'. The relative merits of either side of that equation are weighed in relation to 'What I feel I can afford to give for the transaction' and 'What I feel I want to get from the transaction' respectively. I use the word 'feel' intentionally here because this is a judgement call, not a quantitative analysis, that the buyer is making.

I find it helpful to picture these two factors on a scale, as in Figure 12.2, with 'What I give' on the left and 'What I get' on the right. The role of marketing is to understand the target well enough

FIGURE 12.2 The Net Perceived Value Model. The mental scales people use to assess the value of your offer

What I feel I must give	What I feel I will get
EG:	EG:
• Physical exertion	• Labour savings: physical/mental
• Mental exertion	• Pleasure: sensual/mental
• Risk	• Personal fulfilment/self-expression
• Hassle	• Security/safety
• Reputation	• Health/well-being
• Social status	• Status: social/professional
• Career	• Risk reduction
• Time	• Time
• Money	• More resources/money

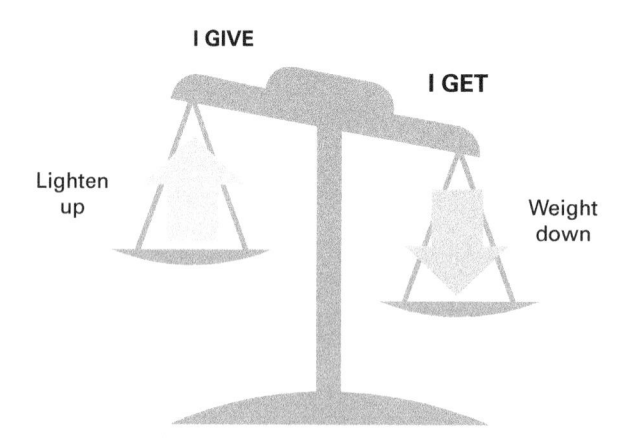

I GIVE — Lighten up

I GET — Weight down

to know what will tip the scales for them. Whichever brand can tip the scale the farthest to the right produces the best net perceived value and wins the sale.

The 'give' side on the left is evaluated in terms of the prospect's resources or tolerances. This isn't always financial. For example, a well-paid but time-starved parent may weigh the time required to acquire a product much more than the price tag. Thus, they may opt to buy a bookcase for $2,000 from the local furniture store rather than get a bookcase with the same appearance and durability at IKEA for $400. For that individual, the $2,000 bookcase offers far greater value than the $400 one. That's because, in addition to $400, the IKEA bookcase will also cost them six hours of driving and assembly time. They value those six hours more than they value saving $1,600.

To lighten the 'give' side of the equation, one must look at the entirety of what acquiring the product asks of the buyer. Sometimes, the option with the lowest price tag, and even the lowest total cost of ownership (TCO) calculation, is not the best value. That's because there are non-financial costs associated with every product. Part of the cost of acquiring your product could be long delivery times, and maybe they feel they can't afford to wait. Maybe your shop doesn't offer parking and they feel they can't afford the hassle. Maybe you have a down-market brand and socially they feel they can't afford to be associated with it. Maybe they have never heard of your brand at all and feel they can't afford the risk.

Just remember that everything you do to lighten up the 'give' side won't tip the scale equally. You need to understand what is important to the target and look for ways to lighten up the cost side of the equation profitably. For this to make a difference, you'll need to find ways that are relevant to your target. For instance, in the IKEA case above, where the buyer has more money than time, two local furniture shops might not tip the scale much with a price reduction. If, on the other hand, one of the local shops could save the buyer a trip to the showroom by providing a great online shopping experience and free delivery, that may be enough to win the sale.

The 'get' side of the equation is all about perceived gains relative to what the target wants, which is not the same as what they need. Needs typically help navigate the buyer to the right product category, but it's what they want that helps them select between brands in that category. For instance, a buyer may need a watch, but if an individual's motivation for buying a new watch is status and not timekeeping, then they are likely to be more influenced by brand image than by a more accurate movement. Sometimes items you add to sweeten the offer may have no value at all. Offering a 3-year warranty on a styrofoam cooler the buyer plans to throw out at the end of the summer probably won't move the needle. The items that you add and subtract from both sides of this scale must be valued by your target buyer in order for them to make a difference in net perceived value offered. Getting this equation right is worth the effort when you consider that net perceived value is the basis of every purchase decision.

At the outset of this part we cited the case of Hans and his component testers. We saw his company invest millions adding bells and whistles to the 'get' side, none of which added any value for his buyers and therefore did not tip the scales in his favour. Had he known his buyers better, he would have actually removed the bells and whistles and got his product to market quicker. He would have done this before his competitors did, and would likely still dominate the market today. To effectively work the scales in this equation, you need to keep your finger on the pulse of the buyer, maintaining a clear understanding of their needs and priorities.

Ask why

Most producers see their product in very concrete, one-dimensional terms: a certain product, that performs a certain function, sold at a certain price. This is very rational but also limiting, because buyers see things differently. In fact, what you think you are selling may bear little resemblance to what people are actually buying. One study on value creation concluded that 'Value, as perceived by customers, is seldom found in what the firm thinks it is selling.'[14]

If you shift your focus from *what* people are buying to *why* they are buying, then value becomes more obvious. Case in point: I just rented Pixar's *Finding Dory* for my six-year-old. I'm not purchasing entertainment. I just bought myself 90 minutes of peace and quiet to write. If Amazon discovered that there are enough other people in my situation, they could use this information to add more value and compete against other online movie rentals. For instance, they could make the presentation of children's rentals more cinematic by adding some cartoons and coming attractions at the beginning of the film and some behind the scenes content at the end to stretch the viewing experience to 120 minutes instead of 90 minutes. Not a particularly strong product development idea but I hope it serves to illustrate the point.

If you are clear on why people buy your product then you can start to augment that value. McDonald's is a good example of this. When people see the golden arches, they are reminded of hamburgers. That's their core product. In fact, McDonald's sells more burgers annually than any other restaurant chain on Earth. But do you think McDonald's offers the world's best quality burger? Maybe it did back in 1940, but today I'd go so far as to argue that very little of the value that McDonald's produces come from its burgers. While I've never considered McDonald's as offering the tastiest burger in town, it is by far the most convenient. McDonald's seems to understand this.

McDonald's is one of the most innovative restaurants in history, but you wouldn't know it by looking at its burgers. In the 80 years since opening, the burger itself has changed very little, but everything around the burger has, from restaurant design and drive-through windows to toys and playrooms for kids, to ordering apps and delivery. That's because they know that I'm not buying hamburgers at McDonald's – I'm buying convenience. When the double whammy of pandemic and economic downturn hit in 2020, McDonald's second-quarter revenue plunged 30 per cent compared to 2019. How did CEO Chris Kempczinski try to attract more diners? He didn't do it with better burgers. He knew that a new factor, safety, was shaping how consumers assessed the value of their dining options. He responded in kind, describing his focus on 'the three Ds: drive-thru, delivery, and digital',[15] because he knew that is where the value had shifted among buyers.

Conclusion

At the heart of your company's profitability is value. Proportionally, no factor can increase profits more than the ability to charge a higher price, which is not driven by 'quality' as the seller perceives it but by 'value' as your buyers perceive it. What makes this realization frustrating for many executives is the lack of control that it implies. The seller has complete control over their offer and its price, but the buyers decide its value, and in a competitive market that means they also decide if the price will fly. If the price you charge tips their mental value scale too far to the left, then they simply will not buy.

Consumer insights are the foundation upon which value is built. They allow you to tip the scale in your favour by providing proprietary value. This requires the company to understand three things about value: a) the criteria used by their by buyers to define it, b) the relative weight of those criteria, and c) how well the competing options deliver it. If we can understand these things, then as marketers we have a better chance of being able to create and use value to compete in the markets we serve.

To help make value less ethereal, we can identify three categories of value where companies can add to their offer. In the next chapter, I explore each category of value further and explain how they can be used to compete when marketing abroad.

Notes

1 T Williams, *Positioning for Professionals: How professional knowledge firms can differentiate their way to success*, John Wiley & Sons, Hoboken, NJ, 2010.
2 Value, dictionary.com, undated. www.dictionary.com/browse/value (archived at https://perma.cc/E3PP-XZXB)
3 M Marn, E Roegner and C Zawada, *The Price Advantage*, John Wiley & Sons, Hoboken, New Jersey, 2004.
4 M Marn and R Rosiello, Managing price, gaining profit, *Harvard Business Review*, September–October 1992. https://hbr.org/1992/09/managing-price-gaining-profit (archived at https://perma.cc/EXF3-WG3Z)
5 M Marn, E Roegner and C Zawada, The power of pricing, McKinsey & Company, 1 February 2003. www.mckinsey.com/business-functions/marketing-and-sales/our-insights/the-power-of-pricing (archived at https://perma.cc/PU7G-APH9)
6 A Hinterhuber and M Bertini, Profiting when customers choose value over price, *Business Strategy Review*, 2011. www.researchgate.net/publication/228129605_Profiting_When_Customers_Choose_Value_Over_Price (archived at https://perma.cc/PVF6-7BVH)
7 A Hinterhuber and M Bertini, Profiting when customers choose value over price, *Business Strategy Review*, 2011. www.researchgate.net/publication/228129605_Profiting_When_Customers_Choose_Value_Over_Price (archived at https://perma.cc/8VG8-48UB)

8 B Ritholtz, United States of America Financial Crisis Inquiry Commission (FCIC) Interview of Warren Buffett, The Big Picture, 26 May 2010. https://ritholtz.com/2016/03/fcic-buffett/ (archived at https://perma.cc/DH8L-X2DU)

9 A Hinterhuber and M Bertini, Profiting when customers choose value over price, *Business Strategy Review*, 2011. www.researchgate.net/publication/228129605_Profiting_When_Customers_Choose_Value_Over_Price (archived at https://perma.cc/8K24-BHDX)

10 F Baltesen, Hoe duurzaam is Tony's Chocolonely? FM.NL, 29 November 2018. https://financieel-management.nl/artikel/hoe-duurzaam-is-tonys-chocolonely (archived at https://perma.cc/K6BT-QJC7)

11 A Myers, Tony's Chocolonely records '0 per cent profit and 100 per cent impact', latest results show, Confectionery News, 25 November 2019. www.confectionerynews.com/Article/2019/11/22/Tony-s-Chocolonely-records-0-profit-and-100-impact-latest-results-show (archived at https://perma.cc/QH2P-ZB3J)

12 A Einstein, Any fool can know. The point is to understand, Good Reads, undated. www.goodreads.com/quotes/72361-any-fool-can-know-the-point-is-to-understand (archived at https://perma.cc/D8EK-GUWV)

13 H Singh, What is the difference between knowledge and understanding? Quora, 27 January 2019, www.quora.com/What-is-the-difference-between-knowledge-and-understanding (archived at https://perma.cc/8DKA-JD6T)

14 A Hinterhuber and M Bertini, Profiting when customers choose value over price, *Business Strategy Review*, 2011. www.researchgate.net/publication/228129605_Profiting_When_Customers_Choose_Value_Over_Price (archived at https://perma.cc/5D37-Y58G)

15 R Williams, McDonald's boosts marketing budget $200m to drive recovery, Marketing Dive, 30 July 2020. www.marketingdive.com/news/mcdonalds-boosts-marketing-budget-by-200m-to-drive-recovery/582573/ (archived at https://perma.cc/FC5M-8X2C)

13

Creating value

How buyers assess value

As discussed in the previous chapter, value is all about finding the right balance between 'give' and 'get' to produce more net perceived value than your competitors. The value your product provides on the 'get' side is only partially represented by your core product offer. Potential buyers assess your product on two additional dimensions of value: value-add features and value-add associations. To provide maximum value to buyers and to exert maximum pressure on competitors, it helps to view your product in all three dimensions of value.

Most mid-sized companies are fixated on their core product features. This makes those aspects of value that lie outside the core product hard to recognize. To help executives visualize and manage this invisible value, marketing professor Philip Kotler introduced a model in his 1967 book *Marketing Management: Analysis, planning, and control*.[1] Kotler's model defines products in three layers: core product, actual product and augmented product. As a young advertising copywriter, I used Kotler's textbooks as my introduction to strategic marketing. I found his Three Layers of Product Model very useful. Over the years, I have adapted this model to suit my own work and observations. It is presented in Figure 13.1 as the 3-D Product Model.

To manage brand value, the company must look at the product as buyers do: in the three dimensions of (a) core product features, (b) value-add features, and (c) value-add associations. Successful brands tend to constantly differentiate themselves across all three dimensions.

FIGURE 13.1 The 3-D Product Model. In this adaptation of Philip Kotler's Three Layers of Product, the 3-D Product Model helps us to visualize the three categories of value that buyers receive when they acquire the products, as seen from their perspective

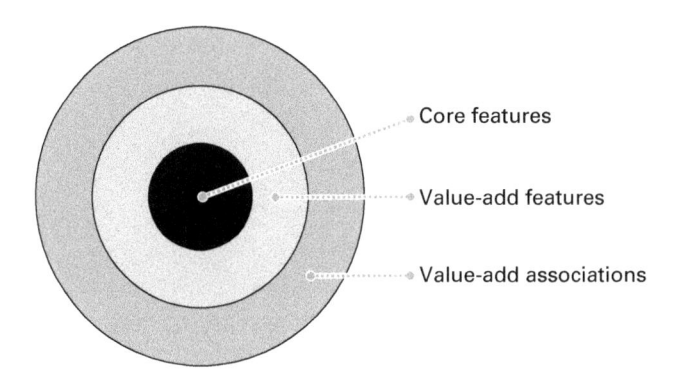

- Core features
- Value-add features
- Value-add associations

You can, too, by using these three dimensions to create an ongoing programme of value development and differentiation. Often you will find you can increase the net perceived value of your offer without altering its core features. Thinking of value in these three discreet categories can make it a lot easier to analyse, manage and discuss value with your colleagues.

All products are 3-D

Every time a consumer makes a purchase decision, whether a new car or a candy bar, they are assessing their options and the value offered to them in three dimensions. The criteria changes from product to product, situation to situation, but the underlying principle remains the same and, therefore, is essential for the strategic marketer to understand.

Take, for example, a product as simple as a Pilates ball. To the producer, it is a ball made from PVC plastic capable of being inflated to 0.6 PSI to 0.9 PSI and supporting an adult's weight without bursting. The ball may cost $4 to produce and can be sold for $30 but chances are that the people who buy this ball see it quite differently. At the gym, they may see the ball and the brand as an expression of themselves, along with their choice of gym clothing and shoes. In fact, they may see the ball as an extension of their outfit. That might be why they chose a particular producer's yellow ball over other options. The point is that there are usually all sorts of reasons why people are interested in products and brands beyond the core function it is intended to perform. Some are rational, many are emotional, but all influence purchase decisions.

Core features

Let's take a closer look at our Pilates ball from the perspective of a buyer. We'll start with core features. These are the tangible attributes that define the category and are required for inclusion in it. These are sometimes referred to as category qualifiers, table stakes, or hygiene elements for the category. For instance, the minimum requirements for inclusion in the Pilates ball category is that it has to be 55 to 75cm in diameter, made of puncture-resistant plastic, and be able to absorb significant shock without rupturing. The core features satisfy those criteria. If your core features are different enough, you can start your own category and be the first brand in. If that difference is highly valued, you will have the kind of competitive advantage that I discussed in Chapter 9 with EMCO.

Over time, core features will be copied by competitors, patents notwithstanding. The barriers to imitation degrade over time as the know-how required to duplicate core functions become common knowledge. This can lead to more parity among all brands in a mature category with regard to core function, making it increasingly easier to substitute one brand's product for another without major trade-offs in functionality.

Think about your company's product in the market you are entering. What basic functionality must a product provide to be included in your product's category? What trade-offs would a new buyer have to make if they chose another brand in your category over your brand? What value could you add to the core features of your offer to better address the wants and needs of your target?

Value-add features

These are tangible features, but they lie outside the primary function of the product, such as payment terms, convenience to buy, warranty, service, support, design, packaging, colour options, etc. They are tangible differences but secondary to the core function. When several producers offer similar core features, they can be expected to move to the next ring in our model and start competing on value-add features.

Like core features, value-add features can also be copied. In fact, when popular value-add features are adopted by enough players in the category, they can come to be considered a de facto standard by consumers (table stakes for the category) while still not being core features. For instance, in 1950 Zenith Electronics introduced the remote control as a value-add feature to its televisions.[2] Today it is part of the core offer.

In the case of the Pilates ball, incorporating ridges along the outside of the ball has become a fairly standard value-add feature, as has offering a variety of sizes and colours. Less common value-add features could be anti-bacterial surface coating, air pressure indicator, or using a more environmentally friendly material (since PVC has a large carbon footprint and is not recyclable).

Value-add features are a brand's primary method for adding value and differentiating as the category matures. Category leaders typically set the norms for their categories with regard to value-add features. They also use them to maintain leadership by keeping the competition off balance. Apple and Gillette, for example, are masters at this. Every year they add new features, forcing their competitors to adapt to their norms. In the case of McDonald's, it can take the time it needs to plan and source materials for its innovations. Over the years this has included things like the first TV ad campaign targeting kids (1966), drive through (1975), breakfast foods (1975), boxed kids' meals (1979), play areas (1987), etc.[3] Working on their own schedule, McDonald's is able to achieve maximum cost-effectiveness and to roll out the programme with minimal disruption. Once launched, if the innovation tips the value scale in McDonalds favour, then Burger King will need to respond in short order to avoid losing customers. Keeping up with ever-shifting conventions set by the category leader can create repeated unplanned disruption and costs for everyone else in the category.

What value-add features does your product offer in the markets it serves? How do they compare to those offered by competitors? How could you augment the value-add features of your brand? Would those additions be unique to your brand? How relevant would those additions be to your target?

Value-add associations

These are intangibles shaped largely through communication and perceived endorsements that reflect on the brand. For instance, a brand may be associated with celebrities, trends, social causes, environmental awareness, groups or a certain set of values. Developing and implementing a brand identity programme is the most direct way to coordinate these aspects of value into a coherent brand narrative. On their own, these types of things do not change the product in any material way, but they can have a significant influence on sales. These associations can also enhance the user's own reputation by association. Luxury brands do this by providing the user with perceived status or prestige.

To use our Pilates ball example again, if a popular celebrity is photographed by paparazzi using a certain brand of ball, then fans of that celebrity may value that ball more even though it has not changed and even if the celebrity did not make a formal endorsement. On 15 January 2007, sales of Wasa crisp bread in the US inexplicably shot up overnight. The Swedish crisp bread company was taken off guard when it learned that US TV personality Oprah Winfrey took a bite out of a Wasa crisp bread on her programme. That was all it took. Within one week of that show, US sales had risen by 25 per cent. Two months later, they were up by more than 50 percent.[4] Nothing about the crisp bread changed other than that it had been momentarily associated with a popular TV personality. Part of that was awareness, but it's hard to imagine that airing one TV spot once could have that effect. It is just as hard to imagine how Wasa could have altered the physical crisp bread product to trigger such a pronounced increase in sales so quickly. The crisp bread's core features and value-add features remained unchanged. What did change was value-add associations created by a third party. Value-add associations may seem ethereal, but they can have a very real impact on the bottom line.

Value-add associations are also shaped by brand identity and the work of brand managers. The more skilful the development and implementation of the brand identity is, the more it will differentiate the product, generate affinity and be difficult for competitors to copy.

Of the three categories of value that companies can use to add value to their offer, this is the least tangible and often the least prioritized. Not attending to value-add associations makes it difficult for customers, employees, investors and other stakeholders to connect with the brand on an emotional level and maintain positive feelings towards the company. As I discuss in Chapter 8, these 'soft' elements have real business consequences fostering loyalty, premium pricing, brand advocacy and long-term revenue growth.

Since the elements on this level are abstract and intangible, they are more difficult to manage. This is particularly the case in foreign markets. Feelings and associations are coloured by culture and other societal factors so are most prone to local differences. Some value-add associations may have universal appeal and, therefore, can be implemented across different markets. Others will not. You will need to manage your brand's value-add associations on a market-by-market basis and develop this value accordingly. If you are dealing with one or more foreign cultures, it will be difficult to 'wing it' even if you were able to do that in your home market.

Brand identity and management is the primary delivery system for value-add associations. For international marketers to provide value in this ring, it helps to have a well-defined, codified brand identity and brand architecture, as well as a marketing strategy that factors in value-add associations. These, in turn, should all be based on a well-defined, codified understanding of your competitors and the people to whom you sell. Having these tools in place makes it easier for the manager to convey these values to the market. As tangible differences between companies and products become harder for stakeholders to discern, competition for the best customers, employees and investors becomes increasingly dependent on these value-add associations.

There is a reluctance in many mid-sized companies to invest in developing their brand. This is most pronounced in companies that have grown through the toil of their sales department without the support of a strategic marketing function. Executives in these companies may not have had reason to consider value-add associations ever before in their careers. Experience has taught them that sales efforts alone are enough to grow and prosper. In such an environment, the value offered by the brand is often narrowly defined as customer support combined with what's spelled out in the spec sheet and warranty. This approach can be enough to prosper in business-to-business markets – to a point. The inflection point is when:

1 the company wishes to reach the 'next level' where they will be competing directly with larger, more sophisticated companies that have started building barriers to entry with strategic marketing and brand management in addition to direct sales support;
2 the company finds that competitors at its own level are starting to complement their sales efforts with strategic marketing and brand management.

If either applies to your business, then it may be time to look into finding new ways to augment the value-add associations of your brand by investing in brand development. This starts by understanding your buyers in the context of the market where they live.

All value is relative

I've made the point that value is relative to the buyer. It's also relative to the buyer's context, which can change. With regard to the 3-D Product Model, different rings tend to be more important to different buyers at different times and contexts. The weighting of the rings depends on this context, which can shape the value priorities and value perceptions of the people to whom you market.

For instance, I was staying at a hotel in Amsterdam one rainy March evening. My flight had been delayed by a storm and it was past 10 in the evening when I got to my room. At 8.30 the next morning, I would be presenting a product launch case study to a room full of pharmaceutical executives. I was feeling a little pressured and still had work to do on my presentation. I was also feeling tired and wanted a Coke. I grabbed one out of the minibar and noticed the price was almost ten euros. I knew there was a 24-hour convenience store a few blocks away where I could get the same Coke for about one euro. But it was raining. And I'd need to get changed. And it would take 20 minutes. I cracked open the Coke from the minibar and kept on working. Value is connected to price, but only loosely. For me, at that moment in time, the ten-euro Coke in my minibar was a much better value than the one-euro Coke around the corner – not because I thought ten euro was a good price, but because in the bigger scheme of things, I perceived my options to be limited. Despite my minibar bill, I had to admire whoever put the Coke there for anticipating that.

Context is often influenced by one of the classic Four Ps: place, as in a minibar vs a corner grocer. Consider this when assessing the value requirements of your buyer. You may find it useful to map the value rings in proportion to the importance your target is likely to place on them. The thicker the ring, the more weight it carries. This can make it easier to explain which ring you will need to focus on in order to compete. For instance, here I've modelled how I would weigh the importance of core features, value-add features and value-add associations for four products from my own perspective.

Rolex watch

There is really only one reason I would buy a Rolex and it has nothing to do with the core function of value-add features. My timing requirements are pretty minimal, so a $20 watch can do that job, plus I carry my phone everywhere and it tells the time just fine. So the core function of telling the time would not play heavily into my decision to buy a Rolex. With regard to value-add features, I like the design on

FIGURE 13.2 Rolex watch 3-D Product Model

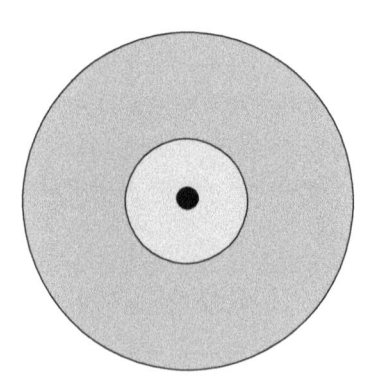

a couple of models but the features I like are not entirely unique to Rolex and not compelling enough to offset the price. The most compelling value that I would find in purchasing a Rolex is brand association. Some of that is the brand mystique that has been created through decades of promotion and product placement, but most are because of memories I have of my Dad's Rolex when I was a kid.

Tesla automobile

This is a product where my interest is pretty evenly divided among all three categories of value. As automobiles go, the Tesla offers reliable transportation that's safe and fun to drive without the pollution and hassle of gassing up. The value-add features like the no-haggling

FIGURE 13.3 Tesla automobile 3-D Product Model

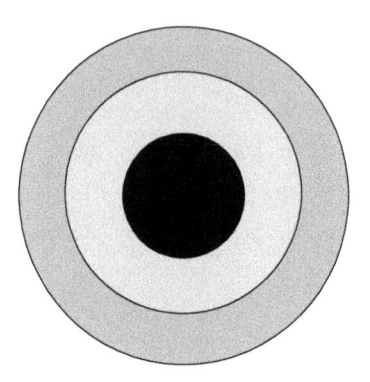

purchase policy, the self-driving functions and cockpit design are also draws for me. I also like the idea of the car and Tesla's mission to accelerate the advent of sustainable transport. The company's brand values, progressive image and innovative technology are all draws for me. My friends who own Teslas advocate for the brand on social media, and I imagine I'd do the same.

iPhone smartphone

What's the first thing people focus on when shopping for a new smartphone? It could be the camera, the memory, the software or the screen size, but it probably won't be how well it makes phone calls. I started with the iPhone because its core functionality was unique at the time and it was compatible with all the other Apple stuff I owned, so there was a strong platform effect for me. Today there are lots of brands that offer similar functionality to the iPhone with regard to phoning and texting, so the core features related to telephony are insignificant. What's most important to me are the value-add features and specifically the seamless compatibility of hardware and software with my other devices. I'm an Apple fan, so the brand plays some role in my choice as well.

IFO fuse

Shortly after moving to Sweden, I was sitting in my kitchen working on this very model. It was a hot summer day and I was trying to think of an item where the core function was pretty much the only reason for buying it. I was stuck. I couldn't come up with one example. At that moment, the power went out in the kitchen. My fridge and freezer had no power. I found the fuse box and realized there were no circuit breakers. It used the old-style ceramic fuses, and the one for the kitchen had blown. My new home had no spare fuses and I had no clue where to buy them. As the ice cream in my freezer began to melt, I ran down to the grocery store and found a fuse branded IFO. At that moment, I didn't care how much it cost, who made it, or how long it would last. I just needed to get electricity from point A to point B. That fuse helped me solve two problems at once that day.

FIGURE 13.4 iPhone smartphone 3-D Product Model

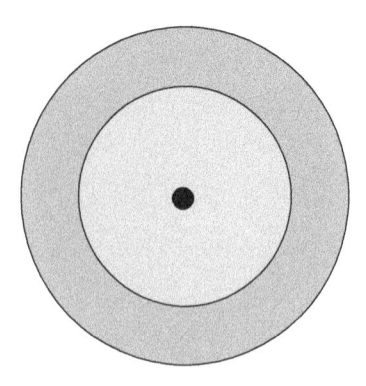

FIGURE 13.5 IFO fuse 3-D Product Model

Bear in mind that these are my perceptions. For example, I bet an electrician would have a much different opinion about that fuse I bought. You probably see the other three products differently as well. So, if everyone has their own take on value, how can it matter for marketing? It matters because there are trends in perception that are usually shared by portions of the market that we can segment and target. These trends change over time; that's why you have to keep in contact with your target to see what they want so you can offer the value they seek.

This is not to say that you need to sit and wait for people to tell you what your next innovation should be. Far from it. Steve Jobs saw his job as figuring out what his buyers would want before they did.

Designer John McNeece, writing about the limitations of customer surveys, reasoned that had Henry Ford asked buyers what they wanted they probably would have said faster horses.[5] True enough, but I'm not advocating asking people what they want from your brand. I'm more interested in 'why'. If Henry Ford had set out to breed a faster horse and sought to understand why people valued owning a horse (eg speedy transportation, independence, convenience), and what they did not like about owning a horse (eg feeding and shelter, falling off, shovelling manure), then I think the results would have convinced him to build a personal transportation machine anyway.

Swedish telecom giant Ericsson provides a textbook example of what happens when you don't keep pace with the value requirements of your buyers. Ericsson created and dominated the cell phone handset market at its inception. It had a perceived advantage focused on the core features of its phones. Back in the early 1990s, handsets were new and cell towers were few. Reception was a big problem with early cell phones. Ericsson had a strong engineering tradition and was able to make handsets that were perceived to address the reception concerns with its proprietary technology and superior engineering skills.

By the late 1990s there were a lot more towers and better software and hardware, so most of the reception problems were largely diminished, at least in and around major cities. As a result, the competitive battleground shifted from core features like the technology used in the receiver to value-add features like form and design. The Finnish company Nokia picked up on this shift and started competing in the second ring with sleeker-looking phones that featured rounded edges, no external antenna, and bigger screens that displayed graphics – all major innovations at the time. Ericsson engineers scoffed at Nokia's design since the internal antenna compromised reception. To their amazement, consumers didn't care.[6] Meanwhile, Ericsson held its ground in the centre ring, as depicted in Figure 13.6, and continued to compete on the technical superiority of its circuit board and reception. In the process it lost the entire market it had built. Ericsson was fighting an engineering battle based on core features, whereas Nokia was fighting a design battle based on value-add features. The more relevant brand won.

FIGURE 13.6 Nokia vs Ericsson. In 1999 Nokia focused on value-add features of its phones while Ericsson focused on core features. Nokia's value priorities more closely mirrored those of the buyers and it stole Ericsson's market share

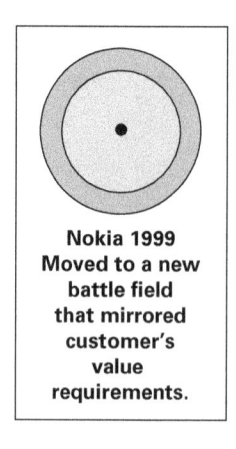

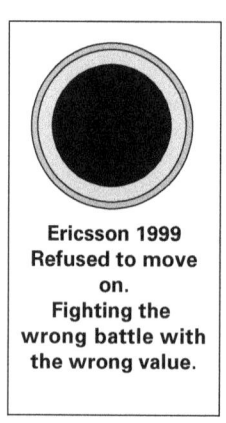

Nokia 1999
Moved to a new battle field that mirrored customer's value requirements.

Ericsson 1999
Refused to move on. Fighting the wrong battle with the wrong value.

Ericsson's own website provides a very candid appraisal of its failing. It chronicles just how out of touch the company was with its customers: 'It gradually became apparent that Ericsson's culture with its lack of consumer contact did not offer the most fertile breeding ground.'[7] Ericsson's strength was in engineering solutions and selling them to national telecommunications monopolies and major service providers. It was completely ill equipped to understand end users, much less compete for them. There was no one in the company who adopted the buyer's perspective or advocated on their behalf. So Ericsson wound up trying to engineer its way out of a marketing problem, with disastrous results.

What goes around, comes around. In 2007 Apple arrived on the scene with its iPhone and gave Nokia a dose of its own medicine. The iPhone was said to be technically inferior to Nokia's top model at the time, since the iPhone was a 2G device (not 3G), didn't support GPS, and its camera resolution was only 2 megapixels. But the Nokia N95 was bulkier and featured over 20 buttons on its face alone, as opposed to the sleeker iPhone with one button. Apple's iOS operating system took user interface to a new level with its touchscreen and then, of course, there were the apps. While Nokia and Ericsson sold phones that did some computing, Apple sold a hand-held computer that did some telephony. This undermined Nokia at a core feature level and ushered in the era of the smartphone.

Value requirements change over time

As categories mature, the value requirements of buyers can evolve in a predictable pattern. When a new category is launched, consumers tend to focus on core features. In many cases, a company need only answer the fundamental question: Does it work? We can see this today in the fledgling consumer space travel market with Virgin Galactic and Space X. The focus right now is on who is technically able to get passengers up and back safely. When space travel is more routine, they will most likely move on to competing on value-add features like seat design, baggage allowance and the in-flight menu.

As categories mature, it's not uncommon to find several players with products that, on a core features level, are close substitutes for each other. This forces sellers to find new ways to add value and typically gives rise to a number of value-add features. Take Apple vs

FIGURE 13.7 Value lifecycle – how the relative importance of the three value categories can evolve over a category's lifecycle

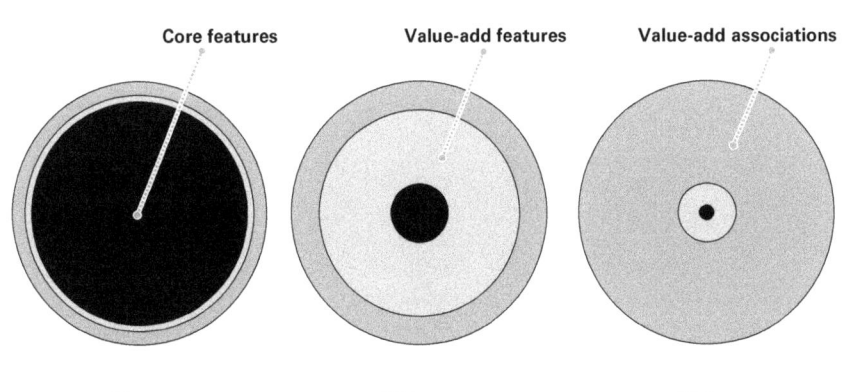

New
Eg Virgin Galactic vs Space X Focus now is on the ability to simply get the public into space and back safely.

Mid-term
Eg Apple vs Samsung Basic smartphone functions are taken for granted and the battle has moved on to value-add features like design, battery life and screen characteristics.

Mature
Eg Coke vs Pepsi Focus has almost left the product entirely and is now on value-add associations with celebrities and causes.

Samsung. The core functionality of various smartphone brands is pretty similar, so now they are competing on value-add features like battery life, design and screen characteristics.

As categories mature, they can begin to rely more upon value-add associations to create new value. Coke and Pepsi seem to be at that stage. Altering the core recipe is probably not going to win anyone over. Coke tried that in 1985 with New Coke, and it was a fiasco. Both brands talk about refreshment and both will run campaigns with the same types of value-add features like novelty bottle design and seasonal flavour variations. At the end of the day, however, the two brands are fighting an image battle using promotion to create value-add associations with trending celebrities and causes.

Reducing cost

Of course there is the flip side to modelling the value priorities of the product offer on the 'get' side of the equation. Just as buyers see your product offer in three dimensions, they also see the cost in three dimensions. Price is the number on the price tag. Cost includes the price but takes a broader view. You can model the cost or 'give' side of the equation with categories of costs: core price, friction costs and associative costs, as shown in Figure 13.8. When you look at costs this way, you will often find that there are ways to significantly reduce the net perceived cost of your offer without reducing the price tag.

Core price

This is the total monetary cost for acquiring the product. That would include the asking price plus any taxes, fees, or finance charges, whether they are charged by you or by third parties. This answers the question: How much money, in total, will be required to acquire the item?

Unless you are striving to be the low-price leader, core price is the absolute last item you want to lower when looking to reduce net perceived cost. How does your core price compare with competitors in the markets you serve? Does it make sense to adopt a different

FIGURE 13.8 The 3-D Cost Model. Shown here next to the 3-D Product Model, the 3-D Cost Model helps us to visualize the three categories of costs that buyers must give up in order to acquire the products, as seen from their perspective

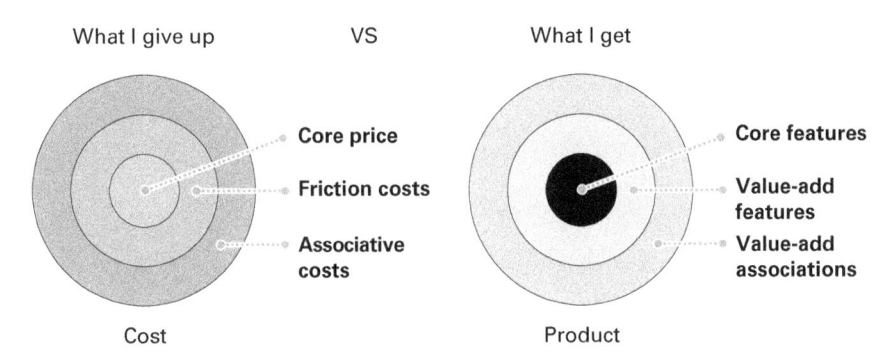

price position in some markets relative to the competition? Do you offer enough value on the product side to increase your asking price without losing market share?

Friction costs

These are the tangible, non-monetary requirements that must be satisfied to acquire the product. They can also be thought of as friction points in the buyer's shopping, acquisition and ownership process. They are tangible and very real to the buyers, just not cash. Common friction costs include time, travel, and hassle, eg ease of getting to the store or comparing alternatives, pick up and delivery, assembly, configuration and learning curve. These costs can also include hassle factors like special payment routines, poor customer service and overall ease of interacting with the seller. Remember the United Airlines example from Chapter 7? They increased value and thus online sales in China by 300 per cent simply by providing ticketing in Mandarin as opposed to English.

What hoops do buyers have to jump through to acquire your product? There are always friction points with buyers. Do you know what yours are? Do you know what your competitors' friction points are? How could you decrease this friction to make it easier for people to shop, purchase and own your product?

Associative costs

These are intangible costs, often in the form of different types of risks based on brand associations. They don't need to be negative to add to the cost. For instance, a brand with no reputation at all can impose a serious risk factor (risk of the unknown) when competing with a known brand. The brand can also have a poor reputation or have recently been involved in a scandal. From the buyer's perspective, these all detract from the net perceived value and serve to weigh down the left side of the buyer's mental value scale. These are the most ethereal of the costs and can be quite subtle. Ironically, if your asking price is too low you can actually be adding to the net perceived cost because perhaps it raises concerns about product quality or safety, or perhaps the buyers feel it would cost them social status to be associated with what they perceive to be a discount brand. 'Reassuringly expensive' was the tag line used in the UK by Stella Artois to explain the price premium it charged on its beer,[8] the idea being that the higher price was indicative of higher quality. This notion underlies a relevant point for those contemplating a lower price. Consumers understand the value ratio to the point that when the 'give' side of this equation is conspicuously low, they generally assume that compromises have been made on the 'get' side.

Are buyers typically eager to be associated with your brand? Why or why not? Is the reputation you have cultivated among customers positive? How would they describe your brand? Are the perceptions of customers known and widely shared by prospects? What negative associations does the buyer have to cope with to acquire and own your product?

Having worked out both sides of the scale, you can now get a feel for how your buyers assess your offer and what you can do about it. If net perceived value were an equation, it would look like this:

Buyer's perceived product value − buyer's perceived product cost = buyer's net perceived value

Although I have phrased this as an equation, this is not meant to imply that you need precise measurements of consumer sentiment to manage net perceived value. This is a heuristic equation meant to illustrate the point and serve as a mental short-cut. Even without pinpoint quantification of the variables, just the process of thinking through how this equation applies to your products, buyers, and competitors will provide useful strategic insight.

Sources of value

In Figure 12.2 I provided a simple model to illustrate the role of the marketer in creating the highest net perceived value possible, which is to lighten up the 'give' side of the scales and weigh down the 'get' side. But how, exactly, can you add or detract value? In Figure 12.2 I provided some examples of the types of things that do this.

Eric Almquist from Bain & Company has taken this one step further and mapped out the individual elements that create value for buyers, called the Elements of Value® (Figure 13.9). This work was inspired by Abraham Maslow's hierarchy of needs, which range from basic physical needs to complex psychological needs. Almquist and his team conducted over 10,000 interviews with more than 50 companies across the US and compiled a list of 30 value elements for B-to-C purchases and 40 for B-to-B purchases.[9] The elements, which span all three layers of value as defined in the 3-D Product Model, are presented in Figures 13.9 and 13.10 with permission from Bain & Company.

Both B-to-C and B-to-B were found to have a positive correlation between the number of value elements a brand excels at and the loyalty and advocacy of its customers. This effect was most pronounced in the B-to-B study. Here they removed factors that they found were table stakes or category qualifiers such as product specifications, price, regulatory compliance and ethical standards. Based on an assessment of the remaining 36 elements, they found that companies that were able to excel at six or more elements had an average NPS that was over 450 per cent higher than companies that did not achieve excellence in any of the 36 categories and 60 per cent higher than the NPS of those that achieved excellence on one to five elements of value. Given the correlation between growth and NPS cited in Chapter 11, a 60 per cent to 450 per cent advantage is significant.

FIGURE 13.9 Bain & Company's Elements of Value® for B-to-C

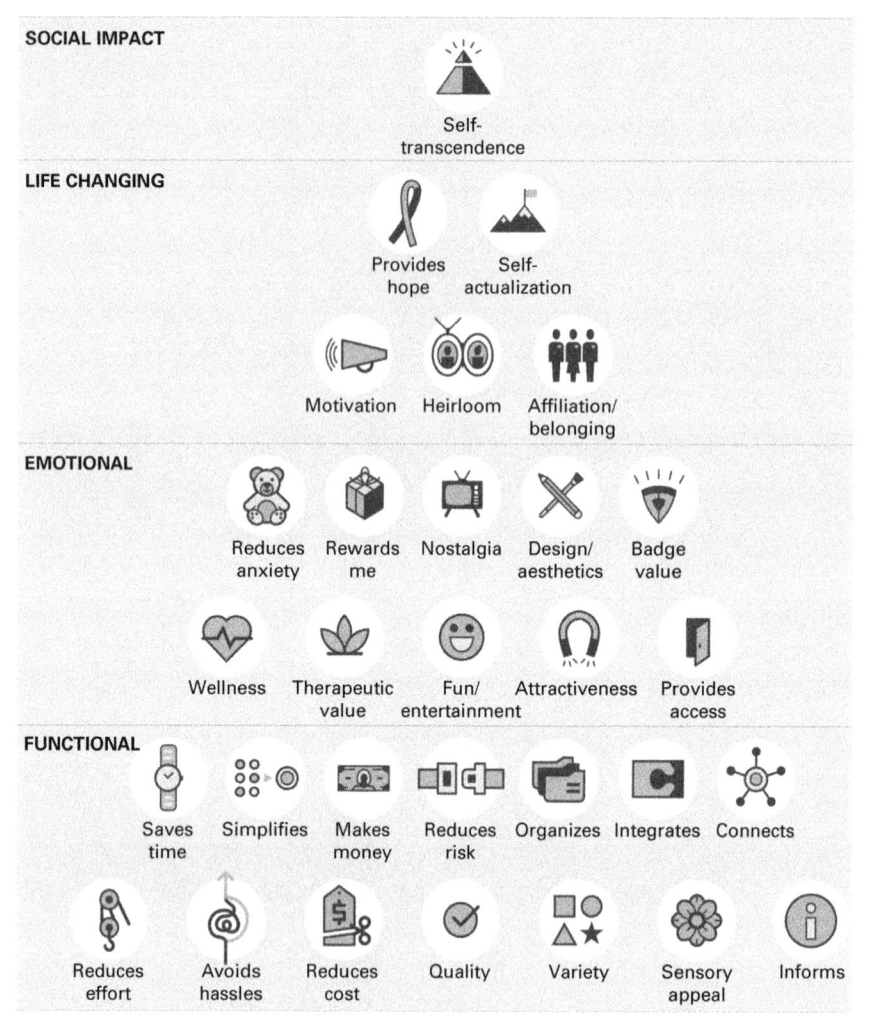

SOCIAL IMPACT
- Self-transcendence

LIFE CHANGING
- Provides hope
- Self-actualization
- Motivation
- Heirloom
- Affiliation/belonging

EMOTIONAL
- Reduces anxiety
- Rewards me
- Nostalgia
- Design/aesthetics
- Badge value
- Wellness
- Therapeutic value
- Fun/entertainment
- Attractiveness
- Provides access

FUNCTIONAL
- Saves time
- Simplifies
- Makes money
- Reduces risk
- Organizes
- Integrates
- Connects
- Reduces effort
- Avoids hassles
- Reduces cost
- Quality
- Variety
- Sensory appeal
- Informs

SOURCE Reproduced with kind permission of E Almquist (2018) and Bain & Company

Reading the study, I could not help but think of all the B-to-B companies that focus on the table stakes as the prime driver of value to their customers. These companies will have the most to gain by moving outside core values and core price to explore other areas to add value and subtract cost.

These studies reinforce the importance of using the full range of value levers that you have at your disposal. Avoid the tendency to focus on core features and price alone and expand your net perceived

FIGURE 13.10 Bain & Company's Elements of Value® for B-to-B

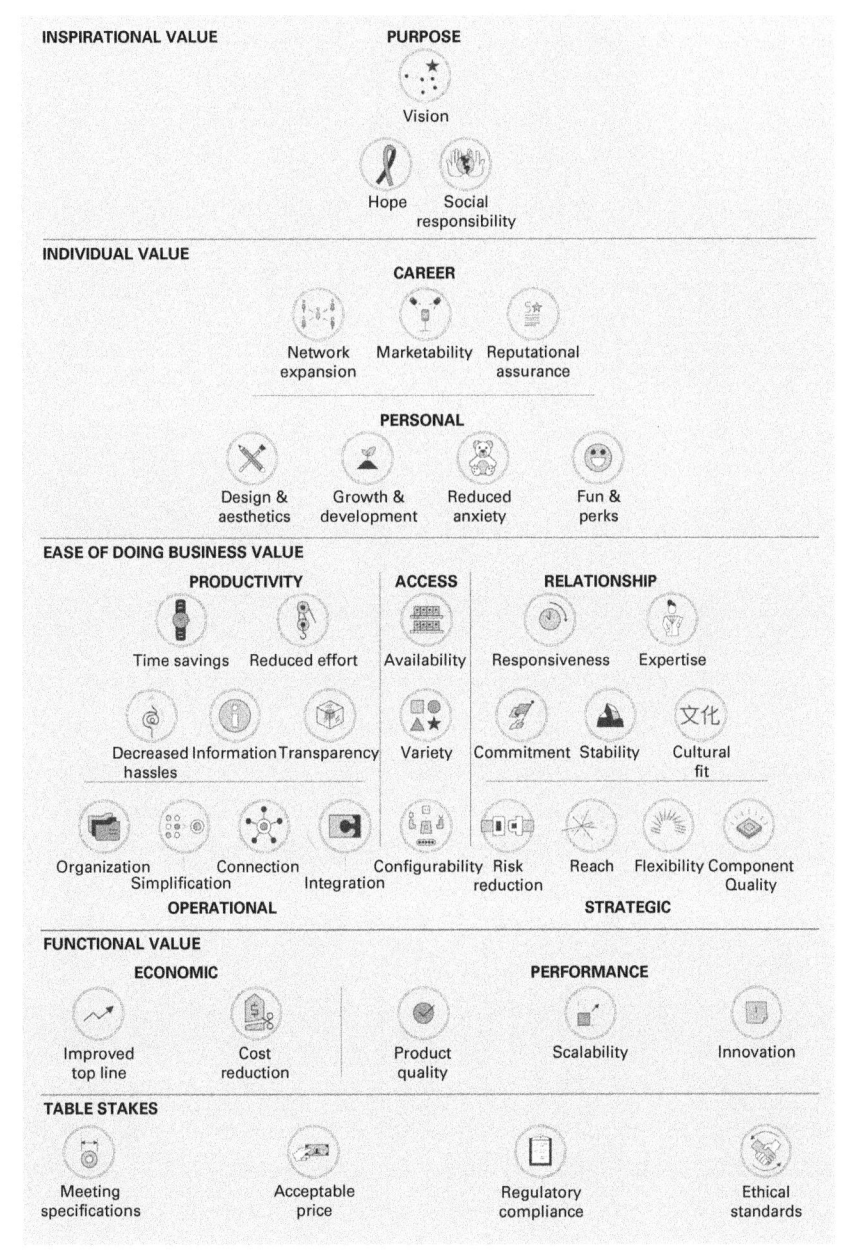

INSPIRATIONAL VALUE

PURPOSE
- Vision
- Hope
- Social responsibility

INDIVIDUAL VALUE

CAREER
- Network expansion
- Marketability
- Reputational assurance

PERSONAL
- Design & aesthetics
- Growth & development
- Reduced anxiety
- Fun & perks

EASE OF DOING BUSINESS VALUE

PRODUCTIVITY
- Time savings
- Reduced effort
- Decreased hassles
- Information
- Transparency

ACCESS
- Availability
- Variety

RELATIONSHIP
- Responsiveness
- Expertise
- Commitment
- Stability
- Cultural fit

OPERATIONAL
- Organization
- Simplification
- Connection
- Integration
- Configurability

STRATEGIC
- Risk reduction
- Reach
- Flexibility
- Component Quality

FUNCTIONAL VALUE

ECONOMIC
- Improved top line
- Cost reduction

PERFORMANCE
- Product quality
- Scalability
- Innovation

TABLE STAKES
- Meeting specifications
- Acceptable price
- Regulatory compliance
- Ethical standards

SOURCE Reproduced with kind permission of E Almquist (2018) and Bain & Company value by working on the outer two rings. There are many ways to increase net perceived value, many of which differ from market to market. You can't pursue them all. To help decide where to focus, start by talking to your stakeholders. Through in-depth interviews and surveys, find out which aspects of the product and cost are most important to them. This will provide a manageable shortlist on which to work. If you are dealing with multiple foreign markets, you will want to repeat this exercise for each of them. This work should inform your value proposition and position in the market you're entering, as well as help you prioritize research and development efforts.

Conclusion

In the introduction to Part Two I said that value is all that matters to buyers and all you have with which to compete. In this chapter I have provided some tools to manage and maximize that value. The hard part for many people is to see value from the buyer's perspective as opposed to the top-down view from the C-suite. This becomes even more of a challenge when your C-suite and buyer don't share a common language, culture or nationality. The only way to get the insight required to create proprietary value in foreign markets is to get to know your buyers even better than the local brands do. This makes it even more important for international marketers to establish a programme of regular interviews, surveys and/or focus groups to keep in sync with buyers.

Net perceived value is not a number calculated by buyers, but rather a judgement call made on the basis of weighing, consciously or subconsciously, the pros and cons of your offer based on some facts and a lot of beliefs, concerns, perceptions, motivations and gut feelings. It's not so straightforward, but then neither are people. The good news is that you have six ways to tilt these scales in your favour by:

1 adding value to the offer with core features, value-add features and value-add associations;
2 reducing the cost of the offer by reducing core price, friction costs and associative costs.

Further breakdown of the specific aspects of value has been provided with the work of Eric Almquist and his colleagues. To put these models to use in shaping your value proposition, position and offer, you will need to find what your particular buyers and other stakeholders value most.

Companies that master the intangible aspects of their offer are better able to assess, manage and grow the net perceived value of their brand. They also start to see the market differently and have more tools with which to compete than companies that do not master these skills. In the next chapter I address a special group of marketers who may feel a bit left out of this whole discussion.

Notes

1 P Kotler, *Marketing Management: Analysis, planning, and control*, Prentice-Hall, Upper Saddle River, NJ, 1967.
2 MeTV Staff, A history of the TV remote control as told through its advertising, MeTV Chicago, 17 November 2015. www.metv.com/stories/a-history-of-the-television-remote-control-as-told-through-its-advertising (archived at https://perma.cc/62KD-Q8EZ)
3 O Nicol, McDonald's innovation timeline, Sutori, undated. www.sutori.com/story/mcdonald-s-innovation-timeline (archived at https://perma.cc/MV98-HW3N)
4 Oprah spikes sales of Swedish bread, Boston.com World News, 9 March 2007. http://archive.boston.com/news/world/europe/articles/2007/03/09/oprah_spikes_sales_of_swedish_bread/ (archived at https://perma.cc/XL6V-453W)
5 My customers would have asked for a faster horse, Quote Investigator, undated. https://quoteinvestigator.com/2011/07/28/ford-faster-horse/ (archived at https://perma.cc/EC7R-3D7S)
6 S Henckel, Så dog den svenska mobile, *Ingenjören*, (5), pp 30–44, 2012. www.ingenjoren.se/media/2012/12/Ing-5-12_low.pdf (archived at https://perma.cc/5WQ7-AJEK)
7 S Karlsson and A Lugn, Problems with mobile phones, Ericsson, 2020. www.ericsson.com/en/about-us/history/changing-the-world/big-bang/problems-with-mobile-phones (archived at https://perma.cc/5ZML-A72P)
8 About Stella Artois, *Stella Artois Blog*, undated. www.stellaartoisblog.com/about-stella-artois/ (archived at https://perma.cc/546D-3SAM)

9 E Almquist, J Senior and N Bloch, The elements of value, *Harvard Business Review*, September 2018. https://hbr.org/2016/09/the-elements-of-value (archived at https://perma.cc/BUA3-MFYE); E Almquist, J Cleghorn and L Sherer, The B2B elements of value, *Harvard Business Review*, 2018. https://hbr.org/2018/03/the-b2b-elements-of-value (archived at https://perma.cc/8YEM-H79K)

14

The commodity caveat

Commodity as a choice

I'd like to include a special note to anyone involved in selling commodities, such as food, building materials, energy or services. If you are selling a product that has been labelled a commodity, then you may think that the notion of adding value or subtracting costs does not apply to you. If you recall from Chapter 12, when companies increase their prices the largest gains in profits are made by companies with the smallest margins, which is often the case with commodity sales. In Figure 12.1 you saw that the companies with the thinnest margins saw increases in operating profit of up to 61 per cent. If you believe you are selling a commodity, you probably have the most to gain from working on net perceived value. All six of the profit levers discussed apply to you as well:

- Adding value to the offer with core features, value-add features and value-add associations.
- Reducing the cost of the offer by reducing core price, friction costs and associative costs.

Even commodities have perceived value

A commodity product is defined as one that has full or partial fungibility; that is, the market treats all these products as equivalent, or nearly so, with no regard for who produced them.[1] For there to be a true commodity market, all suppliers would need to sell an identical product in an identical manner with identical reputations. In such a market, we would expect to see market share distributed evenly among all sellers.

But, as we know, that never happens, suggesting that outside exchange-traded commodity markets, the idea of a pure commodity is more of a theoretical construct than an actual phenomenon. In each commodity category there are players who are able to capture more market share than others. That is because, even though the core features of a ton of copper from one vendor may be identical to a ton of copper from another vendor, there is more to the product offering than the core features alone. Each copper producer will have differences in the value-add services it provides during the buying process, and each will have different reputations. All this will affect the perceived net value offers by Copper Producer A compared to those of Copper Producer B.

Harvard Economist Theodor Levitt is quoted as saying, 'There is no such thing as a commodity. All goods and services are differentiable. A commodity is simply a product waiting to be differentiated.'[2] I agree. When someone says they sell a commodity, I interpret that as a choice of business model, not a category. It is a valid business model for companies that do not wish to take on the risk and expense of developing product brands. However, any product can be differentiated, and thus de-commoditized.

Consider salt, the oldest and most basic of commodities. All salt is essentially the same chemical – sodium chloride. Yet we have a variety of sodium chloride categories, such as sea salt, table salt/iodized salt, kosher salt, flavoured salt, *fleur de sel*, Hiwa Kai, Black Hawaiian Sea Salt, Dead Sea Salt, Australian Murray River Pink Salt, Kala Namak, organic salt, fair trade salt, rock salt, fine salt and pink Himalayan salt, just to name a few. It's interesting to note that many of these categories draw upon nothing more substantive than the source of origin to differentiate and command premium pricing. Source of origin can be a powerful differentiator, even if your location isn't exactly the origin. The 'Hawaiianization' of macadamia nuts and pineapples are two prime examples. Neither of these foods is indigenous to Hawaii. Macadamias are native to Australia and pineapples come from Paraguay. However, those two regions failed to market them. It was the Hawaiian producers who first laid claim to the species and were first to market them globally as their own.

Another characteristic of a commodity good is the lack of pricing power discussed in Chapter 12. Your price is dictated largely by your competitors' prices, since the market assumes you are all selling exactly the same thing; but even if the price (core cost) is fixed, the seller can still affect the net perceived cost by working with the 3-D Cost Model presented in Chapter 13 to reduce friction costs and associative costs. Likewise, even if the core features were fixed, the same producer could still sweeten their offer using the 3-D Product Model with value-add features and value-add associations. These measures could be enacted without branding the core products themselves. The result would still be an increase in the buyer's net perceived value, but not for the purpose of charging a higher price so much as driving higher volume because more commodity buyers prefer doing business with you.

Petroleum and copper are often cited as examples of commodities. The same could be said of food items like sugar, tea, coffee beans, rice, collagen, wheat, corn, chicken, pork, beef and fish, but it can also apply to manufactured goods. A paper from the MIT Sloan School of Management makes this point with the example of the electric bread toaster.[3] The first commercial toaster was put on the market in 1905 and sold for the equivalent of $78 adjusted for inflation. By 1930, toasters of identical function saturated the market and were easy to make, buy and use. By any definition, toasters had become a commodity. One hundred and ten years later, Amazon lists 1,727 different toasters ranging in price from $14 to $4,369. It's interesting to note that the median price is $78, with 50 per cent of the models above the original price point and 50 per cent below. The MIT paper summed up the danger of the commodity myth: 'Executives, entrepreneurs, and investors are too ready to believe that commodity is destiny. The result is a dulling of strategic focus and a narrowing of the business mind.'[4]

The VICO case

My team recently worked on a project that highlights this point. The client in this case was a publicly traded company from Southeast Asia that sold a commodity. We'll call it VICO (not their real name). When the company approached us, it had around USD $350 million in annual sales, all B-to-B, with customers in over 20 countries. Like EMCO, it was first in its category and had maintained amazing growth for over a decade without investing in the brand or, for that matter, any marketing at all. It relied purely on the sales team and scaling production. It called us because sales growth had flattened out and profits were in decline. As the category matured and became more crowded, VICO found it increasingly difficult to maintain a premium price. Customers had very little loyalty. Discounting became the only way it could defend market share from competitors. In the absence of a strong brand image, it also found it difficult to compete for the best employees without over-paying.

This pattern is not uncommon. VICO realized that sales alone could only take it so far. To push to the next level, it need something more. It started with an investment to gain market and buyer insights. That allowed my team to develop a highly relevant marketing strategy and value proposition as well as a new brand identity and communication platform. It transformed VICO's business. It turned what it had previously sold as a faceless commodity into a well-differentiated product based on the corporate brand. Within a year of launching a proper brand identity and strategic marketing programme, this particular company was able to increase its average sales price in all markets globally while simultaneously gaining market share. Sales revenue increased by 12 per cent with a 33 per cent increase in gross profit. Investors also responded favourably to the change, as reflected in a 110 per cent increase in the company's share value over the same period. What's more, these results were all achieved during an overall downturn in its industry.

THE POWER OF PERCEPTIONS: THE HIMALAYAN SALT PHENOMENON

There is a reason I use the word 'perceived' when I talk about value. Value, like beauty, is in the eye of the beholder. The Himalayan salt phenomenon in the US and Europe is a prime example. This is a product with high fungibility, meaning that salt products are very much alike and can be easily substituted one for the other. Himalayan salt was differentiated from normal salt with the lore of its Himalayan origins, its raw, unprocessed purity and its long list of health benefits.

Truth be told, the salt is mostly not from the Himalayas, is incredibly impure (thus the colour), and has no substantiated health benefits whatsoever.[5] Pink salt has always been the cheapest salt because of its impurities. It is what most municipalities in cold regions use to de-ice their highways, commonly referred to as road salt. Despite this, pink salt from any brand marketed with 'Himalaya' as its source of origin can sell at a premium price that is up to 200 times that of common table salt. Part of this is based on rational reasons, like the perception that it is healthier since it is 'raw' and claims to contain 84 beneficial trace elements that would normally be refined out of table salt.[6] However, since it contains only trace amounts of iodine, some critics claim it actually poses more of a health risk since most people get their iodine through salt.[7] Also, there is a reason that trace elements are processed out of normal salt. Of those 84 trace elements found in Himalayan salt, 60 are actually contaminants since they include radioactive elements like radium, uranium and polonium, as well as known toxins like thallium, arsenic and mercury.[8] They are found in trace amounts that don't do any harm, but they are certainly not providing a benefit.

Further, a financially motivated, well-circulated urban legend accompanied the launch of the salt. It is said that workers in the Himalayan pink salt mines suffer no cancers or other modern medical maladies, just from being in close proximity to the stuff. When the salt was first launched in Europe, this tall tale was related to me by at least a dozen people who felt it was credible. This story has never been validated. In fact, the salt mine cited in these stories doesn't even exist. The myth says the salt comes from rarefied mines in the Himalayas. The less glamorous truth is that most of this salt doesn't come from the Himalayas. It comes from the world's second-largest salt mine, the Khewra Salt Mine in Pakistan, situated between Islamabad and Lahore just

> south of the Himalayas.[9] Road salt from Pakistan may be a more fitting moniker, but it's not the type of image that sells premium pink salt.
>
> The truth about this salt is not hard to corroborate, but after raising the issues at several dinner parties, I've concluded that no one really wants to know. It's irrational. But so are consumers. Irrational associations probably explain most of the pink salt's popularity and perceived value. I do not endorse the tactics used by many people who sell this novelty salt, but if they can sell tainted sodium for 200 times more than table salt, imagine what you could do with your product by helping people perceive its true value.

Some products may lend themselves to differentiation more than others. Who would have thought that a sharpened piece of aluminium could have maintained its differentiation for over a century, but since 1904 that's exactly what Gillette has been doing. Fiji water, Absolut vodka, Kobe beef, De Beers diamonds and the myriad brands of Himalayan salt are all examples of would-be commodities that have been successfully differentiated. Even electricity has been branded and differentiated based on supplier reputation and the method by which it was generated (wind, solar, coal, oil, etc). These are all examples of highly fungible products where value-add service and associations were added to de-commoditize them.

How can you de-commoditize your product? Frank Purdue did it way back in 1970 when he de-commoditized the entire chicken industry. Frank Perdue inherited his family's small chicken farm in Maryland, USA. Selling commodity chickens at auction was not working out. He decided to differentiate. He knew everything there was to know about chickens. For many years, that blinded him to the fact that he knew virtually nothing about the people who bought them. So he started his journey by trying to discover what buyers valued.

He left his farm and spent an entire summer in New York City visiting butcher shops. Each day he would hit the streets with his notebook to talk to butchers and learn what customers most valued in chicken. He wound up with a list of a dozen core features such as yellow skin, tender texture and plump breasts. He went back to his chicken farm and began a selective breeding and feed programme to alter the core features of his chicken. He also began an aggressive advertising campaign to build value-add associations with his brand.

It worked. He was soon able to sell his chicken for 14 per cent more than others' chickens. This was not because he created *his* idea of the best quality chicken but because his chicken was designed around the value requirements of his *target*. The business has grown steadily since then and today sells globally with around US$ seven billion in annual sales.

However, even a customer-centric brand like Purdue can slip up. Later in his career, Frank Purdue realized that his target market was concerned with reducing fat in their diets. Once again, he saw an opportunity to tip the value scale, so he created a chicken with significantly less fat and tried to sell it at a premium price. He was eager to beat his competitors to market, so he also decided not to test the idea with consumers. The effort failed because, although his target customers were looking to reduce dietary fat, they did not see chicken as a significant source and were not willing to pay more for a low-fat chicken. Like Hans, Frank invested millions trying to weigh down the 'get' side of the value scales with a value-add feature that none of his buyers actually valued.[10]

Conclusion

If you feel you are selling a commodity, I hope you will take this to heart. While it is true that products can have a broad range of fungibility, I'd maintain that there is no product that is a pure commodity nor any product that is destined for commoditization. Commoditization is not an inherent attribute of any category. It is a decision made by the seller not to invest the time or resources required to differentiate their offer.

Notes

1 Commodity, Wikipedia, undated. http://en.wikipedia.org/wiki/Commodity (archived at https://perma.cc/GCG4-KLBT)
2 P Kotler and G Armstrong, *Principles of Marketing*, Prentice Hall, Upper Saddle River, NJ, 2001.

3 M Schrage, The myth of commoditization, MIT Sloan Management Review, 1 January 2007. http://sloanreview.mit.edu/article/the-myth-of-commoditization/ (archived at https://perma.cc/D3EQ-FEDF)
4 M Schrage, The myth of commoditization, MIT Sloan Management Review, 1 January 2007. http://sloanreview.mit.edu/article/the-myth-of-commoditization/ (archived at https://perma.cc/D3EQ-FEDF)
5 H Hall, Pink Himalayan sea salt: An update, Science-Based Medicine, 31 January 2017. https://sciencebasedmedicine.org/pink-himalayan-sea-salt-an-update/ (archived at https://perma.cc/N6Y3-33RK)
6 Minerals in Himalayan pink salt: Spectral analysis, The Meadow, 2020. https://themeadow.com/pages/minerals-in-himalayan-pink-salt-spectral-analysis (archived at https://perma.cc/74M8-Q2PA)
7 Your fancy Himalayan salt is putting your thyroid at risk. Here's why (and what to do about it), MindbodyGreen.com, 12 June 2017. www.mindbodygreen.com/articles/himalayan-salt-is-putting-your-thyroid-at-risk-heres-why-iodized-salt-is-better (archived at https://perma.cc/D3G9-XWL4)
8 Minerals in Himalayan pink salt: Spectral analysis, The Meadow, 2020. https://themeadow.com/pages/minerals-in-himalayan-pink-salt-spectral-analysis (archived at https://perma.cc/DA28-K8XJ)
9 Khewra Salt Mine, Wikipedia, undated. https://en.wikipedia.org/wiki/Khewra_Salt_Mine (archived at https://perma.cc/TX5L-SA8L)
10 L Snowbridge, How Perdue Farms became the number-one premium chicken product brand in the US, smart CEO, undated. https://web.archive.org/web/20170627073939/http://www.smartceo.com/perdue-farms-became-number-one-premium-chicken-product-brand-u-s/ (archived at https://perma.cc/GX6G-57CK)

Afterword

Time to get started

In this book, we have covered a lot of ground. Reflecting on the previous 14 chapters, two central themes emerge: perspective and value.

As marketers, we tend to define our world in terms of the tools we have to help us do our job: product, price, place and promotion. That hasn't changed, but I hope you now have a better idea of why you are using those tools and to what end. You may see the four elements of your marketing mix, but your buyers see one thing: net perceived value as the balance between give and get. If you can learn to see the world through their eyes, you will see it too, and your company will prosper as a result.

Each marketing success and failure cited in this book can be attributed to how well the company was able to read its buyers and respond to their desires. That's not easy to do, particularly when working internationally. Advertising legend David Ogilvy once observed, 'Consumers don't think how they feel. They don't say what they think and they don't do what they say.'[1] I agree, but this shouldn't dissuade you. There is too much at stake. Your brand's buyers possess the answer to your most critical marketing questions and they are always right – if you know how to ask them. Develop that skill, starting with the art of perspective. An organized approach will allow you to scale the collection and analysis of buyer insights to all the markets you serve.

The title of this book is *International Brand Strategy*. You may have noticed that much of its content applies to domestic marketing as well as it does to international marketing. As noted in Chapter 2, brands fail abroad for many of the same reasons they fail domestically. For that reason, you should strive to understand the perspective of domestic buyers and test the validity of your assumptions at home as well as abroad. If you recall from the Introduction to Part One, Target thought it knew its Canadian neighbours well enough to forego the time and expense of validating their assumptions. They saved eight weeks and a couple of hundred thousand dollars and then lost USD $5.5 billion over the ensuing 14 months.[2] Familiarity may breed contempt, but in marketing it breeds complacency. Target taught us that just because you are familiar with a market segment it doesn't mean you understand them. This is as true for your brand's domestic buyers as it is for international buyers. So the practices outlined in the book should be used domestically as well as abroad. The difference for international marketers is that the bar for success is higher because there are more groups of buyers to understand and more work is required to gain their perspective. Process then becomes more of an imperative in order to address the increased complexity.

In Chapter 10 I advised you not to get too over-confident when entering foreign markets. Assuming the role of the underdog, at least internally, is a good way to keep your team in check, but your outsider status has advantages too. You will have more time to plan your offence than the local brands will have to mobilize their defence in response. Your team will be on a mission and motivated to succeed, as opposed to carrying on with business-as-usual. You will be able to see the market with fresh eyes, as opposed to how it's always been. You will not be complacent. Use this edge to compete.

A final word on strategy. I'm sure 200 years ago some business author writing by the glow of a whale-oil lamp felt the same twinge of uneasiness I feel now as they penned the line 'The accelerating rate of change we see in society and commerce today calls for a fresh look at the business strategies we have inherited from our predecessors.' They were reflecting on the advent of the steam engine. I'm reflecting on the advent of AI and the internet, but the implication is the same: things move faster now, so we need business strategies that can keep up. No matter how frenetic things seem today, I'm equally sure some business author two hundred years from now will be looking back on our era with nostalgia at how things were so simple and slow-paced in the 2020s.

Assuming that yours is the first era to experience rapid change seems to be a cliché in business literature since time immemorial. We are not the first, nor will we be the last, generation to feel as if the world is speeding up around us in an unprecedented manner. In a dynamic world, the relevance of any approach to business strategy will struggle to outlive its author.

Strategist Rita Gunther McGrath has gone as far as to suggest that it is no longer possible for companies today to maintain a sustainable competitive advantage.[3] I introduced her work in Chapter 9. The idea is that since industries are in flux and consumers are so unpredictable, it's impossible for a strategic advantage to last for more than a year or two anyhow. So why bother? The best we can hope for today is to find successive waves of opportunity and build transient strategies for a temporary advantage until we spot the next swell.

There is a lot to like in McGrath's idea of companies shaking off the myopia and rigidity of the past and embracing change and new ideas as opposed to fighting them. I also agree that in uncertain times when the future is murky, it makes more sense to focus on more proximal strategic objectives. But the premise assumes that strategies are a constant and if they are failing at an increased rate today then it must be because the markets have changed to become strategy-resistant. What if the market is the constant and it's the quality of the strategies that are to blame? That would be more consistent with my observations as a practitioner. It's also a lot more plausible than the second premise, which states that consumers today have become unpredictable.

I used to subscribe to the idea that the only constant in marketing is change. Today I maintain the belief that change is constant and that adaptability is vital but there is at least one other constant. Beneath the whirlwind of passing business trends and the shifting fortunes of national economies, there is a still point – a simple, steady constant that can be used to navigate even the most tumultuous of times: value.

Rooted more in science than economic theory, value is the lowest common denominator in business as in biology. Even a single-celled microscopic protozoa trades in value, expending resources in search of net positive value outcomes in order to survive. Same with humans. We are single-minded, unwavering and remarkably predictable in that way. That has not been erased by the digital revolution or globalization today any more than it was by the steam engine 200 years ago. Any company that can more effectively marshal its resources to consistently identify the value requirements of buyers before its competitors, then develop and deliver targeted net-positive value through its offer, will have created a sustainable competitive advantage.

Of course, if everyone can replicate your advantage, then it cannot be sustained. For it to be a sustainable advantage, there would need to be something that prevents competitors from duplicating it. Strategist Richard Rumelt describes this as an 'isolating mechanism', which, in developing a good strategy, is the hard work required to produce one. Few companies are up to it or feel they have time for it. This may be the real consequence of the fast-paced times in which we live. No one feels they have time for strategy. That alone may serve as the isolating mechanism that will keep your competitors from duplicating your efforts. As Rumelt notes, 'The first natural advantage of good strategy arises because other organizations often don't have one. And because they don't expect you to have one, either.'[4]

Notes

1 D Brennan, Don't say what you think, but do what you feel, Mediatel News, 27 November 2013. https://mediatel.co.uk/news/2013/11/27/dont-say-what-you-think-say-what-you-feel (archived at https://perma.cc/3WA5-Z3GB)

2 Financial Post Staff, Target Corp: A timeline of the retailer's failed Canadian experiment, *Financial Post*, 15 January 2015. https://financialpost.com/news/retail-marketing/target-corp-a-timeline-of-the-retailers-failed-canadian-experiment (archived at https://perma.cc/R7JF-45SM)

3 R G McGrath, Transient advantage, *Harvard Business Review*, June 2013. https://hbr.org/2013/06/transient-advantage (archived at https://perma.cc/WK4C-EZSD)

4 R P Rumelt, *Good Strategy, Bad Strategy: The difference and why it matters*, Crown Business, New York, 2011.

INDEX

The 22 Immutable Laws of Marketing 146 *see also* Reis, A *and* Trout, J

Aaker, D 169
advocacy 180–83, *182 see also* articles/papers
afterword: time to get started 231–34
airlines competing on price 160–62
    Laker Airways, Pan Am, British Airways *and* TWA 160
alternatives to translation 92–103
    adaptation: the best of both worlds 97–99
    adaptation checklist 99–102
        do you speak the target language? 101–02
        have you accounted for text expansion/contraction? 100–101
        have you arranged for back-translations? 102
        have you developed your own network of resources? 101
        is the adapter living in the target market? 99–100
        is the adapter qualified to adapt? 100
        is the target language the adapter's native language? 100
        is the writer adequately briefed? 101
        will the adapter work with a partner? 100
        will you be allowed direct access to the adapter? 101
    how to manage language barriers fluently 92–93 *see also* Anholt, S
    the right name for the right job 93
    the right resource for the right job 94, 95, 96–97
Amazon 151, 196
    1727 toasters listed (in 2015) 225
    acquisition of Whole Foods 157
Amquist, E 217 (Bain & Company) 217
Anholt, S 92–93
    and *Another One Bites the Grass* 92

Apple 144–47, 149, 151 *see also* Cook, T *and* Jobs, S
    iPod 144–46
    vs Creative 146
Apple Newton 174
articles/papers (on)
    'Blurring the lines: Is there a need to rethink industrial marketing?' 131 *see also* Wind, Y
    'Does your company have what it takes to go global?' 53 *see also* Quackenbos, D; Ettenson, R; Roth, Martin S *and* Auh, S
    'Distance still matters: The hard reality of global expansion' 32 *see also* Ghemawat, P
    'Even commodities have customers' (*Harvard Business Review*) 142 *see also* Jacques, F M
    'The globalization of markets' 32 *see also* Levitt, T
    'The myth of commoditization' (MIT Sloan Management Review, 2007) 225
    'The one number you need to grow' 180 *see also* Reichheld, F F
    'Toward a theory of medical fallibility' (1975) 20 *see also* Gorovitz, S *and* MacIntyre, A
    'Why the world isn't flat' 32 *see also* Ghemawat, P
Ault, S 53

balancing short- and long-term growth 126–38 *see also* Binet, L *and* Field, P
blurring the lines 131–35 *see also* articles/papers *and* Wind, Y
    between B-to-B and B-to-C marketing 132

balancing short- and long-term
        growth (continued)
    and Honeywell 132–34 see also
        subject entry
    building sales vs building a
        brand 126–29
    the case for B-to-B brands 129–31
Barker, R 26
Bartlett, C 70–72, 74, 75 see also Managing
        Across Borders: The
        transnational solution 70
B-B brands 135–36
    and companies 136
Beecham 42 see also Lucozade
being understood in foreign markets
        (and) 79–91
    the art of adaptation 85–87
    how to translate promotional
        material 84–85
    the link to sales 82–83
        variables and their relative
            importance 82
    localization 87–90, 89
    the power behind your promotion 79–80
    the role of language 80–81
        and three challenges for the
            international marketer 80–81
        working with multiple languages 83–84
        writing for the translator 85
Beltman, H J (CEO, Tony's
        Chocolonely) 191
Binet, L 127–29, 131 see also Field, P; The
        Long and Short of It, and
        research
Binger, J H (President of Honeywell) 133
Bjorner, C 86–87
    and data from IPA Effectiveness
        Databank 127–28
BlendTec 134–35 see also Dickson, T and
        Wright, G
    and 'Will it Blend' videos 135
blogs
    Born to Be Global 90 see also Kelly, N
    Evergreen 148 see also Jorgenson, E
Broadwell, M 24, 29
    and 'the four levels of teaching' model 24
        see also Burch, N
Buffet, W 148, 188
building brand equity 168–84
    adding insight to your net promoter
        score 171–72
    brand equity in action: the CrayOffs
        example 172, 174–83, 182

    advocacy 180–83, 182 see also
        subject entry
    affinity 179
    awareness and an exercise 174–75
    belief 178
    interest 175–76
    loyalty 179–80
    relevance 172, 174, 173
    trial 177–78
    trust 176–77
    understanding 174
    brand management and brand
        equity 169–70
    the mechanics of 168–69
Buehner, C W 134
Burch, N 24, 29 and 'the four stages of
        competence' 24 see also
        Broadwell, M
    1. unconscious incompetence 24
    2. conscious incompetence 24
    3. conscious competence 24
    4. unconscious competence 24

Castaldo, J (Canadian Business magazine) 6
chapter notes for
    afterword: time to get started 234
    alternatives to translation 103
    balancing short- and long-term
        growth 136–38
    being understood in foreign markets 91
    building brand equity 183–84
    the commodity caveat 229–30
    creating value 221–22
    defining a strategy to compete 166–67
    defining your approach 78
    developing a competitive
        advantage 152–53
    domestic vs international marketing 47–48
    introduction 16–17
    net perceived value 198–99
    planning for departure 116
    reducing risk 67
    why brands fail abroad 30
The Checklist Manifesto 21 see also
        Gawande, A
Christensen, C (Harvard Business
        School) 20, 174
Coca-Cola 64, 76
the commodity caveat 223–30
    commodity as a choice 223
    even commodities have perceived
        value 223–25 see also Amazon
        and articles/papers

the power of perceptions: the Himalayan salt phenomenon 227–28
the VICO case 226, 228–29 *see also* Purdue, F
Competitive Strategy 155, 164 *see also* Porter, M
conclusions for
   alternatives to translation 102–03
   balancing short- and long-term growth 135–36
   being understood in foreign markets 90–91
   building brand equity 183
   the commodity caveat 229
   creating value 220–21
   defining a strategy to compete 165–66
   defining your approach 78
   developing a competitive advantage 151–52
   domestic vs international marketing 46–47
   net perceived value 197–98
   planning for departure 116
   reducing risk 65–67
   why brands fail abroad 29
Cook, T (CEO, Apple) 146
creating value 200–222
   all products are 3-D 201–06
      core features 202
      value and features 203–04
      value-add associations *and* brand identity/management 204–06
   all value is relative 206–13
      IFO fuse 210–13, *212*
      iPhone smartphone 209–10, *209*
      Rolex watch *207*, 208
      Tesla automobile 208, *208*
   how buyers assess value 200–201, *201*
   reducing cost 214–17
      associative costs 215–17
      core price 214–15, *215*
      friction costs 215
   sources of value 217–18, *218*, *219*, 220 *see also* Almquist, E *and* Maslow, A
   value requirements change over time 213–14, *213*

defining your approach 68–78
   embracing complexity 70–72 *see also* Bartlett, C *and* Ghoshal, S
   and managers' assumptions on approaching markets 71

global integration vs local responsiveness 68–70
multinational corporation structure (and the) 74, *75*, 75–77
   global approach 75–76
   international approach 77
   multi-domestic approach 76
   transnational approach 76–77
   the Unilever approach 72–73
defining a strategy to compete 154–67
   'but we don't have any competitors' 159–60
   competing on differentiation 162–63
   competing on price – airlines 160–62
   a final note on strategy 164–65, *165 see also* Porter, M
   home-field advantage 154, *155*, 155–57
   planning for profit 157–58 *see also* Porter's 5 Forces
Denial: Why business leaders fail to look facts in the face – and what to do about it 52 *see also* Tedlow, R
Dettman, M (director of advertising, Honeywell Information Systems) 134
developing a competitive advantage 139–53
   building an advantage from strength to strength 144–47 *see also* Jobs, S
   the case of EMCO 139–42 *see also* EMCO
   how to avoid mirage marketing 142–43
   preparing for competition 147–51
Dickson, T (owner, BlendTec) 134–35
domestic vs international marketing (and) 31–48
   culture: domestic reality *and* international reality 36–37
   the difference between marketing domestically and abroad 31–33
   documentation and codification: domestic reality *and* international reality 43–46
   language: domestic reality *and* international reality 35–36
   market input: domestic reality *and* international reality 44–45
   media environment 43–44
   position: domestic reality *and* international reality 39–42 *see also* Dove; Lucozade *and* Ogilvy, D

domestic vs international marketing
   (and) (*continued*)
   and St Patrick's Day prank 41
   the role of marketing *and*
      objectives 33–35, *34*
   brand equity: increases the
      probability of future sales 34
   margin: maintains premium-pricing
      integrity 34
   sales: increases the probability of sales
      today 33
   value proposition: domestic reality *and*
      international reality 37–39 *see
      also* Volvo
Dove 39
   and its value proposition 39
Drucker, P F 128
Duffy Agency 104
Duffy Brand Equity Circle 169–70, *173*, 182
   output 171

Einstein, A 192
EMCO 149–52
*The End of Competitive Advantage: How to
   keep your strategy moving as
   fast as your business* 147 *see
   also* McGrath, R G
Ettenson, R 53

Field, P 127–29, 131 *see also The Long and
   Short of It and* research
figures
   3-D Cost Model (shown next to 3-D
      Product Model) 215
   3-D Product Model (adaptation of
      Philip Kotler's Three Layers of
      Product) 201
   3-D Product Model, Rolex watch 207
   Bain & Company's Elements of Value®
      for B-to-B 219
   Bain & Company's Elements of Value®
      for B-to-C 218
   companies receive two types of value
      from markets, and should
      manage both 182
   the Duffy Brand Equity Cycle, modelled
      from the consumer's
      perspective 173
   four generic phases of marketing work
      that follow ideation when
      entering a new market 60
   IFO fuse 3-D Product Model 209
   integration-responsiveness grid: Bartlett
      and Ghoshal's model 75

   iPhone smartphone 3-D Product
      Model I209
   likely outcomes when pitting your
      strategic skills against those of
      local competing brands 155
   marketing contribution model 34
   Net Perceived Value model. The mental
      scales people use to assess the
      value of your offer 194
   Nokia vs Ericsson phones in 1999:
      Nokia's focus on value-add
      features, Ericsson's focus on
      core features 212
   percentage increase in operating profit
      based on 2% increase in
      price 187
   the value loop 165
   value lifecycle – how relative importance
      of three value categories
      can evolve over a catagory's
      lifecycle 213
Fisher, T (CEO, Target Canada) 1–2, 4–5, 8,
   10, 11, 12–13
Ford, H 211
Friedman, T 32 *see also The World is Flat: A
   brief history of the twenty-first
   century*

Gawande, A 21 *see also The Checklist
   Manifesto* 21
Ghemawat, P 32, 50, 51 *see also* articles/
   papers
Ghoshal, S 70–72, 74, 75 *see also Managing
   Across Borders: The
   transnational solution*
Good Strategy, Bad Strategy 150 *see also*
   Rumelt, R
Google Translate 44
Google+ 174
Gorovitz, S 20, 23, 51 *see also* articles/papers
*The Gutenberg Galaxy: The making of
   typographic man* 32 *see also*
   McLuhan, M

Herman, B 58, 59, 60, 61, 65
Hjalmar, B 87, 96
Honeywell 132–35 *see also* Binger, J H;
   Dettman, M *and* Sweatt, W R
   acquired by AlliedSignal 134

Inglourious Basterds 31, 36 *see also*
   Tarantino, Q
introduction to Part One 1–17 *see also*
   Target *and* Walmart

adapting to the market 9–11
compromised values 3–5
missing the target 1–2
and Part One overview 14–15
preparing for departure 14
price perception 7–9 *see also* surveys
success as a foregone conclusion 2–3
technical difficulties 5–7
under-estimated competition 11–12
what can we learn from this? 12–13
introduction to Part Two 117–25
  building value in foreign markets 123–24
  Part Two overview 124–25
  the problem with quality 117–21
  what can we learn from this? 122–23

Jackett, J 126–27
Jacques, F M (CMO, Lafarge) 142–43 *see also* articles/papers
Jobs, S 144–47, 210 *see also* Apple
Jones, J P 43 *see also* studies
Jorgenson, E 148 *see also* blogs

Kahneman, D 51, 52 *see also Thinking, Fast and Slow*
Kapferer, J-N 169
Keller, K 169
Kelly, N 90 *see also* blogs
Kotler, P 185 *see also Marketing Management: Analysis, planning and control*
  model: defining products in three layers: core, actual and augmented 200
Krebs cycle 170
  output 171

Lafarge 142–43 *see also* Jacques, F M
Larson, E 53–54
Larson, R 53–54
Levitt, T 32, 224 *see also* articles/papers
The Long and Short of It 127 *see also* Binet, L *and* Field, P
Lucozade 42
  repositioned from medical to sports drink and with new tag line 42

McGrath, R G 23, 147 *see also The End of Competitive Advantage*
MacIntyre, A 20, 23, 51 *see also* articles/papers
McKinsey & Company 129–31 *see also* studies

McLuhan, M 32 *see also The Gutenberg Galaxy: The making of typographic man*
McNiece, J 211
Managing Across Borders: The transnational solution 70 *see also* Bartlett, C and Ghoshal, S)
Marketing Management: Analysis, planning and control 200 *see also* Kotler, P
Maslow, A 141
  and hierarchy of needs 217
models
  3-D Cost 125
  3-D Product 125, 206, *207*
  Porter's Forces 157
  Three Layers of Product 200, *201 see also* Kotler, P
Murdoch, R 50–51

Nestlé 190
  Kit Kat bar 77
    re-invented to suit market in Japan 77
    as sold in Switzerland 77
net perceived value 185–99
  ask why people are buying 196–97
  creating scarcity within a category 189–91
  identifying value 193–94, *194*, 195–96
  planning for profit 185–86
  understanding value 191–93
  value in action 186–89, *187*
niche companies 156–57
  Whole Foods 157

Ogilvy, D 39, 79, 231
  and Dove soap 39
Orwell, G 52

Part Two: introduction (and) 117–25
  Alex 118, 121
  building value in foreign markets 123–24
  Hans 117–18, 120–23
  overview 124–25
  the problem with quality 117–21
  what can we learn from this? 122–23
    don't mistake a head start for a competitive advantage 122–23
    don't mistake quality for value 123
    don't mistake ruling the category for leading the category 122

Paul, M 192
    and difference between knowledge and understanding 192
planning for departure 104–16
    bon voyage 104–06
    eight inputs required to localize your marketing mix 112, *113, 114, 115*
    planning checklist 106–15
    what management approach will you use in the foreign market? 106–12
        have you documented core marketing strategies/processes? 110–12
            and suggestions to get you started 111–12
        have you documented steps you will follow to enter the market? 112
        how will the brand identity be adapted? 108–09
        how will the marketing mix be managed 107–08
        how will you adapt your value proposition to be suitable for global use? 109
        how will you ensure you get regular input from the market? 110
        how will you position the brand in the foreign market? 109–10
    localization recommended 106–07
Porter, M 155, 157, 163, 165 *see also Competitive Strategy*
    Generic Competitive Strategies: price, differentiation, niche 155–56, 161, 163
    and his research 163
    value chain model 164
Porter's 5 Forces 157–58, 159
    competition in the industry 158
    potential of new entrants into the industry 158
    power of customers 158
    power of suppliers 158
    threat of substitute products 158
Positional for Professionals 185 *see also* Williams, T
The Price Advantage 186
Purdue, F 228–29
    and de-commoditizing of chicken industry 228–29

Quakenbos, D 53

reducing risk 49–67
    the ABCO case 54–57
    and unanticipated challenges 55
    exit ramps 64–65
    idea 60
    keep things moving 59, 60
    managing risk begins by acknowledging it 49–50
    and braving Niagara Falls 49–50
    overcoming cognitive bias 50–52 *see also* Kahneman, D *and* Tedlow, R
    Phase I: framing 60–62
        criteria 61–62 *see also* Herman, B *and* Siegelaub, J
    Phase II: strategy development 63
    Phase III: implementation 63–64
    Phase IV: management 64
    putting risk in perspective 57
    success begins close to home 52–54 *see also* articles/papers
    what to include 58–59
        reasons; options; benefits and negative consequences; timescale and costs *and* major risks and opportunities 58–59
Reichheld, F F 160, 171 *see also* articles/papers
Reis, A 40, 146 *see also The 22 Immutable Laws of Marketing and* Trout, J
research
    on B2B customers (Google and CEB) 131
    conclusions of Binet and Field 128–29 *see also* Binet, L *and* Field, P
Ries, A 40 *see also* Trout, J
Roth, M S 53
Rumelt, R 150, 234 *see also Good Strategy, Bad Strategy*

safety as value proposition 38, 41 *see also* Volvo
Schroer, J 43 *see also* Jones, J P
Scully, J 145
search engine optimization (SEO) 44
Shaw, H (reporter, *Financial Post*, Canada) 8, 9
Siegelaub, J 58, 59, 60, 61, 65
Steinhafel, G (CEO, Target) 4, 8, 10, 12–13, 20, 66
strategy, final word on 232–33
studies (on)
    brands and B-to-B purchase decisions (McKinsey & Company) 110–11

pricing (*Business Strategy Review*) 187, 187
pricing (Harvard Business School) 187
pricing (McKinsey, using S&P Composite 1500 Index) 187
the relationship between media spend and sales (1990) 43 *see also* Jones, J P
Sumner, W G 37
   credited with breaking his own norms into mores and folkways 37
surveys (of)
   600 B-to-B marketers 131
   Canadian consumers, Target's tagline and low prices (Vision Critical, 2012) 9
   Canadian shoppers: 89% felt Target failed to deliver on promise (2015) 9
Sweatt, W R 132–33 *see also* Honeywell and strategic marketing 133

tables
   options for translating text from one language to another 95
   various levels of localization 89
Tarantino, Q 31, 36
   and *Inglourious Basterds* 31, 36
Target (and) 1–14, 104, 232 *see also* Fisher, T *and* introduction
   Canada 1, 11–12, 14, 64
   'Expect More. Pay Less' promise 7, 11
   its growth - success as a foregone conclusion 2–3
   price perception 7–9 *see also* reports
   United States 11, 12
Taylor, A E 49–50
Tedlow, R 52 *see also Denial: Why business leaders fail to look facts in the face – and what to do about it*
Thinking, Fast and Slow 51 *see also* Kahneman, D
Trout, J 40, 146 *see also* Reis, A *and The 22 Immutable Laws of Marketing*
Tverske, A 51

Unilever 23, 72–73

Vallance, C 126
van de Keuken, T 190
Volvo: value proposition of safety 38, 41

Walmart 2, 3–4, 9, 11, 150–51
websites: Europe, Middle East and Africa (EMEA) *and* India (EMEAI) 88
why brands fail abroad (and the nature of) 18–30
   assumptions 26–29
   competence *and* incompetence, four stages of 24–25
   failure 20–21 *see also* articles/papers through ignorance and ineptitude 20–21
   foreign markets 19–20
   and the importance of knowing what you don't know 18–19
   knowledge asymmetry 26 *see also* Barker, R 26
   marketing 21–23
      lacking characteristics of a profession 22
Williams, T 185 *see also Positioning for Professionals*
Wind, Y 131–32 *see also* articles/papers
The World is Flat: A brief history of the twenty-first century 32 *see also* Friedman, T
Wright, G 134–35 *see also* BlendTec and willitblend.com 135

Zaltman, G 80, 82

CPSIA information can be obtained
at www.ICGtesting.com
Printed in the USA
LVHW070715201220
674185LV00005B/6

9 781789 666298